HAPPINESS IS AN OPTION

Choosing to be happy when life tells you otherwise.

BJ Gidman

First published in Great Britain in 2011 by

Time On Your Hands Publications

www.bjgidman.com

Copyright © 2011 BJ Gidman,
including author's own photographs and those
given by kind permission by the friends
and family of Fiona Crompton.

The author's rights are fully asserted. The right of BJ Gidman to be identified as the author of this work has been asserted by her in accordance with the Copyright, Designs and Patents Act 1988.

A CIP Catalogue of this book is available
from the British Library.

ISBN 978-0-9569209-0-4

All rights reserved; no part of this publication may be reproduced, stored in a retrieval system, or transmitted, in any form or by any means, electronic, mechanical, photocopying, recording or otherwise, without the prior written permission of the publisher, nor be otherwise in any form of binding or cover other than that in which it is published and a similar condition including this condition being imposed on the subsequent purchaser.

Cover design by D-R ink
www.d-r-ink.com

Typeset in Sabon by
www.chandlerbookdesign.co.uk

Printed in Great Britain by
Good News Digital Books, Ongar

This book would not have been written without extensive excerpts from the personal diaries of Fiona Crompton, whose voice is represented by the publication of this book.

Time On Your Hands Publications

Proceeds from this book will be donated to Cancer Research UK and Walk the Walk.

*For Fi: a lover
AND a fighter*

INTRODUCTION
She's Got A Way

IT'S NOT sentimentality that led me to write this book, although no doubt there will be manifestations of slushiness throughout. What began as me simply being compelled to write down how her death made me feel, then evolved into the concept of a book. My thoughts about losing an old friend, her thoughts on being positive and living life, experiences we shared, then developed into more. I found myself with questions to ask to those who were close to her: questions I didn't know if I would dare ask: questions I almost asked her when she was alive but somehow never did for fear of spoiling the moment of just being with her. She wouldn't have minded though, and she would have been totally honest. I knew she would love the idea of having a book written about her (as long as I kept some secrets secret!) but how would others feel? Her husband loved the idea. He gave me her folders, diaries and journals that she had compiled to help her through her life with cancer. Once I read them, all my questions were answered. She always had plenty to say (a slight understatement, as anyone who knew her would testify) and I wanted to somehow put it all together in one place. Others close to her thought it was a good idea too, knowing that people might gain something positive from reading her story.

So many people are living with cancer, either personally or with a loved one, affecting them directly or indirectly. There are plenty of books around on how to beat cancer or cope with a diagnosis; on nutrition, positive thinking, meditation, or even fifty things you should or shouldn't say to someone with cancer, and more besides. This book might touch on some of those things but essentially it is simply about one woman and what happened to her and how she managed to deal with it in an amazing way. She wasn't a celebrity like Patrick Swayze, Farrah Fawcett or Jade Goody, who also lost their battles with cancer in 2009, although she did make a few appearances on TV and in her local press. She was just an ordinary person, like the teacher teaching your kids, a friend you've known since you were young, a neighbour who always has time for you, a mother and wife, a sister, a cousin; just someone like the many everyday people you see shopping in the supermarket - except she turned out to be extraordinary to those who spent time with her.

This is the story of my friend who died too young and too soon, because of cancer. She didn't just cope. She didn't just enable all around her to cope either. She fought. She inspired. She had a positive disposition that guided how she lived her life and how she dealt with the bad things that happened to her and her family. She made all around her feel strong. She had an honesty and frankness that cut through any bullshit. She was strong and tough, loving and kind. She was fun and up for a laugh. She was a downright flirt. Her smile was incredibly powerful and could cure any feelings of negativity. That smile still manages to do its stuff: even now she's gone. It makes things better, but unfortunately it couldn't cure the cancer.

Nevertheless, that didn't stop it trying.

1
You've Got A Friend

September 2009

Hi Hun

This may come out as sentimental waffling but hey, that's what chicks do... So this is from a Closet Chick that would never admit to actually watching Dirty Dancing (me), to the Ultimate Chickster (you)...

Would so love to come and see you and say how much you mean to us and give you a hug and be the 1000th person to say how much we both admire your strength and courage and love of life. When I heard the shocking news and those terrible, terrible words 'a matter of weeks', the first reaction was a selfish one – I want to see you one last time - but actually I wanted more – I'd want to see you again, another time, and another time, and another time... but I know there will be no time now. I know that you are tired and need to rest and a long queue of visitors is not good for that, so I'm sending you these words instead – because if I was actually *there in person, all I could do is hug you and Simon and Sophie and James, and ramble on as usual about S Block, Happy Shopper Vodka nights, Lloyd Cole, About Last Night, Sometimes by Erasure, Portobello Market...*

What a magnificent teacher you turned out to be – in more ways than one. You know how valued you are, and the difference you have made in raising cancer awareness. You are such a great role model, not just to Sophie and James, but to all of us supposed grown-ups too. You are someone who is admired, respected and loved with as much intensity as something that is so intense that it could win first prize for intenseness from the Academy of Intensity, Passion and Strength In General.

I cried the day I heard the terrible news and I'm crying now. Crying for the unfairness of it all, for you and what you have had to go through, for Simon, Sophie, James and your Mum... And there will have been tears and crying from everyone who knows you, not least your own close and loving family.

But you don't want tears, I know; you never wanted sympathy or pity. You needed to be strong and positive to fight this as long as you have, and you couldn't do that without support, love and the normality of life. So you live your life to the full and demand that everyone around you does the same. And really that is why we cry – in shame of ourselves for never making the most of every moment, for moaning about things that don't really matter, for holding a grudge when there is no reason to be hateful, for wasting our time on things that don't make us smile. Not forgetting the fact that we don't want you to leave us and we will miss you like crazy.

You always made me smile. Since I first met you, you were always so up for fun. That's not to say you never got angry or pissed off – but you vented it, disposed of it and carried on with the fun. Even when you had more right than most to be angry – you still never let it get in the way of your own or your family's fun.

So I write because I want to tell you these things, things I left unsaid when I've seen you before. Maybe they should have remained unsaid. Maybe I'm being selfish for saying how I feel. But sometimes it's good to let someone know that they made a difference to someone just by being a crazy chick from college that was a fabulous friend. Maybe one day I will write a book about my fabulous friend who lived her life in an extraordinary way.

Rest sweetie darlin', you are sooooooooooo loved and will be soooooooooo missed – there I've said it.

Luv Babs xxx

I wrote that letter on Monday 7 September 2009, but it was never sent and Fi never got to read it or have it read to her, the latter I suspect would've more likely been the case. It felt intrusive somehow and selfish at a time when there was no need for words anymore. Fi knew how I felt about her and I knew how she felt about me. I knew that the most important people in her life would be with her and there was no need for anyone else. The next day I changed my mind and still wanted to go and see her; after all, I was her mate and if I'd still been living nearby I would've popped in. Despite living in Belgium, it would have only taken me a morning to get to Harpenden. With no commitments to stop me, unable to telephone as our phones were down, I emailed, paraphrasing some of my letter to let her know how amazing I thought she and her husband Simon were, and to see if a visit would be possible. Simon replied the next day.

> *Hi Babs*
> *Simon here. Thanks for your support and love. It has been really good seeing all the lovely things that people have been saying about Fi and it has certainly helped to keep her smiling.*
> *She has deteriorated a bit since last week and isn't able to keep up with emails, Facebook or text messages at the moment but I have been trying to pass on all the messages to her. She is quite sleepy a lot of the time but she is still eating and although she does get tired when people come to visit, it does appear to make her happy. She does like to hear stories of what has been going on and listen to tales from the past; she is just finding it very difficult to concentrate on anything for more than a few minutes. I just don't know how she will be in a few days time as it is impossible to tell what will happen.*
> *It would be a lot easier to fill you in with all the details on the phone so please give me a call when your phones are back up and we can talk about next week.*

Fortunately my phone was working the following day. Simon explained that Fi's moments of lucidity were few now and that in his own gentle way he was putting people off coming to see her. It was time. We chatted about the fact she was being nursed by her mum (a qualified nurse) and how things had been and how it helped him to chat to people, both of us keeping it together and holding back the tears. I put the phone down and realised that I would never see her again and felt immense sadness for Simon, their two children and her close family. I was home alone as my husband Iain was on business in Canada. There was no one to hug and no one to put on a brave face for. I felt numb and in shock. My throat was sore from a huge lump and tears filled my eyes every time I thought of her. On my daily walk with our dog I replayed conversations in my head with Fi. I imagined her walking beside me with their dog Mac. I had a hard time sleeping that night. I probably wasn't the only one.

The next day was 11 September. It is a tragic date in history due to the terrorist events of 2001. A fact that failed to register with me.

Babs

Was going to call you but like a fool I didn't make a note of your number yesterday so I have had to send you an email instead.

Sadly Fi passed away just after 11am today. She had all her family with her and was in no pain, it was very peaceful. I was so proud of the kids and they were able to say goodbye as they had decided not to go into school today.

We are currently planning to have her funeral next Friday at 1pm and I will send out the full arrangements in a general email to everyone tomorrow but I wanted to let you know before I did that, as I am sure that Fi would have wanted me to do that.

Take care, love Simon

I felt honoured that Simon found the time to email when he most certainly didn't have to, indeed it would have been entirely acceptable to have other more significant matters occupying his time. It was truly typical of his nature and kindness. After a little while I replied.

> *Dear Simon*
>
> *So so sorry. I will miss her so much. She was the most sincere, genuine, easy-going friend ever. I always felt so good when I was with her. But my loss will be nothing compared to yours and the kids - what an amazing Mum they were lucky to have had and not many people in this world find the love that you two shared. I've emailed so that I can get the words out, but will speak to you soon. I truly appreciate you taking time out to let me know.*
>
> *All our love, Babs and Iain xxx*

Tears came in torrents for the rest of the day, and for days to come. I had never cried so much in my entire life. Not when my granny died (I missed her but merely snivelled), nor even when my father had died unexpectedly years earlier (I wept every time I heard Andy Williams songs and spontaneous tears oozed every time I saw a silver-haired old man wearing a flat cap). The closest thing that had caused such gut wrenching pain of uncontrollable sobbing was when I met a boy at Trent Polytechnic who, against all reasoning and my better judgement, broke my heart every time he left me to go back to his girlfriend. It wasn't logic that determined what I was meant to feel. My body made those decisions, not my brain. My stomach flipped whenever I saw him, a lump came to my throat whenever he made a cutting comment, my eyes stung whenever I imagined life without him, my cheeks warmed whenever he praised and complimented me, not to mention the strange tingling sensations I experienced in various anatomical regions whenever we kissed. In other words, bodily functions have played more of a role in my response to life's situations than any logical reckoning established by my thoughts. That boy turned out to be my husband.

My body was certainly taking over now, as my head could make no sense of what had happened to my friend; a friend who I had also met, at the same time as that boy, all those years ago at Trent Polytechnic in Nottingham. Words like unfair, unjust and wrong, interspersed with several vicious profanities, ran through my head, as regularly as the tears ran down my cheeks, merging with the intermittent infant-school rivers of snot from my nose. In the week that followed I made travel arrangements and hotel reservations. My husband Iain would fly back from Canada; we would meet at Heathrow and hire a car. On Fi's wishes I had to pack something pink or purple to wear, as those were her favourite colours. I figured she'd approve of a flash of pink fishnet peeping out from my black jeans, little Saucepot that she was.

2

The Time Of My Life

At the Old Cock Inn we had a drink before going to the church, chosen not for the name, which at one time Fi found amusing no doubt (even in our melancholic state we still sniggered), but because it was practically next-door. Slowly more people came in wearing pink or purple and did the same. With a half hour to go we decided to leave. A crowd had gathered outside the church and I recognised Fi's brother Iain in his pink tie and a kilt (McIntosh tartan) and her godson Sam in his naval uniform. I discovered later that they had been instructed to wear these outfits by Fi and she had warned the family that she would haunt them if they did not carry out her final requests to the letter! She would be on show and it had to be right!

We went inside to be greeted by a gorgeous photograph of Fi taken on a photo shoot after her What Not To Wear makeover. The church was almost full. I couldn't look at the Order of Service as I was trying to keep it together and concentrate on finding a seat. I clutched the pink card and sitting down, finally glanced down and saw the same beaming photo looking up at me, and the words 'A Service in Celebration of the Life of Fiona

Crompton'. Her life was indeed something to celebrate, and she'd certainly spent most of it celebrating, but at that moment I felt I was there to cry and mourn her death. The first of three hankies came out ready to stem the flow. Looking around the church, at the hundreds of people, the wooden beams above, the flowers and stained glass windows, I had images in my head of Simon, Sophie and James getting ready this morning for the day ahead. What must they and the rest of her family be going through? I couldn't look at my own husband, whose hand gently rested on my knee. My eyes filled and I swallowed back the ever-increasing lump in my throat. *"Get it over with. Get it over with."* I told myself, but then felt weak and pathetic given the strength and courage shown by Fi. The least I could do for her was to get a grip and show my support by being here for her for the very last time. The moment had come. Suddenly everything went quiet.

The sound of bagpipes playing 'Flowers of the Forest' drifted into the church. Fi's coffin was being brought in. She was very proud of her McIntosh heritage. Her father hadn't been born in Scotland but had extensively researched the family ancestry. Fi's Grandfather was a Scot and she was known by the family to have a very similar temperament to him. My husband, half Scottish, found the sound of the pipes incredibly emotional and moving. We stood, clutching each other's hands tightly, to steady ourselves for what was to come.

Hearing Reverend Christopher Futcher describe Fi's life and its events, it was all the things I knew about her already. It didn't surprise me when he said that Fiona had planned her funeral with him and amongst the seriousness of doing so there had been laughter. I found out later that when choosing a coffin, she had shown her family a picture of a white, wicker coffin. Her cousin Debs had laughed, saying it reminded her of a laundry basket and should they add a special touch with some knickers hanging out of a corner? They all shared the same wicked sense of humour. Other eco basket coffins were rejected as they looked too much like a picnic hamper. They finally decided on a natural wicker coffin. Fi was always a great organiser and we shared the same passion (some would call it Obsessive Compulsive) for lists, cataloguing photos and meticulous lesson planning when we were teaching. This event was organised with the same attention to detail as always.

At this point it struck me that I would never see her ever, ever again. The subsequent hymn and bible reading did nothing to ease this realisation; my atheism meant the words simply washed over me without consequence but my heart recognised how the ritual and faith may be providing comfort and solace to some, as it had done for Fi who had a firm belief in the power of angels. In fact it provided me with a bit of time to catch my breath, which I realised I'd been holding since the Rector had started speaking. But then I audibly choked when they played the song chosen by Fi for reflection: 'You and Me' by The Wannadies. It was a song I knew she loved and I'd used it as a soundtrack on a DVD movie I'd made for her with her photographs of when she and Simon had renewed their wedding vows in 2007. (I made ten movies for her. It took our passion for organising photos to a whole new level). Today, with flashes of pink and purple shining out over the congregation, Revd. Futcher had made the comment that instead of a funeral, the church looked more like a wedding than some of the weddings he had seen.

In my head I had the image from my movie of her walking down the aisle with Simon, and now here I was, facing that very aisle, listening to that very song which coincidentally I had used as a backing track. That image merged with all the times I'd spent with her; laughing, talking, singing, dancing and drinking. The tears fell, knowing they were now forever memories, never to be repeated.

The Time Of My Life

How Fi's cousin Debs managed to read the poem 'When Tomorrow Starts Without Me' (Author Unknown) I'll never know. It was around eight verses long and began...

"When tomorrow starts without me and I'm not here to see,

If the sun should rise and find your eyes all filled with tears for me,

I know how much you love me, as much as I love you

And each time that you think of me, I know you'll miss me too.

But when tomorrow starts without me, please try to understand

That Jesus came and called my name and took me by the hand,

He said my place was ready in Heaven far above

And that I have to leave behind all those I dearly love

But as I turned to walk away a tear fell from my eye

For all my life I'd always thought it wasn't my time to die

I had so much to live for and so much yet to do

It seems almost impossible that I was leaving you..."

Debs obviously shared Fi's ability for courage and strength, no doubt due to the fact that they are related. They would describe their relationship as cousins through family but best friends through love and choice, and true sisters to each other. I began to realise how special Fi made you feel when she became part of your life. All these people here today (the church was standing room only, with around five hundred people) were proof of that.

The poem 'She is Gone' by David Harkins was adapted and read by Fiona's brother Iain, who inserted her name into the poem to personalise it. The beautiful words basically warned against drowning in your grief (something I was doing right there and then) and instead to remember the good times and be happy that Fiona had been part of your life and the difference she had made. I could almost hear Fi's voice as he read. I suspected, correctly, that Fi had chosen these readings herself as they were so close to what she thought. I later discovered that after she had died, Iain had looked for something to say at her funeral about his sister. He found a poem and asked Simon, her husband, if he could read it out. Simon gently informed him that Fi had strictly instructed every detail of the service and anything different was not to be entertained. He did not wish to incur the Wrath of Fi!

But as it turned out, Iain had found the exact same poem that Fi had chosen.

> *"You can shed tears that Fiona is gone or you can smile because she has lived.*
>
> *You can close your eyes and pray that she'll come back or you can open your eyes and see all she's left.*
>
> *Your heart can be empty because you can't see her or you can be full of the love you shared..."*

At the beginning I had been willing this event to be over, and now I realised it was helping me face the loss of my amazing friend. Since Fi had organised every detail, it didn't feel like a generic service or a ritual. It felt like she was doing one last thing for us all. I felt proud that she had been my friend and it felt like her friendship was palpable in church that day.

The coffin, covered with flowers, went out to the song '(I've Had) The Time Of My Life' from the film Dirty Dancing. I saw it, raised high up above the congregation. This image now made it all real. The End. No denying it now. But I was kind of expecting the song. She was someone who loved chick flicks and it was just so her. Fi's brother Iain and godson Sam were quietly singing along as they carried out their beloved Fiona. The other pallbearers were close friends and family, along with someone from the undertakers. Fi had requested the latter in order to have 'an expert' on hand to ensure they all walked properly and in time! Good thinking on her part, as Sam instinctively jiggled to the music (as Fi would have boogied along to this song) but stopped when it wobbled the coffin a bit.

I finally looked at my husband and gave a half smile, before we both left the church, walking past an overflowing donations bowl for cancer charities. Even at her funeral, Fi had somehow managed, against all odds, to make me smile.

Outside was sunny and bright. Those two words could be used to describe Fi perfectly. It was another reminder not to wallow. We took some deep breaths before heading back to the pub to wait whilst the family went to the crematorium for a private service. My husband Iain grabbed something to eat, knowing he would need to soak up the considerable amounts of alcohol he intended to drink in order to get him through the day. As designated driver I couldn't use this course of action, and in any case my body felt empty and wanted to stay that way. Then we walked the short distance to the hotel where we hoped to see Simon, Sophie and James. I didn't know what I was going to say to them but I knew I wanted to hug them Bigtime. As it turned out, we didn't need to worry about what to say. As always, The Cromptons make you feel at ease. Simon, incredibly strong and dignified, chatted about future plans and how the day had gone so well and just how Fi would have wanted. James looked all grown up in his purple shirt and suit trousers. Sophie ran towards me and I got an amazing welcome hug. Fi lives on that's for sure. Her mum Jean told us about the Scottish Clan Gathering Photobook that Fi had helped her make and about funny things that had happened in recent months. I wanted to tell Debs and Iain how much I admired their readings at the church, but they were busy making sure everyone was looked after and I hadn't really met them before. I wished I'd had some of Fi's confidence to do so. I told them later on Facebook, agreeing with her brother Iain's comment that the day was emotional, happy, sad and inspiring all at once. He said, *"Fi would've loved it. The way there was standing room only, everyone was wearing pink and purple, she would have absolutely revelled in that."*

We spent the afternoon talking through memories with friends from college days - the time when we had all first met Fi. When we weren't speaking we were looking at the photo slideshow of Fiona from childhood to now. Simon had made this for her and it was one of those times when words simply aren't necessary. We got a flush of warmth when we saw ourselves with Fi in various places from over the decades, usually with a drink in our hands, always posing and laughing. We all imagined her 'up there' with Patrick Swayze, who had died four days earlier from pancreatic cancer. There would have been scores of women on heavenly clouds queuing up for a heavenly dance with him, but Fi would've flashed her smile,

The Time Of My Life

wiggled her way through and got stuck into the Dirty Dancing routine. Go Fi!

Before leaving, I went to freshen up and someone asked me who I was. I told her I was an old college friend who now lived in Belgium and she exclaimed *"Oh you're Barbara! I've heard so much about you!"* I felt amazed that Fi had talked about me to her other friends (probably something to do with Belgian chocolate!) but it brought home just how big Fiona's circle of friends was. Just for a few minutes, there was a little spark of camaraderie between two strangers who had met on such a sad occasion – it was like Fi was spreading the happy vibe even when she wasn't there anymore. Any friend of Fi's would be a friend of mine. When she left, I quickly checked the state of my make-up and said out loud *"Thank God for waterproof mascara."* A voice behind me said how she wished she'd used it, as her 'cunning plan' of wearing normal mascara in order to stop herself from crying had failed miserably. This sounded exactly like something Fi would say. We chatted for a few seconds before parting, offering consoling half-smiles. There's that camaraderie again. It's the Fi effect.

At the end of the Order of Service, Fi had included an excerpt from 'Farewell My Friend' by Rabindranath Tagore. It was her way of saying goodbye and telling us what she wanted us to do.

> *"At every turning of my life I came across good friends, friends who stood by me even when the time raced me by. Farewell, farewell my friends, I smile and bid you goodbye. No, shed no tears for I need them not, all I need is your smile. If you feel sad do think of me for that's what I'll like. When you live in the hearts of those you love, remember, then you never die."*

H I A O

Fi had requested that we should not send flowers but if we wished to make a donation, to split it between Cancer Research UK and Walk the Walk. Online donations together with cheques and church contributions raised around £10,000.

3

Young Guns

The year was 1986. Wham! had announced they were no more and George Michael was going solo. It was an end of an era too for Fiona McIntosh who was in her final year at Sir John Lawes School, a state run secondary school in Harpenden, Hertfordshire. Daughter of Jean and John, elder sister to Iain, she was Head Girl and enjoyed participating in the life of the school. She kept newspaper clippings of charity events, amateur dramatic productions and articles on pupils she knew. Two such pupils were her best friend Emma along with her boyfriend Iain Sinnott. Fiona also had a boyfriend whom she had met at a party when she was sixteen. On the back of her sixth form photograph are inscriptions, jokes and well wishes from her peers. There are comments about her boyfriend Simon being 'the right one' and good luck messages with 'those horrible kids', a reference to her intention to become a primary school teacher. In the Autumn Term, she would be going it alone at Trent Polytechnic in Nottingham to study for four years on a B.Ed (Hons) Primary Generalist course. She took with her a poster of George Michael to hang in her room on campus. To sit on her bed was a threadbare teddy that used to belong to her grandmother who had given it to her mum and who now had passed it on to her, and a cuddly soft toy puppy dog with big eyes called Sad Sam from her brother.

I didn't catch sight of her sixth form photo until years after we met. It made me giggle to compare myself at the same time, two hundred and fifty miles away, at a sixth form college in Stockton-on-Tees where, instead of a uniform, we had a smoking room. There were no such thing as class photographs and should any peers wish to offer up best wishes for the future, the comments would have been rather unsavoury. As students we didn't raise money for charity very often, we would more likely wash cars in the car park in order to raise extra cash for a drink at the pub at lunchtime. If you were called Head Girl, it meant something entirely different. I too would be attending Trent Polytechnic that coming September, armed with a serious Lloyd Cole fixation (which incidentally and rather disturbingly has never left me) and a burning desire to leave home and unburden myself of my virginity, rather than to actually become a primary school teacher. My possessions included a poster of The Cure, a box of chocolate cakes made by my mum and a small but well-read collection of French literature.

We were miles apart, geographically and demographically, but destiny brought us together on Clifton Campus where we had been assigned a room each along with eight other girls and ten boys in a blissfully basic but beautifully adequate accommodation building known as S Block. That first year was an intense time where friendships were formed quickly and strong bonds were created due to the close proximity of teenagers thrust together, sharing the same experience away from home and grappling to assert their independence. The first thing that struck me about Fiona was her self-confidence.

She was amazingly sociable (an attribute quite alien to me) and I watched agog as she talked casually to gorgeous guys, people in the refectory, anyone who sat next to her, in fact anyone in general! We got on really well, no doubt thanks to her sociability, and I was totally smitten with her southern accent. I was also mesmerised by her smile. I hadn't met many people with straight, white teeth. I realised I wasn't very free with my smile due to the state of my teeth, but a smile, as I learned from Fi, goes a long way. She was the type of person I had been aching to meet: easy going, laughed a lot, not shy, game for anything and someone who seemed to have first hand knowledge of 'it'. We formed a little gang with two other like-minded S Block girls, sharing clothes, gossip and cigarettes as we danced endlessly to 'Don't Leave Me This Way' by the Communards. Soon Fiona became Fi after a day when, with nothing in particular to do, we decided to paint pictures of all the S Block girls in the style of an infant school child. I don't think the intention was actually to replicate the artistic efforts of a seven year old but the end result looked exactly that. We labelled each painting with nicknames. First I was 'Lloyd', which just didn't seem right, and then, avoiding the obvious 'Babs', chose 'Bobs' just to be different. Needless to say it didn't really catch on except with Fi. As the first term went by, Fi was also referred to at times as Flirty Fi. To Fi, she was merely doing what comes naturally and loved nothing more than spending time with people, even better if they were male and good-looking. To the rest of us who had to rehearse what we were going to say to the opposite sex for fear of staring blankly or becoming a gibbering wreck, this behaviour seemed a blatant invitation to be more than a platonic, casual acquaintance. Given the fact that she had a boyfriend at the University of Leicester this was, at first, seen as rather naughty. We had met Simon, along with his housemates Jon, Dave and

Julian, when they had visited S Block for her birthday. We all thought Simon was lovely, and that she should be a little subtler in her flirting. What we failed to recognise was that the flirtatious behaviour actually was part of her nature, a way of making people feel at ease with her, of lightening a situation and of sending out a friendly vibe. She and Simon were quite a well-established item, unlike the rest of us in our primitive or non-existent relationships. They knew each other very well and certainly knew each other's intentions. It was us that misread her flirty behaviour and Fi put us straight on such matters. She knew what she was doing. I asked my computer Thesaurus to expand on the word 'flirtatious' and up popped 'playful, engaging, enticing, coy'. It's Fi exactly.

But that's not to say she didn't partake in a bit of rumpy-pumpy given half the chance.

Fuelled by a trip to the cinema where we witnessed, our jaws open and dribbling slightly, a 20ft naked Rob Lowe and a strategically placed fridge door in 'About Last Night', I began to feel a little left out of the rumpy-pumpy game. Whereas I could merely wonder impatiently as to whether I would ever find myself picking my underwear off some bloke's floor like Demi Moore tiptoeing round a sleeping hunk, Fi made a mental note that she really should try re-enacting the bathroom scene. Only a true friend would listen patiently as I droned on about getting onto the first rung of the 'sex' ladder, and only a true expert like Fi could help. Did she know of any good-looking blokes willing to help me out? Of course she did! For not the first matchmaking time in her life, she enlisted one of Simon's mates for a good-natured cherry-popping encounter. If it hadn't been for Fi's little 'bunk-up the ladder' I would have been wandering aimlessly through a virgin wilderness for years. With her intervention, my confidence improved and I was free to focus on finding Mr Right (which I did, eventually).

For that, Fi has my eternal gratitude.

When it wasn't about sex, it was about alcohol. The Trent Bridge Inn, or TBI as it was known, offered a sophisticated array of cocktails and rather nifty glasses which always made their way into our handbags at the end of the session, I suspect rather less subtly than we imagined at the time. It was here that we learned the valuable life lesson that although cocktails tasted yummy, they will render you paralysed when it's time to go to the toilet. If you are ordering an Elmer Fudpucker but in fact you find you have just swore at the barman, then it's time for a lime and soda. When one eye shuts of its own accord, then it's time to go home. Happy hour cocktails often started off the evening but never led to anything but an early night and a hangover that made your hair hurt.

Alternatives to cocktails were the 'make-your-own' evenings spent in my room in S Block. We would return from the off-licence with cheap vodka, Happy Shopper orange juice and a packet of Marlboro. Bang on some music and we were ready. In the era where music video reigned supreme, we often dramatised our own productions to our favourite tracks. During a particularly protracted rehearsal to 'Sometimes' by Erasure, the repetitive effect of re-enacting the first verse culminated in slipping on the rug and dive-bombing whoever was posing glamorously with a Marlboro on my bed, giggling till we ached.

Of course there was also the joys of the Student Union Bar with its discount prices and lager that seemed to find its natural habitat sloshing about on the floor by the end of the night. It was there that we saw such music greats as Deacon Blue, It Bites and the lesser-known Edward and the Deckchairs. We also frequented a bundle of favourite pubs in the city centre and the best evenings would be those ending with a dance. Choice venues were either the Irish Club (cosy) or Rock City (the ultimate) or maybe Ritzys (for a change). With a kebab or pizza to finish and a mad dash for the campus bus or taxi queue we spent our time very, very happily, with the innocence and exuberance of youth running through our veins (along with rather high levels of alcohol).

In between hangover management and crumpled duvets, we actually attended lectures and went on teaching practices, as well as working in school one day a week. Our psychology lecturer was an Anthony Hopkins lookalike who left us with 'older man' fantasies while he tried to teach us about child development and the influence of physical, mental and emotional growth on cognitive progression. He made it all sound very sexy and, like Hopkins, was extremely watchable. Our philosophy lecturer on the other hand, was not so charming. He was rumoured (probably entirely scurrilously) to be slightly inebriated during Friday afternoon's double session, but we didn't mind the irony since that was the state we would be in only hours after his lecture. Fi and I, and the rest of the gang of four, often worked on assignments together, to share the workload and increase the probability of getting the books out of the library before anyone else. If you were clever it also had a bonus effect of getting a better grade: my essay on the value of play in learning got me a 'C' but by the time Fi had worked on it, she got a 'B+' for hers. Fi always strived to do her best so that she could achieve her full teacher potential. Proud of training to be a teacher she stuck the letters of the alphabet round her room, when the rest of us thought this was naff. But that was Fi. She did what she wanted regardless of what people thought. She actually enjoyed being with the kids and being a good teacher. This was obvious when we all had a week in Anglesey, camping with primary school children from mainstream and special schools. Allergic to tents and the outdoors in general, I suffered dreadfully during the week and spent most of my time avoiding sunlight, children and anything referred to as 'fun'. Off went Fi to organise teaching activities and socialise in the pub at the end of the day. From her photos, most of which were of the children painting or playing, she obviously enjoyed the experience, unlike me, who from other photographs look like I've been kidnapped with no hope of a ransom coming through.

Fi and I would spend time with the others from S Block or just the two of us doing silly, girly things together ('silly' and 'girly' were new experiences for me). Whenever I hear 'Caravan of Love' by the Housemartins I am taken back to my room in S Block and the hours Fi and I spent using my latest gadget of a double tape deck and various tape recorders trying to create our own version. Endless corpsing occurred especially when it came to singing our 'hilariously' incorrect version that included the line 'we'll be living in a world of peas'. Laboriously we counted out and sang the 'aahs', doing harmonies and backing vocals before taking turns to sing the lead. Using the two decks to overlap our voices became rather complicated and the final result was a complete disaster. But I don't think I have ever laughed so much over a sustained period, without the aid of alcohol, before or since.

When the time came to move off campus in September 1987, my assumption (and Fi's) was that our gang of four would simply find a house with a few of the lads next door (including the one I would end up marrying). I remember there being a bit of a panic trying to find somewhere with enough rooms. When we had one too many housemates for the house we eventually found, then one person had to go somewhere else. No one volunteered. The lads mistakenly seemed to think Fi's flirting would cause problems of countless male admirers sniffing around the house and since we girls couldn't find a house for four, and Fi was friends with so many more people, she would easily be able to find a house with others. This decision was rather strange when I look back, made effectively by the lads without consultation with us, let alone Fi. There was little discussion about it due to the urgency of bagging accommodation. I remember having to break the news to Fi, and us both being in tears. I think everyone assumed that as she was so sociable and confident that it wouldn't really bother her. But just because you smile all the time doesn't mean you don't feel insecure or upset. She never showed it to the others, she made it look like water off a duck's back. Putting on a brave face was a skill she was very good at. The decision may have been due to the selfish ignorance of youth and a distinct lack of girl power, but it didn't make me feel very good and when I got older I apologised persistently to her for this time. Of course she forgave me.

So we ended up living apart in our second year, although both in houses in West Bridgford, a suburb in between the city centre and the campus. We hadn't fallen out, but we were obviously spending the majority of our time with other friends. Love lives, teaching practices, assignments, washing-up rotas and other important matters took up most of our time. We still met up in clubs of course and the friendship was always still there, just more diluted as we moved in different circles of friends.

Like me, Fi kept a diary during our time at Trent, documenting events of the day, imparting any gossip and worries, and then hiding them away under our beds. Fi had been writing a diary since 1981, which must mean that she actually had something to report on (she had a love life for a start). My early attempts at journal writing inform the reader that I breakfasted on Ready Brek and lemon barley water, went to school, came home, watched telly and went to bed. I had to wait until 1986 before anything remotely interesting would be worth writing down. We both ceremoniously burned all our diaries after graduation, perhaps to erase the cringing agonies of our youth and just remember the good bits manually. Selective memory is a wonderful thing. But Fi kept one diary from her time at polytechnic, from 1989, the third and penultimate year of our degree course.

Her lovely boyfriend Simon had already graduated from his B.Sc Engineering course in 1988. In 1989, he was living at home with his parents in Harpenden and whilst looking for a job he worked in a local pub. When he finally got a job, he carried on working at the pub at weekends. Up to this point, their relationship had not been constant. They had been 'on a break' but now were seriously back together. Like an early Bridget Jones (but one who happens to be training to be a teacher and sporting dodgy 80's fashion) the main focus in Fi's diary is her love life. No longer a 'Singleton', and yet to join the ranks of the 'Smug Marrieds', Fi could be classified as a different breed of female - an 'ACE', if you like, meaning 'All Consuming Engaged'. But she also took a keen interest in other people's love lives and had a recurring obsession with how tedious her philosophy lectures were, amongst other things.

Over to you Fi. I know you've been trying to get a word in.

4

Good Life

From these entries, you will discover the student teacher Fi. She is careful with her money. She is studious and keen to do well on her final Teaching Practice. She knows a lot of people and takes notice of their opinions and actions. Swearing forms a natural part of her vocabulary. She gets drunk regularly on extremely cheap drinks. She thinks that 'cut glass' is a design classic. She thinks about her engagement ring a lot.

Life at Trent Poly was one thing, at home in Harpenden was another. The former was fun and exciting, but lacking the much-desired presence of her now-fiancé Simon. The latter was more routine and often frustrating, as the promise of spending time with Simon wasn't quite as she imagined. At this point I was in a relationship with the aforementioned S-Block-boy-who-I-would-end-up-marrying, called Iain, who was away on a work placement as part of his degree course. As a note to the reader, Fi's best friend Emma was still with her sixth form boyfriend, also called Iain (Sinnott). To confuse matters further, Fi also mentions her brother, also called Iain. Hopefully the three will not be confused as the same person. That would be just bizarre. I'm all for the unconventional, but that would be too weird.

The diary is also a great insight into teacher training in the late 1980's. We had to make everything we used in school including games, cards and books for children to work in. No photocopied worksheets, no commercial resources. It's amazing what we did with a *Banda machine, sticky-back plastic and a pair of scissors. Mobile phones were in their infancy and not for the likes of poor students, so communication methods consisted of going to a phone box armed with a bag full of coins unless your student accommodation was luxurious enough to house a phone and you could afford the high charges laid on by landlords. An old fashioned system involving paper, envelopes and something called postage stamps was the most common way of communicating over distances but this had an irritating time-delay aspect which mingled with a sense of anticipation, euphoria or plain disappointment.

*A spirit duplicator. Look it up on Wikipedia. Inhaling recommended.

HIAO

1989 BT (Before Texts LOL)
Sunday 1 January
Well, I hope this year will be better than the last eh? All the prospective in-laws coming over today! I went out last night and saw in the year with Si, Em and Iain, Paul and Nichola. Em and Iain bought us an engagement pressie – some lovely glasses. I spent the night at Si's last night. Today was OK really. Si and I went to the Engineer at 4pm until 10pm! Riveting it was. Got back here and had a cry on his shoulder. Funny thing is I don't know why I cried either. He almost cried too and assured me he loved me and nothing would come between us. I do love him so much but sometimes I can be cruel. I really didn't feel like socializing and it looked like I was bossing him about but I told him if he wanted to stay at the pub I didn't mind. HE'S QUIT SMOKING! For now at least.

Monday 2 January
I think the root of my problems is that I want to spend time just Si and I together without going out just so we can talk. We've decided on 1 April 1991 as our date if we can book the church! Today Si came over at 11.30am and stayed for a while. He came back after lunch and we said bye to Nan (as she left today) and went to Habitat. We bought some champagne glasses in the 'cut glass' style. They're flute ones. Went to Si's this arvo. This evening he had to work, as Lee was ill. Iain, Em and I went down there too. Stayed till 11.30pm and I got very merry!! Came back here for Chinese and Si left at midnight. He's so cute I really do love him so very much! I'll miss him even if I shall see him Friday.

Tuesday 3 January
Back to wonderful Trent today. Theresa's Xmas pressie was Body Shop stuff. A good £6 worth! She said we can pay £25

rent from now on! Oh and the oven is broken therefore no hot meals till the new one arrives on Friday. Sue had brought me some flowers and written congratulations by them. We've also got Meche the one-eyed cat with us now! Jon rang to confirm Friday so I've got to fetch him at work at 5pm. I wonder what Simon did tonight? Did he think of me and is he missing me?

Wednesday 4 January
Back to Poly. Got up at bloody 8am and went to Poly only to find the sodding lecture wasn't till 10am so I came back again. Nichola has fucking blabbed to everyone that I'm engaged. I saw Karen but she never said a word to me all morning. Hels came over and said congratulations and thanks for the letter! Theresa went and bought me a card – same as Iain and Em's. It was bliss driving to Poly! Mum booked the wedding for 30 March 1991. Rector Neil says the Saturday is OK with him.

Thursday 5 January
I must tell Si about the 30 March 1991 wedding option instead of Monday 1 April 1991. It would give us a longer honeymoon and we'd be married two days earlier!!! And before the new tax year!! Had an exhausting day at Poly. I was however surprised to realize I had done the work covered in sociology when I summarized a book in November! Got sarky comments from a few folk about being engaged. Si rang tonight. He was really short on the phone. He said he couldn't afford to come up on 21 January to go to Peterborough. Charming. He even sounds keener to see Jon than me. Great. I won't see him for ages after Sue's birthday what with his hols and all. Went to Lynne and Claire's at 9.30pm and stayed till 12.30am and had a really good chin wag with them. If Si can't afford to come and see me how can he afford to go boozing most nights?!

Friday 6 January
Home today. Picked Jon up at 5.30pm after much hassle trying to find him. Got on M1 and did 90mph. Got home at 7pm. Had tea at Simon's. Had a mini ruck about him not coming to see me in Nottingham. I got to the point where I said that what was the point of being engaged when we only see each other three days a month! So he said he'd come up on 21 January!! HE'S STARTED SMOKING THE BASTARD! It made me so mad.

Sunday 8 January
Got up 11.30am. Si and Jon went for drinks with Dad in the Old Bell. I've hardly been home all weekend. I feel guilty about it really. Mum said she'd book the Moat tomorrow. We had a lovely meal at lunchtime then went to Susan and Bill's and then briefly back to mine and then to Simon's before getting the train to Nottingham. I can't wait to see Si in twelve days. I miss him so much at times it's unreal. I wonder if he's the same about me or if he knows how much I love him and miss him. Got to Nottingham at 10pm.

Tuesday 10 January
Philosophy! Wow!! What a waste of time. Barbara asked about the engagement and where was the ring etc. She said Dave had rung her so she'd told him about it too. Got home about 10.30am. I did some psychology and philosophy this afternoon. Mum rang tonight. She's booked the reception and is going to Habitat tomorrow. Dad's got a new job – director of something, therefore he'll be travelling and therefore I can't have the car for TP *(teaching practice)*. SHIT that means for six weeks I'll be up at 6.30am, if not earlier, to get a crappy bus at 7.15am to get to school for 8.15am.

Monday 13 January

School! My sciatica is back and really painful. What a day. I overpaid my bus fare on those shitty green buses *(green buses required the correct change as they had no conductor on board to take your fare, as on the blue buses)*. Then I had a migraine at lunchtime right through till I got home. I had to go straight to bed. School was great. I really enjoyed myself. I'm going in for a half day next Friday. Lots of kids in my class have emotional problems that affect their behaviour. Got letter from Mum. Iain's *(Fi's brother)* car's broken so guess whose he's borrowing! Fucking brilliant.

Saturday 14 January

Got a phone call from Jon. Dave rang him and asked to come to Nottingham because Lorraine has chucked him, as she doesn't want to be in a serious relationship. Even though I didn't know her I was pretty shocked and felt for Dave. Still felt dodgy so did no work all day. Went for a drink with Jon and Dave. It was lovely seeing Dave again. I've invited him up for next Saturday. We had a good laugh about the old days and various funny escapades. My headache has moved round to a dull ache at the back. Vision rather impaired all day.

Monday 16 January

I must go to the opticians this afternoon and get a check up. Today I really MUST start my sociology. Had rather inactive workday. Yes, I did sod all. Dave rang me tonight and asked me to look out accommodation in Nottingham for him because he's leaving Leicester! He said he tried to phone Bobs but she was at Iain's!! Bloody hell!! Made popcorn in the wok.

Tuesday 17 January

Loads more people asked me today if I was engaged. I wish I

had my ring now! Today at 3.30pm ish Simon and I will have been engaged three weeks! Still no fucking post. I haven't had any for bloody ages! I started my sociology assignment today!! I spent ages in the library too! Sue and I made pizza for tea. Yummy it was too.

Wednesday 18 January
Today, well I did fuck all really. I had psychology, what a laugh. Barbara and I gossiped about Dave etc. I went back to hers after at 1.30pm, stayed for lunch and generally had a good chat from then until 6.30pm! It was nice really. Got back here and went to Lynne and Claire's. We had lasagne and cheesecake for tea. Sue had this ace peach wine from Marks and Spencer. Lovely time we had. No post again.

Thursday 19 January
Yes, no post. Story of my bloody week! Nearly fell asleep in sociology today. Collected my resources *(paper/card etc to use on teaching practice)*. Had a word with JP *(course leader)* about 'X' and her sudden weight loss. He was glad we'd brought it to his attention and I only hope she never finds out it was us who said anything. It's only because we'd hate anything to happen to her that we're showing an interest. Did an hour's work in the library. Had computers till 4pm. Went out with Theresa and the lads tonight. Si rang. He's coming up by train therefore arriving here at <u>9pm</u>. Still, at least he will be here.

Friday 20 January
My baby is coming to stay! I went into school this morning for half a day. No post. In school, M was a total shit and P had a fucking tantrum on me! *(Children's initials used, rather than names.)* I worked with half the class and I almost felt

put in at the deep end because I didn't know all of Shirley's *(class teacher)* rules etc. Dave rang at 2.30pm. He's phoned Si and they arranged to meet in town! Cheers Si! Dave phoned Barbara again last night. I bet that pleased Iain!!

Saturday 21 January
Si and I had a good laugh down the TBI last night. We had a good chat and quite a bit to drink! Woke up this morning at 8am! What a way to be woken up too! Had a shower and went into town. Met Dave. Met Jon in Yates's at 2pm. I swear I give up ever having Si to myself, bar in bed. Em rang from Peterborough. Had a good gossip. Went to the Irish tonight. Felt drunk then after a while felt claustrophobic and I had a sore throat so was ready to go at midnight. Came back here at 1.30am. Si was IMPRESSED by the basque!

Sunday 22 January
Dave stayed for lunch and he and Si went off to Sneinton to look at houses. Yes, I have got a stinking cold probably due to being caught in the rain on Saturday. Si and I had a shower together and that was nice. Lunch was ace, including champagne! Si and Dave left on 7pm train. Nearly missed it and I didn't get the chance to kiss Si goodbye at the station in the rush! Sue has invited Dave to stay next weekend for her birthday. Am I selfish? Now I know how Si felt when I went to Leicester and we were always with a crowd.

Monday 23 January
Took a day off Poly as I feel lousy. I can't believe of the whole weekend I saw Si to myself from 9.15pm Friday until 10am Saturday, then 2am Sunday until 10.30am Sunday. Shit I must be getting possessive. What a role reversal to 1987. I think Barbara had Iain all to herself so why doesn't it work like that

for Si and me? I really could've cried coming home on the bus last night. Did bugger all work. Si rang. He apologised for not saying a proper goodbye yesterday. Went to get more Trinovum *(contraceptive pill)* and they've redesigned the packet. Very trendy, plus also in each packet there's a free pill envelope to keep them in!

Wednesday 25 January
Si picks up the ring today. Mum will have got her letter today! I'm going in to psychology today! What joys!! No fucking post again! I had a boring hour and a half psychology lecture and then did three hours in the library. Came home and did a bit more. Lynne and Claire came round for tea tonight. Dave wrote Bobs and said he's coming to Nottingham to Lenton and Jon's. Bobs didn't really want to chat. She was more interested in Louise.

Thursday 26 January
Piss awful day. NO POST. My first lecture ended at 11.30am therefore had a three and a half hour wait till IT. That only lasted half an hour. Then I got fucking stuck on my sociology assignment and to cap it all Si rings and said he went to fetch my ring yesterday and guess what, it's STILL at HQ being done!! It may be here Saturday. I told him to get on the phone tomorrow and demand that it be here by Saturday or else cancel it. I can't believe they'd do that to an engagement ring. Rock City was a laugh! Saw loads of peeps we knew. Jon and Hels are going great. I'm dead pleased for them. Ah!

Friday 3 February
Had an ACE DAY in school. I really enjoyed myself with the kids. Boy was I surprised! I've got the letter 'C' for my topic. Should be fun – clowns, computers etc. Got home at 1.30pm. Fell asleep! Went to video shop and got '9 ½ weeks' and

'Shag'. I also bought Sue 1.5 litres of wine and Si six cans of bitter. He arrived at 7pm and gave me my ring. It's even nicer than I remember and it fits. It's quite heavy to wear and sticks up quite a lot so I catch it on jumpers etc. Si's car is gorgeous. I want one! It's got stereo etc. Brill. Got arseholed tonight.

Saturday 4 February
Si has quit smoking!!! I got woken up in a rather interesting fashion. Simon is certainly getting adventurous in his old age!!! Had a shower and went to Asda. Si drove us in his Metro. It's a really smooth car, really lovely. Went and visited Hels in the afternoon. Jon arrived there for tea! Had an ace chicken kiev for tea then went into town. Me and Hels, Jon, Penny, Cheryl and Adrian. Went to Fellows. Who should be there but Lesley, Jo, Mark *(Hels' ex)* and girlfriend! I really admired Hels' courage especially when they came to the Irish too. Hels and Jon got pissed!

Tuesday 7 February
Bloody philosophy again. Lesley saw my ring in the lecture and was highly critical, Mark was gobsmacked... not bad for a bloke's reaction. Nichola thought it was 'cute', Karen said 'um' and Barbara raved about how gorgeous it was. It felt bloody strange walking into Poly with a 'ring' on!!! Wonder how Jon and Hels got on tonight.

Tuesday 14 February
No post when I left this morning. Philosophy was dead boring so I wrote a letter to Simon. Got home and Sue had bought me flowers! Si had sent two Valentine cards and they were both ace. He said forever seems a long time but it's not too long for him! Ah. Had a homemade Chinese meal for tea. Rather nice. Tried to ring Simon but they were all out.

Thursday 2 March
Iain and Emma have got here! They put in an offer for the flat and by the sounds of it, it's theirs. Sociology revision and IT today. Didn't go to sociology because I heard that my philosophy had to be in tomorrow!! Shit. Mass panic. I sat in the library and worked my arse off till 2pm. Went to IT. Nich gave me a card. Si arrived at 7pm. Went to Sunset And Vine then Rock City. Ace night. Saw John B, Phil, Rav etc.

Friday 3 March
MY 21ST BIRTHDAY! Decided to wear my beige skirt/black skirt and my new top for the meal out tonight. Got up 10am. Opened my cards. I even got one from Barbara, shock surprise! Vanessa and Paul got me some Thornton's chocolates; Theresa and Sue got me my all time favourite piccie! MEGA. Went into town. Si bought me a hat and a really gorgeous necklace. £60 from Samuels no less! Had a ruck with Jon about his attitude about Helen and how they couldn't be separated. Iain and Em arrived at 8.20pm. Went into town. Meal was excellent. Got well pissed. Got to bed at 2am.

Monday 13 March
Got up at 10am. I had all good intentions of doing loads of work BUT no! I washed Em's blouse and ironed it. I chose my fourth year options. Watched Neighbours. Made some phone calls and then tidied out my desk! Great! NOW I feel really guilty. I could have done my PE assignment, but the motivation wasn't there. Went to Em's tonight. Watched 'Three Men and a Baby'. Si felt guilty for not being able to take me to the station and promised to take me for a meal at Easter to stop his guilt! Ah bless him. I do love him.

Good Life

Tuesday 14 March
MUST DO SOME BLOODY WORK. NO LATE NIGHT OR DAYTIME TV anymore! Only an hour or so allowed until after these bastard exams. Just think, this time next week they'll be over and done with. No post. No assignment results.

Thursday 16 March
No post again. No phone calls either. Went to Poly at 11am. I did my sociology notes and had a tutorial with Maurice, for what it was worth. We left the library at 5pm!! Got some assignments back today. Sociology B-, Psychology C-, IT B- Not bad eh! Sue wasn't happy with C for Sociology and a D+ for Psychology. Very unusual for her to ever get a D+. She was really pissed off with it all day. She's never had a D before. I've had four or so!! So far this year I've had three B- 's. Philosophy will counteract all that. I just have to do ace in IT and PE assignments now and get at least a C for my exams.

Saturday 18 March
Irish tonight. Meet at TBI at 8.30pm. That's £10, £1.50 Irish, £1 taxi. Guess who phoned at 10.30am? My baby! Ah love him. He'd spoken to Dave who persuaded him to come to Nottingham! So Si will be up this afternoon. Sue and I went into town and bought some Body Shop stuff. Came back and did some philosophy and Si arrived at 4pm. It was lovely to see him. We went to TBI for 8.15pm. Barbara, Jon and Hels came too. Had a few in TBI and had a mega night at the Irish. Dave got arseholed! Had a really spicy pizza and got home at 2am. Si and I never got to sleep until 3-4am ish.

Monday 20 March
Doomsday 9.30am-12.30pm! Meeting with Ray G *(tutor)* at 1.30pm. What a knackering day. I was dead nervous. I got

up at 7am to check notes then back to bed until 8am. Got to Poly and had half an hour to wait until the exam. Went for a pee then into exam. At first my heart was pounding, then looking at questions, sociology and psychology were a gift. I ballsed up philosophy but as long as I passed I don't care. The three hours went dead fast. Sue and I pigged out on a cream bun and watched a video this afternoon. Went to town at 8pm. Got absolutely rat arsed. I could hardly walk!! Had a mega evening – all for £2.80!! Drinks dead cheap for triples. Committed a sin: two fags tonight. Si rang tonight love him!

So that was the Spring Term. Doesn't time fly for an ACE?! It was a 'shock surprise' for me too when Fi mentioned that I sent her a 21st birthday card. I don't remember doing that. I don't even remember my own 21st birthday. It passed without celebration I think. Either that or it was that time I got so drunk I... No, I won't mention that.

After the Easter holidays, the Summer Term was going to be our Final Teaching Practice. This terrified me, as it did Fi, but for different reasons. Fi was anxious and nervous and keen to do her absolute best. She worried that she wouldn't be a good teacher. I, on the other hand felt that there was no way I should be let loose on society's offspring at this stage of my training without causing some sort of mental scarring. It wasn't that I was a danger to children it was more that my philosophical, non-conformist attitude meant I would be inclined to have creativity lessons all day long involving large tins of paint, empty cereal boxes and Sellotape. With a game of non-stop rounders after lunch.

Wednesday 22 March

Got up at noon. I couldn't be bothered to get up any earlier. Don't get me wrong, I love spending time at home but everyone here has something to do and I'm bored. Yes, I've got TP to plan, books to make and two assignments to write but apart from that I'm doing fuck all that's of any fun for the next two weeks. Simon was working (surprise, surprise) and is on Saturday too. I went out, just Em and myself, for drinks tonight. A whip-a-gram came into the pub! Very slaggy. I visited Si at closing time but when he asked why I was pissed off I said I was bored. He said everyone went through it after Poly term ends and to stop feeling sorry for myself!! Thanx. I've got time off and fuck all to spend it with.

Thursday 30 March

In two years time I shall be married! What a thought! Mrs Fiona Crompton. Today was a beautiful day. It was quite hot. I took Charlie *(the dog)* out for a walk in the park. I helped Dad to bath him. I went round to see Simon at 5.30pm and saw him for about an hour before I went babysitting. He didn't come with me. It's crazy this holiday. We've either rowed or seen each other for about an hour or two. We've been out once. That was a week ago. I've been out two nights since I've been home, excluding babysitting.

Sunday 9 April

Last night I was so pissed off. I hate that pub. Why do I keep going down when Si is at work, when I just get bored and lonely? Why? Because if I don't, when do I fucking get to see him? Christ it's like having to make an appointment in advance. He works in the day and at night. Christ it was my last fucking night at home in ages and he was fucking working and too busy to want to spend time with me today because of that fucking quiz tonight. We ended up having a massive row with both of us in tears and I just stormed off home. He came round and we talked it out. I said it was because I loved him I was upset. He drove me up to Nottingham. Si left here at 8pm. Yes, he missed his quiz for me. It feels weird to be back. I think Si was as scared as me that we might call it a day about the engagement. Both Mums said, "You are still engaged aren't you?"

Friday 14 April
Sorted out my TP into areas and then began the attack. I wrote my general outline, my cards for Ray *(TP tutor)* then I began to list the activities for each heading. Then it's divide them into curriculum areas and finally write the first week's lesson plans which basically involves the young group and a lot of observations. Simon rang tonight straight after 6pm!! Ah, he's missing me. He said that he wants to take next Friday off work and come to see me Thursday night! I told him I'd written to him and I'd bought him a pressie! Went to see 'Working Girl' at the Odeon. Bloody fabulous it was too.

Saturday 15 April
I actually got some post today. I had an engagement card from the Hays, a refusal letter from Our Price and then a letter from Mum and one from Richie. Went round to see Helen and Jon. Jon is encamped there for the weekend. They were still in bed when we went round. Charming. They did come to the TBI but not into town. Met Dave in the TBI and after leaving Jon and Hels to be sickly, we went to the Irish. Sue and I both pulled on the dance floor! Well embarrassing. Was I a nurse? What a chat up line. I eventually got rid of him and we hastily left before the slow dances. At the FA semi final, Liverpool v Forest, ninety-four people, Liverpool fans, died in the stands from being crushed because too many people were in!

Monday 17 April
Must finish curriculum areas and begin key concepts and vocabulary list. What a day. I went to the bank, housing benefit arrived today and Sue's cheque! BT man came to fix the phone. Sue and I did four hours work on TP. I've still got to finish my curriculum areas and do lesson plans for week one. I phoned school. Shirley *(class teacher)* was in a flap because I hadn't been in yet. I asked to see her Wednesday lunchtime and she suggested I came in Wednesday afternoon! She didn't think it would benefit me talking and discussing at lunchtime! Cheers. Now I'm panicking. Si rang and we were on the phone for ages, I didn't feel I had much to say. I guess I'm tense about TP. Paul S, who I went out with before Si, was at the Liverpool v Forest match on Saturday and is in hospital with internal bleeding because of the crush incident.

Wednesday 19 April
Got up 9.30am went into school at 1pm. I had M, M, R, P and J. What nightmares. P was as ever totally awful and I just can't cope with her. My class is now 28!!! Bloody hell. It's chaos. Even Shirley admits it's bloody hard work. She'd done my Clever Cat idea as a display. She says Ray can believe it's mine! What a laugh. I showed her my plans. I left at 4pm. Got home and spent six hours on TP. I wrote lesson plans, made word banks and topic covers for books!

Thursday 20 April
Exam results out today. I've got a tutorial with Ray. Si is driving up tonight. I must make topic books, Banda sheets, go to SU *(student union)* shop for paper and pens! Tutorial too. Chaos. Lesson plans for next week too. As ever Trent fucks up! The exam results weren't out. Had my tutorial with Ray and he seemed OK about it. I got C- for the psychology

question. Went to Resources *(department)* and made books, did Banda and photocopying. Work tonight. Feel lousy. Si came up at 7pm. It was ace to see him.

Friday 21 April
Got up at 11.30am! Went into town at 2.30pm after watching Dirty Dancing on video. Si bought some talc and I bought a pair of Next earrings. Went to the Irish with Dave, Sue and Si. Got arseholed. It was really hot in there. Had a pizza afterwards. I decided to wear Si out and I succeeded in my attempt! He knows what NO means now! Talk about 'let's fall fast asleep straight away'. I think he was rather surprised.

Saturday 22 April
Got up at 12pm ish due to many subtle comments from Tree *(Theresa)* and Sue. Helped make the fillings and snacks for the party tonight. Dossed this afternoon. The party was OK. The food was great. I got pissed. Si was quiet until he got to know the lads etc. Theresa and Eddie almost got it together but not quite! Jacks – when Si offered her the mattress thing – wondered if he and I slept together! Sue and Tree died laughing.

Sunday 23 April
Got up at 11am and cleaned the debris up. Watched The Waltons and Si and I came back up to bed until 4pm! I fell asleep and he read his book. Ah! I do love him, I really do, he's so cute. Next week is a long weekend because the Monday is May Day. Brill. It felt really weird when Si left. Relaxed tonight in preparation for the dreaded Monday. Mum rang up and Debs is pregnant again. Due in November.

Monday 24 April
The dreaded final TP begins! Well, I got up at 7am. I felt nervous. Mrs S picked me up at 7.45am and I was in school by 8.10am! Brilliant! I spent ALL DAY doing window painting. I observed Shirley doing drama. Very in depth. I got home at 4.30pm and dossed till 5.15pm then I worked from 6pm solidly until 10pm! I made Cuisenaire clowns, lesson plans and bloody hell it takes half an hour per evaluation and reflection! What a joke that is. It makes you feel disinclined to write lesson plans.

Wednesday 26 April
Building my shop today *(for role play in class)* and taking two groups. Going to the pictures tonight. I got visited by Ray. He was very impressed! At least that's something. I came home tonight and cried. I had stacks of work to do and I didn't get home till 6pm. Si rang tonight love 'im. I won't see him until Saturday night.

Thursday 27 April
I worked my arse off last night. Two hanging displays, books and work cards. I've still got to paint the shop inside window. I've got to do a rainbow window and introduce rainbow bibs next week, plus change the colour table. Next week I've been told to plan for two groups and take two groups. Then in week three it's plan for three, take two, week four plan for three groups, take three with Shirley, then in weeks five and six it's ME sole teacher! Fucking hell. Today Sue A *(the Head teacher)* saw my teaching file. I did number and handwriting with a little group. I had playground duty too. Got home at 4.30pm, worked until 7pm, then Sue and I went to see 'Rainman'. It's a really good film.

Tuesday 2 May

TP, week two. A four day week, thank you God. Had a good day. I was really busy all day. Window painting went well, Topic work not bad. Got home at 5.30pm. Saw Barbara on the way home. When I got in I did some work until 8pm then went out with Sue, Dave and Julia. Had a great night. Five shorts and a Britvic 55! What a rebel on a Tuesday night. Thought Si might ring but no. No post today either. Roll on Friday.

Saturday 6 May

I got up at 10am, had a bath, did some washing, went to Asda. Then Sue and I spent the rest of the afternoon cooking and making sarnies for the rest of TP. I tried to phone Si tonight but the phone was engaged. Sue and I downed a bottle of wine before heading off to Helen's, then to the Irish. We met Jon and Dave and Paul in town. Went to Gordon Bennet and the Navigation then onto the Irish. I was quite drunk. Jon and Hels in a world of their own. No post today.

Sunday 7 May

Got up at 10am. Did some more washing. I phoned Simon and did some work. I lay in the sun for a while. It was a beautiful day. It took me an hour to write my records, and then I spent three hours doing my TP prep. Si rang me this afternoon. Oh I do love him so much. I missed him a lot this weekend. It's only eighteen days till I see him again. Dave came round tonight so that was a nice break. Mum rang and we chatted for ages. I told her I was frightened about failing TP.

Monday 8 May

I fancy writing a class poem about a clown then the kids can do pictures around it. What a day. It started well. Then when I took the whole class, chaos ensued. It was awful. I was run ragged and the groups were demanding. After that I felt terrible and a failure. I had to compete with the builder's noise during drama but the session went really well despite it all. Got home at 5pm knackered. Sue had the day off due to a sore throat.

Friday 12 May
I put up my Park display. I took some photos of the displays. I was in charge without Shirley there until 11am. It went really well. The kids were brilliant and the top groupers did some brilliant work. I felt knackered at the end of the day. Shirley told me I was doing very well and I'd made a sound start. Got home and had letters from Richie and Mum. Mum's letting me have the Fiesta up here for two weeks!!! For my last week of TP and the following week! BRILLIANT! I can't believe it. Got two videos out: 'She's Having A Baby' and 'Rita, Sue and Bob Too'.

Thursday 18 May
What a day! It started OK. Shirley and I did a science session then I did a language one. G and G decided to have a punch up! I had no one to help me! Cheers. After dinner Ray came in. Poor Shirley had to keep an eye on Class Six. Anyway, Ray watched my PE session and loved it despite the builder's noise etc. The kids were great. Ray asked me to have an external examiner in (I had a feeling he would because he's fascinated by this school). I cried when I got in and phoned Mum, Si etc. He says he can't find any faults with my teaching! Funny that, because I don't think I am that good.

Saturday 20 May
Got up 9.30am. I had a shower, did some washing and all the washing up downstairs. Sue came down about 11am and

I could tell we were in for a talk. It began with the 'my life is crap, you've got so much i.e. a man, a good TP grade because you're such a perfect teacher and I've got nothing, my career is everything and I'm obviously crap etc.' So me having an external examiner is bugging her, I think she was hoping for one. If it were vice versa I'd be pleased for her not jealous. Had a picnic by the river. Went to the Irish, we both pulled TWICE!

Sunday 21 May
Simon rang at 1am but I wasn't in yet. I sunbathed from 11am till 3pm and consequently burned about 2pm. I look like a panda with white eyes in a red face. My front is more burnt than my back. Did TP prep tonight and Si rang. Dave was there too. Apparently Jon was meant to come round yesterday! Sue apologised today for her outburst at me and said she had been jealous but realised it was crazy and she was proud of me.

Tuesday 23 May
I felt really tired when I got in school. I also felt grouchy because it was so hot. Dance went OK. This lunchtime I worked my arse off to make the colour slides. I got really mad with my maths group because they were pissing around. We wrote a class poem today – something else for me to write up for the wall. I phoned Ray and said yes to the external examiner. Apparently he shouldn't have told me about it yet. No one is going to fail according to Stuart *(a lecturer)*. Sue keeps hoping she'll get an external examiner I think, with the way she keeps hinting to Stuart. Karen and Nick have split up! It was either get engaged or split!!

Thursday 25 May
Up at 6.30am today to catch the bus. Must buy the staffroom some chocolates and Shirley and the children too. Today was

much cooler so the classroom was better. I took the little groups and then PE. Shirley told me to take it easy and enjoy my last week and I could do whatever I wanted i.e. swimming etc. Jon rang tonight!! He said Hels is having an external examiner in! He felt left out because Hels is very busy with TP. Selfish git.

Saturday 27 May
HALF TERM! Si and I went into town. Si bought me a yellow t-shirt and about six tops for him and I bought a Winnie the Pooh t-shirt. Went to Pete's tonight. Jon and Hels decided that they're going to spend the rest of their lives together and proceeded to tell everyone BUT they aren't engaged. I think Hels is just looking for a ring. Got home at 12.30pm. Sue and Dave spent the night together... just TALKING.

Monday 5 June
Back to school. I felt really nervous driving to school. It was really scary. Got to school shaking like a leaf. I didn't do anything until 11am because it was singing! I had the whole class totally alone for an hour without Shirley being there!! I left school at 4pm and was home by 4.20pm!! BRILL. Went to see Dave tonight. Stayed till 11pm. Had a laugh.

Tuesday 6 June
What an awful day. I was seconded by Sue A and ordered to go swimming with the kids! I was given someone else's swimsuit and towel. Charming. I felt absolutely disgusting all day. I had to hurriedly plan a maths lesson for all the middle groupers and get the rest of the class sorted too. As I left school the snotty PGCE student made it clear she wanted a lift so I had to offer her one. I felt that if it had been them, I wouldn't have been offered one. Si rang tonight love him!

I wonder if Sue is having an external examiner in because Theresa sent her a good luck card for tomorrow and Sue is being cagey about it all.

Thursday 9 June
END OF TP. Got into school and felt quite weird as it was my last day. We did some work and then we finished so I could go to see Sue A who gave me my report which was excellent and said if I wanted a reference to ask her and if I chose to stay in Nottingham to ring her for a job!!! I couldn't believe it. I got into the classroom after playtime and burst into tears as they had organised a party. They gave me a scrapbook full of pictures and writing and some of the kids cried too! They gave me cards and a cuddly toy. Malcolm the caretaker bought me a huge bunch of flowers. Shirley took me out to lunch and then it was jelly and a cake after with the kids!! It was incredible. We played some games too. After story came the hardest bit. Saying thanks to Shirley. She bought me the Jonathan Livingston Seagull story. It's about staying the same. She said it was an honour and a pleasure to work with me, and any school or class who gets me will be so lucky! She loved her pressies and phoned me later to thank me for the champagne!! We both cried!! Even Sue A!!!

Monday 12 June
Went into Poly. I had an hour's tutorial with Ray. He said he was most impressed by me, my file and my teaching. Found out today that Sue had had an external examiner last Wednesday. Cheers mate. I thought she had. It felt great to find out through someone else. Well, it's what she wanted so FINE. I got a C- for PE and philosophy assignments. I wrote to Mum. Went to the Test Match *(pub)* tonight.

Good Life

Tuesday 13 June
I was thinking a long way ahead. Si and I could have our first dance at the wedding as 'Endless Love', Lionel Richie or 'We've Only Just Begun', the Carpenters?? Sue and I rushed to Poly and sat through the psychology lecture instead of sociology. Whoops. They keep heaping all this vacation work on us! In Education Common Core they are preparing us for interviews and they told us we are now B.Eds just waiting for our Hons! I reckon I'm on a 2:2. We went into Sue's school and I was well impressed by the classroom. She'd covered every available display space. Mum rang, so did Si.

Wednesday 14 June
Went into school this afternoon and it felt really strange. I felt left out. L and M rushed over to me and it was lovely. Even J and some of the others rushed to give me a hug! Lizzie the NQT is pregnant! So that's it for her! It made me think. I want to work two years before I stop to have a baby.

Saturday 17 June
What a nightmare. I weighed myself. Shit I nearly died. Sue and I went into town at 12pm and looked at wedding dresses. I showed her Emma's. Went to Dave's for a meal and it was lovely. We had a good laugh and watched Quadrophenia on video.

Friday 23 June
END OF THIRD YEAR. Into school today. It was a lovely day. Shirley and I get on so well. I stayed until hometime. I felt really sad saying goodbye to N, L, M and the top groupers. I got home and tidied my room and started packing.

> *That's the Summer Term finished, with only one academic year left of our degree. I too remember*

those Sunday mornings with a hangover and The Waltons. Happy Days. Did you catch Flirty Fi's appearance in those entries? Possessively head over heels in love with Simon, planning when she will stop work and have children, saving money for a big wedding and she STILL makes a note of when she's pulled! ('pulled' refers to someone chatting her up, nothing more, I hasten to add!)

In case you're wondering, I actually managed to pass my teaching practice in a lovely school in West Bridgford, within walking distance from my house so there were no early starts and long bus rides for me. My strategy of simply acting like a teacher seemed to convince the kids to have a jolly, whizzy time and I didn't appear to impede their educational development. I hope.

Most of us went home for the summer holidays, although some students headed off to work lucrative shifts in the local Pork Farms factory. At home, I could stock up on chocolate cakes and get my washing done for free. I would 'sign on' and receive unemployment benefit and do nothing, unlike Fi, as you will discover, who worked hard over the summer. In my defence, although I'm the first to admit to suffering from lazyitis, I did work during term time in a Launderette. It was there that I perfected the ability to iron and fold a shirt in seconds. It is a skill that I carry with me, even today.

So whenever I went back home I would consider it leisure time and go out clubbing at the Kirklevington Country Club, AKA The Kirk, (now sadly demolished and a housing estate) where I would stand shyly, stare sultrily at the Robert Smith lookalikes, dance like Claire Grogan and drink vodka and cokes until I found the nerve to smile at someone. Thinking of what song to have as a first dance at my wedding would be something I would never do. When I finally did marry, our first song wasn't for dancing to but for karaoke, and it was 'Suspicious Minds'. Weddings were very much a theme during Fi's summer, as you will find out. Taking mental notes on dresses, receptions and hen nights was a natural instinct of an ACE.

Thursday 29 June

Blue Arrow rang and I ended up in this shitty canteen job in London Colney Industrial Estate. It was God-awful. Really disgusting. The time really dragged. The worst thing is I have to go back tomorrow at 8.30am. Yuck. I got in at 4pm and went babysitting at 6pm till 11pm. I got £8. Not bad considering that I was broke and I've got £30 cash plus Dad's £50 cheque for 'being a clever girl'.

Sunday 2 July

Nan came to stay. Simon is on a Fun Run this morning. He told me yesterday that he felt like he was only passing time when I am in Nottingham i.e. work, eat, sleep. He has nothing to look forward to whereas when I'm home he looks forward to seeing me at the end of the day. It was really sweet. Mind you I feel more alive in Nottingham and a prisoner in Harpenden without a social life, transport, money and freedom. What a strange life. I just feel confined at home. Did nothing today.

Monday 3 July

What a day. It passed quite quickly really but by God it was tedious. The patients at the hospital just wander around loose!

It's frightening and often difficult to tell the staff from the patients! Some of them are ex-patients. Saw 'Indiana Jones and the Last Crusade'. MEGA.

Wednesday 5 July
Worked really hard today but it was so boring. The kid I work with brought in his tape recorder and I had to endure bloody heavy rock all day. No way tomorrow, I'm taking in my Walkman. Si went ski-ing tonight.

Friday 7 July
Work was crap. I got clocked on for forty hours therefore made £120 for just folding smelly clothes. Brill. I collected Emma after work and we called in at Blue Arrow. They had nothing for me for next week. I got £34 for last week minus £8 tax therefore about £26 put aside to go into Halifax. Got home and had a massive row with Simon because he was working tonight and I didn't know anything about it. I was really mad. I phoned Sue and invited myself up for next Saturday without Simon.

Saturday 8 July
Ruth gets married at 3pm at St Nicholas' with the reception at Sir John Lawes!! Steve and Di get married at 5pm, St John's. Claire got a First, Andy 2:1, Browney 2:1, Farris got a 2:1. Ruth looked like... Ruth. Her dress was very simple. The bridesmaids looked lovely. We went to Steve and Di's and it turned out to be a really nice do. It was strange having a buffet, I wasn't keen on that, but the disco was good. I've now decided that Si and I should go for Billy Joel 'Just The Way You Are'. Stayed at Simon's.

Friday 14 July
Went for an interview about a childminding job in August. Banked my £117 wages from Blue Arrow. If I get this two

weeks and nine days job I'll get £130. Well, it's going to pay for the hols even if I save nothing, unlike Sue who can earn £'s tax-free. She'll have saved £300 already no doubt.

Saturday 15 July
Got up at 9.30am. I left the house at 10.30am only to be met by an hour's slow crawling delay up to Milton Keynes because of a 10 mile cone off of two lanes for fuck all reasons! Got to Sue's at 12.30pm. Went into Leicester, bought some earrings and a top. Went to Sector 5 with Ju, Sue, Dave, Julie. Bloody hot. Despite the quarter bottle of vodka I had, I was so hot I fainted in the club! Embarrassing or what?!

Saturday 22 July
Alison and Peter's wedding, Bristol. Got up bright and early. I wore my blue dress and new jacket and Em's hat. I was still absolutely boiling so I pitied poor Alison and everyone all dressed up. The bridesmaids' dresses were beautiful and all hand made by Brenda. The day was really too hot. We stood around for ages with the photos. The wedding was at 1pm but we left the church about 2.40pm! It was a nice do in a country club but we passed on the evening's barn dance!

Tuesday 1 August
Not the most exciting day, but then on this vacation not many days have been that way. Yes, boredom struck again. I got my photos back, I banked a £50 cheque from Si only to learn I've got £28 to owe Theresa for bills. I walked the dog, did a quick saunter through the village. Emma and I decided we couldn't be bothered with aerobics. Si and I went out for a quiet drink just the two of us. I just feel so listless at the moment. Boredom has zapped any life.

Friday 4 August
Si's parents away for a fortnight. Went to Si's and had dinner there. Stayed in and Iain and Emma came round. Stayed the night, much to Ali's obliviousness.

Tuesday 8 August
Got up at 7.15am and had a shower. I left the house with Si at 8am. First I had met his Nan who came in for the newspaper! Embarrassing. Mind you the car parked outside must have given it away. I had a letter from Sue delivered to Si's house today. She mentioned Rob *(her new boyfriend)* briefly – in other words I've got to ask all the questions. Maybe I won't, that'd shock her. Slept at home tonight.

Monday 14 August
I'm getting my hair permed today at 11am. That's another £18 gone. I was quite nervous what the perm would look like. It's turned out OK. Not as curly as I thought. Si likes it at least, so do Ma and Pa, Kay and Sam. Dave rang Si tonight. I guess Si isn't counting on me going to Nottingham for the stag night. I wonder if Em is planning anything this weekend. My wedding music tape arrived.

Tuesday 15 August
My hair had shrunk by this morning so I washed it and tried to blow dry all the curls back. Oh this is going to be fun. Sue rang me this afternoon especially to talk about Rob. I think Dave may have rung her saying I was peeved at being the last to know. Typical when I'd just sent a letter! I must ask Em if Sue is invited to her wedding because I think she reckons she is. Em has asked me to plan her hen night for 25 August.

Wednesday 16 August
I must get some tie-on L-plates for Em! Em hasn't invited Sue to the wedding. Now all I have to do is tell her! Went to Ann and Keith's at Walton. Their bungalow is great. Saw Debs and Hannah *(Debs' daughter)*. They've both grown but in different ways!! Saw Debs' new house which is lovely too. Debs has invited Si and I to stay, or me if I want a break from being bored. Went to Em's tonight, left at 10.30am. Si needs early nights now as he's leaving for work at 7am so I didn't stay.

Monday 21 August
Oh God, what a shit day. The kids were so indecisive it was unreal. *(Fi had taken a job as a childminder)*. I took them to Verulamium Park. We did mini golf, football, walked, had an ice cream. This arvo we did bugger all. Got home at 6pm. Si came round at 7.30pm. I hardly had time to turn round and catch my breath. Went out with Iain and Em.

Wednesday 23 August
What a piss awful day – I am beginning to regret applying for this shitty job. One kid is always tired and moody whereas the other is trying to assert his independence and is introverted. We went to see the Roger Rabbit film. J wanted to come home 'because I'm tired' half way through. He's obviously used to getting his own way. Never a please or thank you for taking them out. Rang Sue today as I had a letter from her. I felt awful telling her she can't come.

Friday 25 August
Emma's hen night. I felt so depressed when I took a look at myself. I must diet. No sweets, no snacks and more exercise especially tummy and thigh ones. Thank God it rained today so I was able to leave the boys to their own devices. Em's hen

night was great. She had a silly hat to wear and lots of condoms appeared!! There were Em's workmates, relatives and her mum etc. We had a kitty of £100+ and therefore everyone got pissed! No stripper – well the Salvation Army appeared but they were for real. It was a fun, drunken and often-rude evening.

Monday 28 August
Lousy Bank Holiday. I felt really tired and off all day. Mum and I had a massive row and she says it's the Pill making my hormones all confused and me unbearable to live with. I didn't go out with Si to John's and this also led to a row. So I stormed off to bed. Si came back at 10pm to apologise. I ate my slice of humble pie too.

Friday 1 September
Wedding rehearsal tonight. I'm trying to persuade Si to go for a meal with me at the Engineer afterwards. I can't believe that Iain and Em's wedding is a few hours away now. It'll be weird that Emma will now be Mrs Sinnott. The rehearsal went OK. I felt really weird, happy, sad, excited. God knows how Em must feel!

Saturday 2 September
Iain and Emma's wedding, St John's 3pm. Dropped my stuff off at Si's at 9.30am and went to Em's at 10am. I'd woken at 6.30am! Em and I picked up Kirsty and went to the hairdressers. We almost got locked in the car park by key operated bollards but it was a private car park really. Luckily a bloke arrived and we got out. Em was remarkably calm all day. We did our make-up at 1pm, watched the flowers arrive and also Paul with a red rose, pearl brooch and a letter for Em from Iain. Claire arrived at 2pm and it was us bridesmaids who weren't ready when the cars came. It took Claire ages to pin the flowers on the back of my dress. Em looked fabulous. It was really exciting travelling in the big car. Si's eyes nearly popped out when he saw me.

Iain waited nervously for Em who was five minutes late. I felt nervous and emotional. Em had a little cry. Iain boomed out "I WILL" and it was over so quickly. Mum and Liz cried. We had loads of photos taken. Our flowers and headdresses looked fabulous. So did all the lads in top hat and tails and Browney in a kilt! The reception was great. Iain mentioned Si and I's wedding in his speech. All the speeches were good. Had a good laugh at the disco. Iain and Em left in a much-decorated car for the Moat House Bridal Suite. Em and I had a good cry. Si and I stayed and got pissed with Si and Jake. Visited Nan to show her flowers and dress. Went to see Wendy and the pressies and ended up at the airport for a drink with Mr and Mrs Sinnott because their flight was delayed so they rung us.

Monday 4 September
Si said if we weren't already engaged he would have proposed on Saturday because I looked so beautiful. Ah. I've been asked to collect Mr and Mrs Sinnott from the airport when they get back at 7.20am! Si arrived at my house armed with a dozen red roses! I nearly died. The reason was he loved me!!

Wednesday 6 September
Si and I are going to London Zoo today. We arrived at 10.30am and the journey didn't take too long. We saw everything there was to see and my feet were aching by the end of it all. It was a lovely sunny day and I enjoyed myself. We spent ages looking at the monkeys. I had hoped to hold one in a 'Meet the Animals' session but they had a virus and couldn't be brought out. Really good day.

Tuesday 12 September
Going to Debs'. Had a good day. Got there at 11.15am. Had lunch with her and chatted and watched Hannah playing. Went

to Auntie Ann's for a couple of hours then Si and I left at 5pm to encounter rain, thunder and lightning all the way home.

Friday 15 September
Alton Towers today. It pissed down whilst we were trying to get to Alton Towers. The journey took two hours! Through rain, fog, sleet etc. Luckily when we got there it started to brighten up. We got our free tickets and went in. We got soaked on the log flume and rapids but it was a good laugh. We went on all four rollercoasters. We eventually got back at 6pm and went to the Irish and had a few drinks with Dave, Ju, Sue and Rob.

Saturday 16 September
I don't know what to make of Rob. Sue is besotted. Very 'couple' all of a sudden. She and I haven't really had a good gossip at all. It's as if she's built a wall around her and Rob. Went into town but Sue said we should split up and meet later. Went out on a pub crawl tonight. Dave and Si got arseholed. Rob passed out. Dave threw a pint of water over his head. Si was aggro-d tonight.

Sunday 17 September
I can't get over how three months has made strangers of Sue and I or is it because we've both got boyfriends here? It took three hours on the M1 to get home. Ali's 18th meal at Harrow was lovely. I ended up finishing Ali's Irish coffee too.

Friday 22 September
Took Charlie out. Visited Mavis *(a neighbour)* today. I didn't realise how badly ill she was from the radiation therapy. She has to wear a wig nowadays. I read my Times Ed and I also got my Trent Poly Graduate Teacher applications book! Shit, how

to write a CV etc. I guess I ought to draft one up next week in practice. Si came over and we watched 'Cocktail'.

Saturday 23 September
Went to Iain and Emma's at 9pm. Si and Jake came along too. We had lots to drink and watched the wedding video. Si and Jake left but Iain asked Si and I to stay so we did. We slept on the floor in the lounge.

Sunday 24 September
Woke up wondering where I was. I was in a double sleeping bag with Si. I slept well considering I was pissed but Si felt the floor! Had breakfast with Mr and Mrs S and then came back to mine. I showered, changed then we all went out for Dad's birthday meal. I hardly ate anything due to hangover and weight consciousness. Si and I discussed money and the lack of it. I wrote my CV and Liz advised me to visit local schools about jobs. My 21st birthday pressie (a necklace from Si) has broken. I'm well pissed off.

> *And so, Fi's diary comes to the Autumn Term. By this stage, you have some idea of the young Fiona's personality. She is extremely family-orientated and the strong link to Harpenden is obvious. No wonder it would be the place she would settle and have a family of her own. She considers the loyalty of friends important and gets bored easily when she is not able to socialise, chat or communicate with others in some way (even by letter). She's also a bit of a film buff and her love of a good chick flick is resolutely detectable at this stage.*
>
> *This final academic year, was the 'Honours' part of the degree which basically meant not many*

lectures and no teaching practices because students were to write and research a dissertation about their area of educational interest. For those eager to get into a classroom it felt a bit like killing time waiting for it all to start. For me it was a case of filling time easily, putting off the inevitable of having to go out into a world of work, responsibility and mortgages. I was frankly in my element, writing 10,000 words on the importance of creativity to a child's development and intelligence. I proudly gave my dissertation the title 'Sticky Fingers', much to my tutor's dismay.

Sunday 1 October
Back to Poly. Had lunch at home. Went to see Mavis to say goodbye. I went round to Si's to say bye to Liz, Rog and Co. It was quite sad. I almost cried as Si and I left my house. Got to Nottingham at 5.30pm and unpacked. Poly seems ages away yet. Went for a drink with Jon and Dave. Got in at 11pm. Sue has decided to live in sin next year with Rob in Nottingham, but not here in Portland Road!

Monday 2 October
The start of the fourth year and the downhill path to the end of student life, whilst trekking the uphill path to final exams, jobs and the beginning of my life's career! Well, registration was very quick and easy. I have an eleven hour timetable: two hours on Monday morning, three hours on Tuesday afternoon, none on Wednesday, two hours on Thursday, four hours on Friday. What a pisser my Friday isn't free. When Si came to pick us up his windscreen got chipped by a stone so he decided to leave tonight. Si and I cried our hearts out this arvo whilst everyone had gone out. I didn't want him to leave. He was

really upset too. Si left straight after tea and I cried buckets again. He rang when he got home.

Tuesday 3 October
Si was so sweet yesterday. I found out how much we really mean to each other. I just love him so much. Yet it sounds corny. I spent two hours before Poly making up my T. Ed file. Today we had two hours Core and two hours National Curriculum. Boring! I have tomorrow off and Thursday because Decision Making is cancelled. Got a video out tonight and Dave came round. I couldn't believe it! I got an A- for my crap IT assignment! Wicked! No D's in last year's marks. All C- or B-.

Saturday 7 October
Didn't bother going into town because it was a miserable looking day. Si rang to tell me to video the 'Young Guns' movie slot on BBC2 tomorrow. It's 'ABOUT LAST NIGHT'!! I can't believe it. Brill. Si, bless him, I can tell he's bored because he's phoned three times this week. Had a lazy day in, watching videos and doing my T.Ed file. Sue is still very quiet and wants to be alone. Went to see 'Dead Poet's Society' tonight.

Sunday 8 October
I must read my IT stuff and finish T.Ed. Went to Julie's and had a good gossip and a look at the wedding photos. Si rang again to say that 'About Last Night' was now on at 10pm! Bless him. Mum rang to tell me about it too. Little bruv was going to video it for me. Oh it was brill. I LOVE that movie... oh MEGA.

Tuesday 10 October
Boring Education Core today. Actually it was quite interesting, it was the National Curriculum that was boring. No post

according to Sue but I know she got a letter from Rob. He arrived with an apple pie he'd made and a huge bunch of flowers! He's totally in love. It's weird. Si is not so demonstrative. Hel and Jon are practically engaged or they will be when Jon asks Hel's dad's permission soon! I feel jealous, like they're stealing my thunder of a summer '91 wedding.

Thursday 12 October
Rob is coming up again tomorrow. I want Si and I to go into town on our own shopping and maybe go out one of the evenings on our own. It would certainly make a change. He's decided he wants to see the Beautiful South at the end of October. What an awful day. Sue and I are barely speaking. I got a phone call from Simon and arranged for us to spend Friday night out on our own. Iain rang me tonight also with the saddest news. Mavis died today. I was devastated. I still can't believe it. I can't believe that she won't be around next door anymore.

Sunday 15 October
Got up at noon! Watched The Waltons. Jon and Helen called round. They invited us out to Ritzy on Tuesday. We were all waiting for the BIG announcement but none was forthcoming. Rob left at 5pm, Si went round to Dave's and brought him round here. They left at 8pm. Si forgot his work gear so I peddled furiously round to Dave's to get it to him before he left Nottingham.

Monday 16 October
I have decided FUCK IT I shall go home this Saturday until next Sunday. I wonder why Sue bothers to stay here. Last night she came in for a chat to sort out our decaying friendship. I think it's her that's changed. She can't accept being tied to me and a

boring life so wants lots of friends etc. She says she doesn't feel she has anything left to say as she knows me so well. She stayed at Sue C's. Dave rang about 'Ritzy at 8pm Tuesday'.

Tuesday 17 October
Sue was in a great mood today. I was just knackered. I didn't get to sleep until 1am as I had Julie round. Went to IT and Education Core. We skived off National Curriculum because the lecturer was fifteen minutes late so we left. Went to Ritzy with Jon and Hels, Dave. Jon and Hels left early. They were OTT and so I just ignored them. Sue was being ultra nice.

Friday 20 October
Iain's 20th *(Fi's brother)*. No post again. Had sociology and sat working in the library from 12pm to 1.30pm. Had two hours of verbal computing! Nightmare. Got in 4pm shattered. I rang Iain. Our house is packed this weekend and Keith and everyone are in my room! Si rang. He didn't realise I was pissed off because he hadn't written.

Saturday 21 October
Off to Harpenden for eight days. Si bless him, came to pick me up in Nottingham! I felt lousy. Really thick with my cold. Iain and Em invited us for dinner. We had a fondue with lots of dips, salad, baked spuds etc. It was all very posh with candles, best china etc. We had a great time. Si and Iain got arseholed and Si and I stayed over. I got four hours sleep because I couldn't breathe.

Sunday 22 October
Went out for little bruv's birthday lunch with Nan, Jo, Iain, Heather, Mum, Dad and me. Had a good nosh up. Went to Si's this arvo. His mum and Nan were very sympathetic to me

and my cold! So was Si. He sent me home with his TV and told me to go to bed and stay in it all day tomorrow. Gosh I'm lucky to have him for life now.

Thursday 26 October
Today I walked Charlie. Read some Hopkins. Riveting stuff that. I've not really done much study at all this week.

Sunday 29 October
Back to Nottingham. I can't believe how time has flown this week. I don't really want to go back but I must. Went to Si's this morning and then to Em's this afternoon. I felt really sad saying goodbye to Simon and I couldn't face the goodbyes to his mum etc so I didn't. Got back here by 8pm. Hels and Jon are engaged as of Wednesday.

Tuesday 31 October
Wonderful Core Education and National Curriculum today. No post today. Saw Helen and the engagement ring. Blue topaz and diamond. Penny confided in me and she's not wearing her ring anymore! Went to a wacky maths lecture by Ken D. I actually enjoyed it. It's weird; I had a dream about my ex's for the past few nights. Maybe it's because I realize that I'm almost married and that part of my life is dead.

Friday 3 November
Only six weeks to go till end of term. Shit! I ought to get some work done!!! I want to grab a bath before we go to Ritzy tonight. My legs think my razor has died. I dyed my hair and it's gone a lovely red brown. Sociology is cancelled Monday. We've got to read a novel instead. IT was short and sweet. Went out tonight and onto Central Park which opened at 11.30pm. It was shit. Met Craig and pal, and John B and pals.

Saturday 4 November
Felt really rough after last night. Dave came round at 11.30am and stayed for lunch and watched a video. I did some sociology in my freezing room. My radiator still doesn't work. Si rang. He's been out on the piss. He doesn't know what to do about jobs. Sue and I got plastered on Tigermilk and went to Dani and Co's bonfire party. I left after an hour to be sick but I wasn't.

Sunday 5 November
Ali's 21st birthday. I was so drunk last night I locked Sue out by accident. We got chatting to these guys in a band called Scarlet Tuesday. They're all Welsh! Slept until 2pm today and then feeling less hung-over I got up and did some work for IT. Wrote to Mum, watched TV and went out for a bike ride.

Wednesday 8 November
Went into town. I got quite a lot of things for Xmas including Si's birthday extra pressie. I treated myself to a lacy bra and knickers. I might buy Mum some too!! Went to see Scarlet Tuesday at the Narrowboat. They were really good. They're playing Yates's on Tuesday too. The freezer was turned off so all our food has to be chucked away.

Friday 10 November
My sweetheart arrives today. A whole weekend just the two of us, and no hassles or am I not counting Dave and probably Jon. Went out to TBI with Sue, Dave and Jon. I didn't feel like drinking much so I didn't really. Saw Jon on the way back. Went to bed about midnight.

Sunday 12 November
Stayed in bed being decadent until 2pm!!! Got up and showered. It was really nice having the house to ourselves. I

never felt so comfortable and loved as I did just lying in bed snuggling with Simon. Sue and Rob came back at 4.30pm. Her parents had let them sleep together in her room at home! Rob stayed the night. Si left at 7pm. He's coming up again on 24 November.

Monday 13 November
Really foggy today. Oh bloody hell. Got to bus stop and waited forty five minutes for a bus. In the end as we were about to give up and go home, Louise gave us a lift! I got a 2:1 for my sociology report on 'Iggie's House' *(a book by Judy Blume)*. I also got a £97.29 housing benefit cheque! I also got a surprise! A cuddly bear in a tin from Simon. I phoned him lunchtime to say thanks. I didn't go into school, it was too foggy. I went into town, got Si's ring and lots of cards plus Theresa's Xmas pressie. Si rang tonight and put me in a state of shock about seriously moving up to Nottingham and living together. I wrote him a long letter saying I don't know what to do. We'd need so much for a house i.e. money, furniture etc. Then bang goes a brill wedding.

Sunday 19 November
I actually began my IT assignment and have more or less done the introduction. I really missed Si this weekend so I sat and watched 'About Last Night' until bedtime. I had a long soak in the tub tonight.

Monday 20 November
Our tutorial this morning was crazy! I'm still no clearer about Action Research. Went into school and actually got all my questionnaires answered! Sue A was great when I asked her to be my reference and she said if I wanted a job in Nottingham to phone her to see if there were any vacancies because she

liked NQT's and she knew me and how well I had done! Si rang tonight, love him.

Tuesday 21 November
Mum is coming to stay. I had two hours IT in which Julie and I made our traffic lights flash with Control Logo. I had Education Core which was really in depth and then one and a half hours of National Curriculum. Mum got here at 5pm. We had a good chinwag and had the casserole she brought up. Vanessa came to dinner too. We got a bottle of wine and 'Buster' out on video. It was weird having Mum to stay. I hadn't seen her for a month so it was really nice.

Thursday 23 November
I MUST begin my IT tonight without fail. Wrong! After Decision Making, Sue and I were in the library until 3.30pm getting books out for our seminar. When we got home I helped her finish off her multi-cultural/action research assignment. Simon phoned me tonight bless him, he's staying over until Monday morning. God, right now I feel so tired and listless. I must get some multi-vitamins.

Saturday 25 November
Finally got into town at 1.30pm. We went everywhere. Finally got in at 5pm. We went out with Jon and Helen tonight. They were all 'darling' this and 'darling' that. Dave and Rachel turned up at 10pm.

Friday 1 December
Last night at Rock City everybody looked so young and it was full of snogging couples. Bunked off sociology today. Went into IT. It's cancelled now until next term. Not bad eh!! Mum's 48th birthday, so phoned her tonight. I forgot to tell

her about my 2:2 predicted grade. If the lecturers' strike over not setting exams goes on next year, we could leave without doing final exams!

Sunday 3 December
Watched 'Rebecca' on video. Si rang and we chatted for ages. Dad rang tonight to say that Debs had a little boy last night at 7pm. He also said he'd pay my Poll Tax whilst I lived at home. No sociology tomorrow so I'm going to the doctor first thing.

Monday 4 December
Got up 7.30am. I queued until 8.30am at the doctors'. I was seen at 9.45am!! Yes I have officially become my mother! I am allergic to cats. He put me on a Beconase nasal spray! I feel much better now and I can breathe! Went to school at 1pm. Shirley gave me a whole load of stuff to do in my NQT year for maths. She's also letting me copy a couple of computer programs. I wish I could get hold of a BBC computer for Xmas to use.

Tuesday 12 December
I went to Poly early to do some photocopying, £2's worth! Sue felt ill so she didn't come into Poly today. Dave and Rachel came over tonight. We've arranged to go to the Irish on Friday and invited the DARLINGS. Had a good chinwag with Barbara today which made a change. No post. Si will no doubt ring me tomorrow. A letter would be too much!

Wednesday 13 December
Hair permed and cut into a bob today. Stuck in hairdressers from 11am till 1.30pm!! My bob is great, my perm is like a bloody Afro. It's just a little too tight.

Good Life

Friday 15 December
Break up for Christmas. Into school all day. Excellent day. Got in at 9am. Shirley gave me a miniature Xmas tree as a pressie. The children gave me a card. The party was hectic. The whole area was taken up with tables and decorated for all the children. Father Christmas came when they were all in the hall. They loved it, especially collecting presents for the class. Brill day. When I got home I had a bath and Si joined me!! Went to the Irish and got in at 2am, having waited ages for a taxi.

Monday 18 December
It sounds awful but I've been wondering why I was so keen to get engaged. Our relationship has become routine now that we're engaged, nothing exciting happens because we're supposed to be saving money. That's a laugh! We've not exactly got a lot to shout about and £100 of that was my non-income contribution. Went to Iain and Emma's tonight. Saw Simon B too. We're going to the Engineer on Xmas Eve.

Friday 22 December
Si's 23rd birthday! I took Chas for a walk and then decided to dye my hair. I thought that ten minutes would be long enough but it's only really come out brown so I'll evaluate it again tomorrow and maybe have another go. Got a massive cold today and so I was hardly able to taste the lovely birthday meal Liz had prepared for Si. He loved his ring and jumper. We didn't go out tonight we ended up just spending time together at each other's houses.

Sunday 24 December
Xmas Eve. Yes I've still got my cold. Came back home at 11am. We're all meeting down the Engineer tonight at 8pm. Iain, bless him, is driving so he's promised us a lift home.

Excellent night. Well pissed, with Barry and Andy and Claire, Pete, Browney, Sinnotts, Farris and Neal and Kathryn. Oh boy it was a laugh! We played drunken pub games. Kathryn and I discussed Clive and his engagement. We all had a good laugh. Si, bless, was adorable.

Monday 25 December
Got up 9.30am. We opened our pressies at 11am from Mum and Dad. Xmas day was terrible. I got bitten by Charlie and Xmas has lost all its magic now. It could have been any day. The best fun I had was watching people open my pressies to them.

Wednesday 27 December
Si and I have been engaged for a year. He brought me some flowers today on his way back from Luton. He promised to take me out for a pizza tonight. Pizzaland was really 'off'. They closed early, didn't have any mushrooms or bread for garlic dishes and the dessert I had was off. The cream was sour. So we didn't pay for my coffee or Si's dessert.

Saturday 30 December
Neither Sue nor I have written to each other. I wonder what she's been up to? No, I don't really. Went to Habitat this morning but didn't buy anything. Saw a nice bed and a nice duvet. I'm now skint. £1.60 in the bank despite my statement saying £52!

Sunday 31 December
Si came over for dinner and we had roast beef. We're all invited to theirs for drinks tomorrow. Had a deep bath and got ready for tonight. Got some booze and went to Iain and Em's at 8.30pm. Si looked rather horny. Paul and Nichola arrived after us. Had a lovely fondue meal and a few laughs. At midnight

we all had champagne which was yucky. Although tonight was nice, it was much more refined than riotous Xmas eve.

Monday 1 January 1990
This is my final year at Poly, my first teaching post and the last time I keep my diary up. Got home at 3am this morning after a £15 taxi to Paul's. We (Si and I) walked back to mine. Met Crombie on the way. Got up at 11am today and went for drinks at Si's at 12.30pm. Iain and Em popped in. I stayed for dinner at Si's. Spent the evening here at my house. Si is back to work tomorrow.

Farewell diary! I shall miss my constant companion and close confidante! Farewell 8 years of diaries.

Farewell maybe, but not farewell forever.

5

Love Is All Around

At the B.Ed Graduation Ball in the summer of 1990, Fi and I said goodbye, to go our separate ways. She sat hugging Simon, all set to embark on their life together. I too had decided to take the plunge and live in a serious relationship with Iain, our mutual friend from S Block. It seemed like our friendship had come to a natural end. Since neither of us had addresses to pass on, as our locations would be determined by where we got a job, we chatted and left it as a kind of 'all the best for the future'. We were moving on. A new chapter in both our lives had begun.

Fi married Simon on 30 March 1991 at St Nicholas' Church, Harpenden. She was Mrs Crompton at last. The first dance eventually was decided (although Simon has no recollection that there was so much debate about the choice of music!) and the couple selected 'Because' by Julian Lennon. Choosing a halfway point between their two jobs, they lived in Hoddesdon in Hertfordshire at first. Moving to Harpenden wouldn't happen until 1997.

Settling down to domestic bliss, Fi became pregnant and

gave birth to their first child on 13 June 1994. The excitement and joy of the occasion was unfortunately tainted with anxiety, as Emily Zoe Crompton was born prematurely. Caught up in the world of special baby units, incubators and tubes, it was frightening and distressing. But they had each other and the support of their friends and family, as always. Love surrounded them and helped them through this really difficult time. Fi, of course, documented the whole period with photographs. Years later, she transferred them into a Photobook to tell the story of their beautiful daughter Emily. The pink Photobook contained two hundred and thirty eight photographs, with Fi's words accompanying every single one.

This is the story of Emily, also known as 'The Bean'.

This was her at nineteen weeks and six days. She was very active. 24 March 1994.

Born at 11.30am (Monday), 5lb 7oz. QE2 Hospital, Welwyn Garden City.

Emily, you arrived nine weeks early. I was in labour for eight hours and they whisked you off to the Special Care Unit. We decided to call you Emily Zoe. Emily means beloved, a fighter. Zoe means life.
   This was the first picture we had. Our first cuddles. Five days old. Daddy's first cuddle. Revd. Neil Collings came and baptised you in the Special Care Baby Unit on Friday 17 June. It was a very special moment for all of us. You were really calm and despite all of your tubes our beautiful baby girl, Daddy and I were able to help care for you. We changed your nappy and sang to you. Lots of cuddles.

H I A O

Father's Day Sunday 19 June. Emily had to have a blood transfusion. World's Proudest Mum - I love you so much Emily Bean. 23 June. You are ten days old. You tried hard to breathe by yourself but it was too hard. You liked being on your tummy. Tiny hands, more cuddles and trying to breathe triggering the ventilator.

You looked so peaceful when you are sleeping. Thirteen days old. 25 June. Daddy even changed your nappy.

Tube feeding. 5 July 2.20pm, you breathed on your own. We were so proud of you Emily. It was such a big step to make. You managed to stay off the ventilator for thirty-two hours. My first cuddle with you off the ventilator. Saturday 9 July. You managed to do twenty hours in the O^2 Headbox. You coped well on trigger, then back to the Headbox and finally onto CPAP (a type of ventilator). Our favourite day. Sunday 17 July 10.30am. You surprised us by breathing unaided in air.

Granddad John's first cuddle. You had a dummy to help you learn to suck. First cuddles with your Grandma Liz, Granddad Roger and Grandma Jean. They had waited five long weeks. Your first bath. You tried to breast-feed. Thirty-seven days old, 48cm long. Here are the wonderful nurses and doctors who helped to make you well. They were amazing.

I spent every day with you when you were in hospital. Daddy fell asleep there! 30 July. My favourite babygrow. Your first BIG nappy. Mummy's turn to bath you! Then cuddles with Aunty Emma.

Forty-nine days old. You weigh 3.440kg / 7lb 9oz. What a big girl you are.

All ready for bed. Sweet dreams Emily. Fifty days old. First time in a bouncy chair. We think you enjoyed it. 4 August. I loved choosing your outfits. You recognised Daddy's voice. Your first bottle feed, 9 August.

On your due date 12 August 1994. Relaxing in your comfy chair. Daddy's turn to give you a bath. 15 August you were transported to Great Ormond Street hospital to have tests. Emily you were so brave, you really were our 'Super Baby'. You were there 15-24 August.

Your first dungarees. It's lovely to be back at the QE2. You could have visitors! Iain, Em and Matt came. 27 August, weight 10lb 6oz. You had your fingers tied. Just waiting for them to drop off.

Back to Great Ormond Street hospital to have your shunt put in on 5 September. You brave girl. On 5 September at 8am you went down to theatre. You wore a Tom and Jerry gown. The Doctors gave you some magic medicine to make you go to sleep. Daddy went down to theatre with you. I was so scared. You woke up three hours later and your shunt was in. It was going to help you stop having headaches and stop your head swelling. You had to lie flat for 48 hours. You were on Parrot Ward at Great Ormond Street hospital. There were some famous people visiting the hospital. We met Mr Motivator, the exercise man from GMTV.

Your extra finger on your left hand fell off on 4 September. The right one on 7 September. You made a good recovery and were allowed to go home!

HIAO

Well, home was QE2 hospital. You left Great Ormond Street hospital on 9 September.

Your first sleep in your own pram. Showing off your shunt wound but lots of cuddles from Daddy. Sunday 11 September. Smart new hat for your first outing to the park. Spot the oxygen cylinder. 14 September, you were thirteen weeks old. Jeanette took your shunt clips out. You were very brave. You had sixteen clips, five in your tummy and eleven in your head. Trial run at going home! We were so excited. 'H' day. Monday 3 October. Sixteen weeks old and going home for good.

Welcome home Emily. Sweet dreams. We are so glad you are home. Your first night in your own cot. Life at home. You had your first taste of solids on 22 October. Three teaspoons of baby rice! You met your Great Nan. On 9 October you went on a visit. You met your Great Granddad.

After a calm two weeks at home you had breathing problems and ended up in St Mary's P.I.C.U (paediatric intensive care unit). You were very poorly. It was three weeks before we could cuddle you. 20 November. The mad crew of nurses from St Mary's P.I.C.U. They were so wonderful. Daddy bought you a Paddington Bear baby grow to remind you of St Mary's. Then on 4 December it was back to Great Ormond Street hospital for your third shunt operation. We met Arnold Schwarzenegger! Jacinta came to see you too. You went back to QE2 on 12 December. You needed an O^2 tent but you surprised us by eating three meals a day. Oat and apple for breakfast. Carrot for lunch. Apple and banana for tea.

This was the last photo I took of you. 19 December 1994.

We will miss you so much Emily Bean.

You died at 7.45am on Wednesday 21 December. You died before we got to the hospital. We hoped it was because you didn't want to say goodbye.

We had lots of flowers and cards. We took prints of your hands and feet and a lock of your hair. Daddy made you a promise that he would carry you into the church and he kept his promise. We put a photo, a letter and your favourite toys in your coffin.

Your funeral service sheet.

St Nicholas' Church, Harpenden.
Emily Zoe Crompton.
13 June to 21 December 1994.
Friday 30 December at 11.00am.
Officiant Revd. Neil Collings.

The Lord is my Shepherd.

Reading: *Mark 10. Verses 13-16.*

Address.
Time for Meditation: 'Love is all around' by Wet, Wet, Wet.

Prayers.
Away in a Manger.

The Committal.

The Blessing.
Donations in memory of Emily may be placed in the basin as you leave the church for 'Help the QE2 Child'.

A poem follows, from Terry, who was born a few months before Emily. His mother Jacinta became friends with Fi and Simon when their children were in either the QE2 hospital or Great Ormond Street hospital together.

> "For my friend Emily.
> I heard about you before we met, the stories of bravery I'll never forget.
> You touched so many people in such a short time; you brought love into hearts especially mine.
> The time we spent in London together will stay with me forever and ever.
> My brave little friend you didn't complain, through all your discomfort and all of your pain.
> Your lovely face has a place in my heart; we were destined to be friends from the very start.
> I'll miss you so, my angel Em, but I know one day we'll meet again.
> My special angel baby, my love I send.
> Sleep peacefully now my little friend.
>
> Love from Terry."

A tribute to Emily read by Revd. Neil Collings

> "Fiona and Simon have asked me to read their tribute to Emily. One of the Special Care Baby Unit nurses gave them the poem 'Footprints' by Mary Stevenson. It seems so appropriate to start with that.
> Although Emily was only with us for such a short time, Fiona and Simon feel that there is so much to say about her. Her names were chosen with much care and were so appropriate. 'Emily'

means work, ambition and victorious. 'Zoe' means life. The name books say that 'Emily will always strive to achieve her desires in life, she will be persuasive so will always get her own way. Her generosity is legendary. She has a passion to help others, but in the process, she herself suffers a lot. She detests injustice and disharmony.'

All of us who knew Emily, or knew of her, will know how right the books were. Before she was born, Fiona and Simon had called her 'The Bean' because she looked like a kidney bean when they first saw her on a scan. The name stuck and she became Emily Bean, a term of much endearment, especially on monitors at St Mary's. Emily was in a hurry to get into the world and make the most of her time in it. Everyone who nursed Emily will remember she never liked to miss out on anything, always keeping them on their toes. She was notorious for always trying out every bit of equipment both in Special Care and Tewin Ward.

Emily was simply Emily. A very unique and courageous baby with her own personality and strong character. In spite of everything she was still able to smile, except in the mornings. She was never a 'morning person' as many nurses on an early shift will remember. She was the only baby who loved getting into a bath and cried when she was taken out. She liked to be the centre of attention and even chose hand-over time to take her final bow. She never liked big occasions, weddings, and going home especially – so "this was a bit drastic to get out of Christmas Emily!"

Fiona and Simon asked me to come and baptise Emily in the Special Care Baby Unit a few days after she was born. They were unable to acknowledge her Godparents at the time, but they would like to mention them today because they played a very important part in Emily's life. They are Iain and Emma, and Sue. Fiona and Simon will always treasure their support and friendship throughout that traumatic time.

Emily achieved so much. She came through two separate periods of intensive care; the latter one at St Mary's was nothing short of a miracle. She endured three operations for her hydrocephalus. She made a lot of progress after that. You have never seen anyone devour carrot puree in quite the way she did. She became more alert and active. She always recognised and responded to voices especially her Mum and Dad's. She most definitely had a sense of humour. Even her cry was finished with a little giggle. She enjoyed hearing laughter and people joking.

It's incredible to believe that someone so young who has lived such a short life could have touched the hearts of so many people. Fiona and Simon have decided Emily was only on loan to them and they were so privileged to have had such a wonderful daughter. Not many parents can say how proud they are of a six-month-old baby and really mean it. Without Emily they wouldn't have met so many caring and dedicated nurses and doctors who looked after Emily with so much love and respect.

Emily was and always will be a very special baby. There are still so many stories that can be told about Emily and many of you here today will have your own special memories of time spent with her. Fiona and Simon ask that you always think of Emily with a happy thought because she will always be their happy thought. Emily has brought so much happiness and joy into the lives of her family that far outweighs the tears and they shall always be thankful for the time they had with her. Every moment was treasured especially those two brief weeks spent at home as a family. The song Fiona and Simon have chosen is 'Love is All Around' by Wet, Wet, Wet. It was Number One when Emily was born and the words are just so 'Emily'.

Emily was easy to love and gave so much back too."

Iain and Emma, the couple's close friends, remember how Fi and Simon spent months travelling to and from the hospital and then actually living in the hospital with Emily. They always saw Fi and Simon together, with the four of them spending evenings together, sharing holidays and celebrations together. To them, Simon and Fi were a very special partnership that had the strength to find their way through some very dark and challenging times. They remember the pain of the funeral, of watching Simon carry the coffin through the church and how the two of them led everyone in a celebration of having the good fortune in spending just a few short months with Emily. They remarked that *"Some couples are torn apart by such trauma but they were truly two halves of one entity."*

After Emily died, Fi bought herself a locket where she kept Emily's photo and a lock of her hair. She wore it constantly at first, then less often as the years passed by, bringing it out for those times when she would especially think of their cherished little baby girl.

A year later, in 1995, Fi had given birth to Sophie, followed by James in 1998. Sophie was given the name Emily for her middle name.

Emily has never been forgotten. Her photographs cover a wall in the living room even today. Sophie and James can tell you all about their older sister. The family go to see Emily's grave on her birthday each year with flowers or a balloon to release up into the sky.

And I'll never forget her either, because 13 June is my birthday too.

6

Back For Good

In 1996, ten years after that pivotal year when we started our degree courses at Trent Polytechnic, it was time for a reunion. In the days before social networking and alumni websites, it was miraculously through word of mouth that people found out about the rendezvous at Byron Bar in Nottingham city centre one Saturday night in October. It was a great night. I remember seeing plenty of familiar faces and there was Fi! I was dying to find out what she had been up to. Married to Simon, of course, teaching, living in Hoddesdon, she then told me about Emily and Sophie, showing me pictures of them. We had a great time catching up and this time made sure we swapped addresses!

Over the next few years we corresponded by letter, but things changed in 1998 when we moved to Hertfordshire due to a job relocation. Now Fi and I could meet up very easily. She often came over to see me, bringing Sophie and James. I would drive over for a good gossip or a hearty meal, often cooked by Simon. She looked after our gerbil when we were on holiday. It was like old times except instead of Thunderbird, we were drinking more refined beverages. I guess, like old friends do, we slotted back into being comfortable around each other as if no time had passed at all.

Just as we were getting back into seeing each other regularly, my husband got a job up north and we moved to Teesside in 2001. But this time I wasn't going to be losing touch. I had too good a time with Fi to let it go again. She wasn't what I called 'high maintenance' as a friend. Some people I knew, made me feel I was treading on eggshells, depending on their mood, or they would depress me if they were down, instead of allowing me to cheer them up or just be there and listen and hug. Moody, needy friends I could do without. Mates that took an interest, loved to chat, share things, give you their trust and reduce you to fits of giggles – they're the kind of people I liked to hang around with, and the type of friend I tried to be. Fi, no matter what her mood or circumstance, was always great to be around. You were always welcome. But if you pissed her off or if she was angry, she'd let you know. You'd sort it out (have a bit of a 'ruck') and then move on without dwelling on it. She and Simon were two of the most genuine, easy-going people I knew. You never failed to smile when you were with them.

Although we were now back full-circle to our original 1986 sixth form geographical position, we were now in possession of cars and a disposable income which meant a visit was hardly a difficult task. After settling into our new house and getting established in my new job, I planned to drive down and stay for a weekend to get my fix of the southern climate and have a good laugh with the Crompos. Life was good. I had found my old friend again.

But before I knew it, a year had gone by. For me, 2002 had been taken up with family matters since my father's death, dealing with the politics of being a Deputy Head and sorting out our new house. A year goes by so fast in teaching, broken up as it is into three terms, with half-terms spent catching up with paperwork and the holidays soon over; suddenly it's the Autumn Term and another year has gone by. For Fi, teaching in Harpenden in a primary school, it was the same. In her school diary, which is one of the few freebies you are given in this profession, 2001/2002's academic year starts with all the usual entries noting assemblies, staff meetings, training days, parents evenings, deadlines for assessments, harvest festivals and Christmas productions.

But just after half-term in the Spring Term 2002, the diary changes and for the first time in thirteen years Fi resurrects her old confidante.

7

What It Feels Like For a Girl

Fi had been on a health kick working on her upper body. Something didn't feel right on her chest, above her cleavage. She described it feeling a bit like a muscle that had built up and thickened more than it should. It certainly did not feel like a lump in her breast, which is what we are all looking out for when we self-examine. She thought she had strained a muscle, but her mum, being a nurse, told her to get it checked out with her GP. The GP referred her to the breast clinic.

2002
Wednesday 27 February
BUPA. Diagnosed. *(Simon had private healthcare cover as part of a job package but when he changed jobs this wasn't available. After this diagnosis, her treatment was NHS).*

Saturday 2 March
James' 4th birthday. Party 3.30pm – 5pm. Mum and Dad had kids tonight, out with Iain and Emma.

Sunday 3 March
My 34th birthday. Lunch at Mum and Dad's.

Monday 4 March
Oncologist, Mount Vernon hospital.

Tuesday 5 March
MRI Mount Vernon.

Wednesday 6 March
Decided to keep a diary of feelings, symptoms, emotions. I WILL BEAT THIS BECAUSE I LOVE MY FAMILY – THEY LOVE AND NEED ME TOO MUCH.

Monday 11 March
Chemo starts. Not as bad as I thought. Painless cannula *(tube insertion)*. Cold cap tolerable. Hope at 5.15pm. Felt light headed, hungover!

Tuesday 12 March
Took medication as directed. Walked up to school to get the kids OK. Tidied toy cupboard out. Felt nauseous at teatime. Did manage to eat tea though and felt better. Slept OK.

Wednesday 13 March
Woke up and remembered I am in this nightmare. I just want it to all be a bad dream. Felt sick at 12.30pm. Took extra tablets given. Managed banana and toast for lunch. Didn't feel 100% all day. Head/tummy sickly.

Thursday 14 March
OK day, woke up shaky, nerves back, dreaded feeling sick but hey, just shaky. Head fine, tummy still food apprehensive.

Managed breakfast, elevenses and had sarni for lunch with Emma. Enjoyed my Jamie Oliver salad for tea. Didn't take anti-sick pills so I guess it was a good day then. Early days but a better one. Liz had the kids.

Friday 15 March
Got scan dates for next week. It just has to be good news please. Felt OK today, just that knot of worry back but that's all. Saw Maureen briefly – she was in good spirits. Went out with Simon to the station to sort out his tickets – popped in on Dad. Did the nursery pick-up. Liz came round and helped out. Had a lovely roast chicken for dinner and ATE it!! I love you Simon... love my soulmate!

Monday 18 March
Simon went to work. Liz came round and sorted out the kids and took them to school. Feeling OK. Went to Em's, Dad's and watched Sophie's ballet, which was really lovely. Ate well today. Enjoyed getting out of the house. Didn't feel too tired but then I didn't do much either!

Tuesday 19 March
Bone scan, chest scan 11am. Dad took me to L&D *(Luton and Dunstable Hospital)*. Had injection. Didn't realise I'd be radioactive and wouldn't be able to hug the kids for 24 hours. Kids slept at Liz's. DRANK TONS OF WATER.

Wednesday 20 March
Felt OK. Went up to school. Did Waitrose shop with James. Whilst Sophie was at a party, James and I had tea at Sally's. Hungry today.

Thursday 21 March
3.30pm, upper-abdomen scan. Stopped eating at 11am. Dad took me to L&D. By 3pm had headache due to dehydration! Scan was CLEAR. LIVER OK. Thank you God. Had orange juice at the hospital, came home and threw up in the kitchen sink. Had a super steak and salad for tea. YUM!

Friday 22 March
10am Dr M *(oncologist)* ALL CLEAR. ALL SCANS ARE CLEAR. Had Indian meal to celebrate!

Monday 25 March
Felt OK today. Had a picnic in the park with Hils, Amanda and kids. Mind you Amanda thought Wood End Park not Rothamsted so I had to go and collect her! Later after picnic went up to Wood End Park and kids had a play and an ice cream. Went to see the 'Full Monty' in St Albans with Julie, Emma and Suzanne. It was very funny and lots of naked men! Kids had a lovely day too.

Tuesday 26 March
Another sunny day. Feeling OK. Managed to put on 3lbs so far since last week. Hopefully the tumour will begin to shrink now. The moulting effect has begun with my pubic hair. Hopefully the hair on my head will stay put. I think it is perhaps going to thin a bit.

Wednesday 27 March
OK. Lovely sunny day but hair on head thinning I fear. I daren't wash or brush it at the moment. Had lunch at Norma's with the kids.

Thursday 28 March

Hair still coming out. Hopefully just thinning not going away! Saw Maggie S this morning. Went for a bike ride with the kids and went to Post Office too. Saw Maureen briefly to deliver Easter goodies. Decided that I will burn the top I got from Emma and Iain that I wore on diagnosis day.

Friday 29 March

Went to the gym with Emma. Felt good to work out again. Did about 40 minutes I guess. Hair still thinning. Wore a baseball hat until I could face washing my hair. Beautiful day.

Saturday 30 March

Went to Sheldon's Brasserie for our anniversary meal. Lovely food and a nice evening. Kids went to Liz's for the night. Hair still falling. QEQM *(Queen Mother)* died.

Sunday 31 March

Easter. Lovely lunch at Mum and Dad's. Lots of eggs. Hair still falling out!

Monday 1 April

Went to see 'Ice Age' at the cinema. James and Sophie really enjoyed it. Had lunch at Liz and Roger's today. I washed my hair and it came out a lot and my scalp hurt with it all. Must ask chemo nurses what to do. Am going to book appointment with Marion White's clinic re: wig perhaps! Better to be prepared I think.

Tuesday 2 April

Bloods 10.30am at surgery. Mum is taking my bloods!! Bloods taken OK! Went with Emma to Marion White's to choose a wig. Had a right laugh and ended up buying two!

One short, one shoulder length. Very realistic but £303 with shampoo and head to put it on!!! But I feel better about myself and Sophie thought they were OK too.

Wednesday 3 April

Tricia had a baby girl, Helena Ann, 7lb 11oz. Chemo 2, 11.30am and clinic. What a farce! I got a call at 10.20am saying my FBC *(full blood count)* was low! Could I come in early to have another FBC done? My level was 1.3, baseline 1.4! Anyway it takes half an hour to get results! So I asked if I could visit Tricia in Maternity. Special permission and off we went. Liz and I bought baby gifts on route from the hospital shop and stayed for nearly an hour. Helena is lovely and Tricia looked well. Went back to chemo at 12.15pm. They wanted their lunch then so Liz and I had lunch in the canteen and went back at 1pm. Chemo finally at 1.20pm but didn't go for cold cap. Home by 2.30pm. Feeling a bit nauseous. Cannula more painful and drugs very cold. Ate tea OK but feel light headed/migraine type. Wearing a scarf to bed for fall out!! Liz liked the wigs. Sophie asked about 'CANCER' and if you die. I said I hope not but explained it to her. Sophie struck me as open and knowledgeable as she asked about cancer. I asked where she had heard about it. "Penny's Granddad had it and died". I explained it was different as mine was breast cancer and my special medicine is there to shrink it. What can you say to a six year old? I can't/won't lie to her, I love her too much and I want her to be 'OK' with this. I want to be better so we can all put this behind us. Dare I say 'Roll on 2003'? Please God let it be better than 2002.

Thursday 4 April

Took tablets at 8am. Slept in till 9.30am. Kids came in and watched TV whilst I dozed. Went to Julie's for the day at 11am.

Liz came in and cleaned my house, brought my washing in and ironed it too! Came away from Julie's at 5.30pm. Spent the day enjoying the sun in her garden in my hat! Dropped the kids in at Liz's for overnighter. Stayed for pizza and salad. Feel tired today. Maybe it's the fresh air/chemo! Parting getting wider!

Friday 5 April
Hels had George, 4lb 13oz. Both well. Had lazy day today! Woke up 9.30am, took tablets. Put washing on and had breakfast. Watched Queen Mum procession in bed. Phoned Liz B. Had shower, braved washing my hair!! Big fall out. Dressed then it was lunchtime. Lisa called round. Showed her my wigs and decided to go to Waitrose... in my wig. I ended up doing banking, shopping etc and felt OK, not too self-conscious. Maureen came round for a cuppa and loved the new look. Liz and Rog returned kids at 7pm. They thought the wig was OK too. Good day. <u>Big step</u>.

Saturday 6 April
Felt FINE TODAY. DIDN'T GET UP UNTIL LATE!! Rested most of the day. Went to LADIES NIGHT in my long wig. Everyone was great. Only one person couldn't stop staring! All the blokes - no worries. Boogied until 1.15am!! Home by 2am!

Sunday 7 April
Felt tired today. Got up at 10am. Went to Costco and then came home to rest. Hair very fine, very thin but can't really brush it anymore. NO EXTRA SICK PILLS NEEDED.

Monday 8 April
School. Walked up to school with the kids (in a baseball hat). Good to see everyone again. Went to Harpenden to get Helen a baby outfit for George. Collected James from school and he

rode/walked to Post Office. Got Sophie from school too. Felt very peckish today, bloaty, possibly PMT!! Bit light headed too. Started taking vitamins.

Tuesday 9 April
QUEEN MUM'S FUNERAL. Felt less bloaty. No period though! Need to rest a bit more/sit down/do nothing to build up for after school stint! James is wearing me out! QM funeral very moving – amazing scenes of pageantry etc. Taking vitamins. Drinking lots of water.

Wednesday 10 April
Vitamins are like horse pills! Felt tired today. James and Sophie went out for tea this afternoon and I just slept. Must take it easy. Still no period. Went out tonight to Linda's for a curry. Had a good laugh and cuddled Sarah's baby Matthew.

Thursday 11 April
Wore Cath's Burberry baseball hat! Very stylish... if Posh Spice has one!! Gilly came round this afternoon for a chat. She got the nursery job. Really pleased for her. Had a restful afternoon and took it easy. Less tired today which was good.

Friday 12 April
Managed all on my own today. Walked up to school and Hils said we should go to Sarah's for coffee. Went with Pat, Hils, and then went into Harpenden with Hils. Met up with Claire and Tricia. Bought some bits for Sophie from the Barbie Sale then went to Slug and Lettuce for coffee. Hils paid, I had no cash on me!! Collected James then Rosie, Chris and Stella came back to mine for lunch! After school, took kids to the park and had a few mums come up to say hi etc!! Good day. Had pain in left armpit?! Still no period!

Saturday 13 April
It's 18 years today since Simon and I first met! Felt sleepy today. Had dinner at Iain and Emma's. Played Taboo. Found out Iain goes commando under his kilt!

Sunday 14 April
Stayed in today. Poor Simon did all the shopping, cooking etc. Haven't heard about MRI yet. Felt tired – managed ironing. I am less patient. Don't like this. Lisa trimmed my hair for me. Looks better shorter. Still very thin on top and falling.

Monday 15 April
Took kids up to school. Had coffee with Trish and cuddled baby this morning. Went down town and got a few bits. Feel OK, just a bit tired. Had a sleep this afternoon. Went to visit Maureen briefly this morning too. Mum and Dad had James for me. Feel more tired in the afternoon these days but <u>not</u> sick. Eating OK. Lots of breast cancer scare stories in the news! Dad has to go for X-rays.

Tuesday 16 April
MRI Mount Vernon hospital 10am. More blood, needles. Why did I agree to this? Six weeks! Period finally here. MRI was OK. 10am appointment and home by 12.30pm. Dad has offered to pay for me to go BUPA. Lovely offer but I am not happy about it costing so much! Very tired today.

Wednesday 17 April
<u>Heavy</u> period. Found out L&D has Cobham Clinic which has nine private beds therefore surgery NHS transfer to private. Fair compromise I think if I can do it. Had lunch with Emma. Slept a lot. Very tired.

What It Feels Like For a Girl

Thursday 18 April
REALLY CRAP DAY. Dad had his X-ray back. He has a lump. 99% to be cancerous. FUCKING SHIT. Now he has to have bone scans etc. Results week Wednesday. This is NOT fair. He's talking chemo as it's inoperable but Mum and I can see the larger picture. This is not good. I'm really scared I think my Dad is dying. Why? Why him? Why now? What will we do without him? He's my Dad. Sophie and James' Granddad. I know we thought we'd lost him five years ago but <u>no</u> not now. Dad I love you so much, whatever you need, I'll be there for you. Cried myself to sleep.

Friday 19 April
Mum came here last night to tell Iain *(Fi's brother)* and Lisa. Iain was totally gutted – we all are. Totally useless today. Hilary popped in, Emma called too. Sent Dad an email to put in words how special he is to me. Cried as I wrote it. Liz came in and we cried too. She collected James for me. All I've done all day is cry. Managed lunch and the ironing. Man came to do the floor. Looks good. Went to see Dad with Simon this afternoon. He looks OK and was chirpy. I'm worried for him though. I think he knows it's not good and is trying so hard to be brave. Love you Dad.

> *Subject: especially for you*
> *Dad*
>
> *I am putting this on paper so to speak because I know you check your email all the time! I also want to find the right words and want you to have them there to see when you feel low. This will make you cry as I am now, but you have to read this.*
>
> *You are the most amazing Dad and have always been there for me as we are all here for you now.*

I love you so much and I know we never say it as often as we should but I guess that is the McIntosh way! You are not to worry about me as I am OK and dealing with my situation just as you must focus and deal with yours.

I am so lucky to have you just round the corner to pick up my son and fix my domestic crisis! Sophie and James adore you and no one can make the chocolate button tree grow things like you! They love you because you are kind and you teach them about things that Simon and I haven't got round to as parents. They love you for you, because you are Granddad John and James' mate! I guess what I'm trying to say is you are the best Dad a daughter could want and I love you.

This is not easy to begin to understand why but together we can fight this and WE WILL YOU AND ME!

Love you always, Fi

Saturday 20 April
Took the kids to the gym for swimming and Sophie for dancing. Simon did all the shopping today. We're having everyone to lunch tomorrow. I went to see Dad. He is in pain and that makes me sad. I know he's scared even if he says he's not. Wednesday is his bone scan, Friday CT scan.

Sunday 21 April
Felt sick today. Hardly ate – nerves? Simon cooked all the lunch. Mum and Dad, Ewee *(Fi's brother Iain, a deviation on his name which arose from Sophie not being able to pronounce his name*

properly when she was little) and Bird *(a nickname for Lisa because she could sing)* came to lunch. It was really nice. We had a 'memories' session! Dad and Mum came to watch Sophie in the parade. We went to theirs whilst she was in the service for St George's Day. Mum thinks Dad is beginning to come to the conclusion this is serious. He didn't seem in so much pain today.

Monday 22 April

Still felt sick this morning. I'm sure it's nerves about Dad. He phoned to see how I was. I went round and did some shopping/banking for him. That made me feel useful and less weepy. Called in again after lunch and left James there for a while with him and Mum. Collected Sophie and popped back. They ended up having tea there. Felt more normal there, as that's what they do. Sophie read her book to Dad and he liked that. Saw Hils and Amanda today. Everyone is being so great. Felt better by tonight! Moving forward I hope.

Tuesday 23 April

Spent today on my own really. I didn't do very much. Liz had the kids after school and for tea. I had a sleep this afternoon. Phoned Dad. Managed not to cry today.

Wednesday 24 April

Dad's bone scan etc. Had breakfast, didn't feel as nauseous today. Trying hard to eat again. Went to Liz B's sweater sale. Had lunch in The Fox with Hils, Claire, Colin and the kids. The boys played nicely. Spent an hour or so in the park after school as the sunshine was lovely. Sophie had her school walk round the local environment! Phoned Dad. He seemed OK about the scan. Said it was painful to sit for so long. Results next week. Iain took him there. Went to Steve and Alison's house. Very nice, rather beige but spacious!

Thursday 25 April

Mum came and took Bloods. Felt better today: accept/adjust, don't know. Poor Dad must be feeling shit just like I did waiting. Watched Sophie do sponsored skip. Saw Maureen today too. Went round to Dad's with Dyson to do their carpets. Spent afternoon with them. Hope Bloods are OK. Won't be surprised if they're not what with all this going on. Dramatic hair loss today.

Friday 26 April

Dad's CT's. Chemo 3. Had a look round Cobham *(clinic)*. Very nice and will be £4300. Not bad eh. Actually saw Dr M *(oncologist)* today! Slight panic at first when he said he wanted to discuss scans!! No…. they're all CLEAR and he felt and measured the lump and it's shrunk. Took me off Dexamethasone as it gives me heartburn. Bloods good, had chemo. Felt <u>really</u> crap tonight, sick and very tired.

Saturday 27 April

Didn't get up till 11am. Felt nauseous. Managed to eat OK but spent day lying on bed dozing. Wearing wig now as hair is going fast. To make matters worse I have a huge pile!! It's really sore.

Sunday 28 April

If Dexamethasone made me feel good I want it back. Feel really tired, and not much with it at all. Must go to doctors re: pile! Not eating much and poor Simon has had to do everything. Dad's chest hasn't been good today.

Monday 29 April

Felt slightly better. Pile still painful. Got appointment for 4pm. Liz had James all day. I just vegged out. Didn't do anything really. Watched TV and rested. Still felt sickly but felt headachy too. Went to see Dad this afternoon. His back was really sore. I'm scared for him, gave him my Healing Angel to have. Used foam stuff on Farmer Giles.

Tuesday 30 April
Wet and rainy day. Walked up to school. Lots of looks after the announcement in the school newsletter! Felt better today. Ate OK today. Emma came by too. Sophie went round to Joshua's for tea. Phoned Dad. He said he's slept a lot today. Less pain but used heat pad for four hours. Really worried for him now. Hope he sleeps OK tonight. Dosed Farmer Giles again, less painful.

Wednesday 1 May
Dad's results. Had reflexology with Louise today. She managed to spot my problems! She even made me get to the loo again! Went to see Dad. He was really scared and he and I both cried a lot. I promised him whatever they said, I'd be there for him. Stayed for lunch then went down town whilst they went to BUPA. I popped into St Nicholas' *(church)* for a quick word! Thankfully results not all doom and gloom. He needs extra O^2 in the house, plus has deposits on left hip and right shoulder. But liver and brain are clear. Radiotherapy to prevent spread. My Healing Angel has helped today. Thank you. Iain has said he'll drive Dad to radiotherapy. Dad sounded more upbeat and I think he now knows what he's fighting. None of us knows how this will really affect him but at least they didn't say *"Sorry, you've only got XYZ months"*. I know that is what really scared him – thinking of all the things he would miss. Mum is still down to earth and not as optimistic but I guess as a nurse she sees the grey side. Thank you God for giving me back my Dad.

Thursday 2 May

James was off nursery today as he had a temperature and dodgy tummy. Washed hair today – tons fell out. Wore my short wig today all day. Maureen visited me today, which was nice. Sarah made me spag bol for the freezer. Felt OK. Dad was still in pain this morning but better this afternoon. He will get O^2 at home now. Went out to see Hils this afternoon. Had a nice chat and wore wig too!!

Friday 3 May

Jubilee Day, no school. Didn't bother going out somewhere with the kids. They were happy to play out with Odette, Penny etc. Went to see Dad. He wasn't too good today. He needed O^2 whilst I was there a few times. He is still sleeping downstairs in a chair. He has deteriorated so much in three weeks. I'm still scared. He sees an oncologist next Thursday. Sophie was lovely with him. Covering him in kisses and fetching and carrying. Mum said to Simon yesterday that lung cancer can do this to you in a matter of months. Certainly not out of the woods <u>at all.</u>

Saturday 4 May

Felt OK. Wig wearing now a necessity. Went to the gym with the kids. Mum said Dad was much brighter today. Went to Paul and Julie's for takeaway tonight. Andy and Sue were there too.

Sunday 5 May

Si went on bike ride. Ewee and Bird came round and Bird cut my hair for me. Met Si at pub and then Elliott and Laura came round to play. Went to see Dad. He wasn't too good. Mum said we should expect the worst and tell him what we want to say sooner rather than later. He seems to be in pain and so fed up. I'm scared he's just going to give up now. Really scared. It means that I could lose my Dad in a few weeks. How do I explain to Sophie and James?

Tuesday 7 May
This has almost become Dad's diary. I went to see him today and he got breathless so easily. He is still in so much pain and just wants the specialist to do something. Mum is bearing the brunt of his anger, frustration and temper. They have a Macmillan nurse coming tomorrow, a district nurse on Thursday. I know the Rector will bring communion to him on Thursday. Lisa came to babysit. Whilst we went to say goodbye to Colin and Claire, Iain said that after seeing Dad tonight it could be days not weeks. He knows Ann is coming on Friday.

Wednesday 8 May
Where to start? Dad had a really bad night. He and Mum sat and planned his funeral etc. He was on O^2 all the time. When I went round I thought that was it. I got there at 9.30am and stayed until 3pm. He had communion with the Rector and Mum and I. We _all_ had a cry and I think he felt much brighter. The Macmillan nurse came and was excellent. She said he needed steroids and to be in Mount Vernon hospital having radiotherapy. So tonight he is in a private ward there. He seems much more relaxed and Mum will have a rest too. Went to visit him, Emma babysat for us.

Saturday 9 May
Poor Dad had another bad dream with hallucinations. Mum had to go over at 4am to calm him. He was really upset. Didn't know/trust anyone. Had a good day otherwise. He liked seeing the kids and they really liked seeing him. They gave him bone-strengthening drugs today.

Tuesday 14 May

Dad was tired today. He had a busy morning with treatment and physio. He had a lot of waiting about and was left unattended without O^2. I saw him for an hour, as he was sleepy. He panicked at 8pm and phoned me as he was struggling for breath and I was the only one who could help him do his exercises. Simon and I drove up there, Iain and Lisa were on their way before us. So I had to calm him down again. Got back at 11pm. I really want to help/be with him but I'm so tired.

Thursday 16 May

Bloods. Jackie has found another lump. That's another thing I'm going to dread. My bloods are low so no chemo tomorrow. I am not sure if I need to go to the clinic either. Had nails done with nail art. Went to Amanda's for lunch with Linda and Hils. Went to Dad's. He was really low. He is scared again and was talking about dying. I want him home so we can be nearer to him. I really am frightened he'll just give up soon. Why is this happening to my family?

Friday 17 May

Didn't have chemo 4 as my blood cell count is 0.74. Very low. I must be really careful as my immunity's almost nil. I spent the day on Emma's sofa and then on my own sofa. Dad phoned me and Iain had said I'd had chemo so he wouldn't worry about me. I couldn't tell him that I was so tired. He has a chest infection so I really can't see him right now. Hopefully he'll be home on Monday.

Wednesday 22 May

James to Alex's. Emma popped in today. Stayed for lunch. James not 'right' at Alex's. Liz collected him. I went to Mum's to set up a bed for Dad in the dining room. Sophie had tea at

Bev's with James. After tea and putting James in the shower it all becomes clear. He has chicken pox. Sent him off to Liz's for a few days. Dad came home. It was so GREAT to see him. He looks 'better'. Very scared. Spent evening with him and helping Mum.

Thursday 23 May
Bloods were OK! Why oh why is chemo so yuck?! Spent day popping in and out of Mum and Dad's. Dad was very panicky. Then he gets all sorry and down. I wish Iain wasn't going away on holiday in the Caribbean as he could help Mum. I am worried about her and all the work she's doing for Dad. She needs rest too. Poor James has 38 spots and counting. Yes it's chicken pox for sure. Dad used zimmer frame to have a bit of a walk. It's really sad to see him a scared and fragile old man when he should be vibrant, mobile and full of life.

Friday 24 May
Chemo 4 – yes, my blood count was a massive 5! Saw Dr M *(oncologist)* who was pleased. Got Dex plus three days Ondansatron and a huge bottle of Gaviscon! They reduced the chemo dose so I wouldn't feel so crap and recover faster. Feel ropey tonight but at least I have eaten well. Dad saw Macmillan nurse who said radiotherapy takes a week or two to kick in and lasts for six weeks. So hence O^2 is better. That perked him up.

Saturday 25 May
Feel OK today. Went round to Mum and Dad's at 1.30pm as Dad's O^2 not good. He did however perk up and I stayed for the rest of the day. Simon and I slept over there to help give Mum some sleep. I stayed up with Dad until 3am. He was very restless and stubborn. Mum got up at 3am to be with him.

HIAO

Sunday 26 May
At 1.10pm my Dad died. He'd had a good wash, breakfast etc and finally decided that was enough. He lay in his bed and drifted off in an hour. Mum and I were at his side and so was DP *(a doctor)*. He was ready to go. Sophie had been in before and was very grown up and told him she loved him and he could be with his dog.

We couldn't get hold of Iain. Then we realised that today was Nan's birthday too. Mum was very brave. I'm glad I was there for her and Dad. He had really had enough and it was almost as if he had decided that the time was right. The Rector came and was really nice. They came to take Dad away at about 3.30pm. His funeral will be Friday 7 June at 2pm at St Nicholas'. Then a private cremation. Weston's have agreed he can be interred with Emily which makes me happy for both of them to be together. We had Mum back here for some tea with us. It's all been so fast. Six weeks from initial doctor visit to this. I promise you Dad I will beat this bastard for both of us. I love you Dad. All my love, Fi.

Monday 27 May
I don't know how we got through today. I walked Sophie to school and got bombarded. I had a coffee with Sarah S and then went round to help Mum. We organised the funeral arrangements then went to St Albans to register Dad's death. We also put an obituary in the Herts Ad. We then went out shopping! Strange as it may seem but we bought black jackets, tops and a hat for Mum too. Finally got hold of Iain and Lisa at lunchtime. They are coming home on Saturday. Mum and I are still in shock. Had some lovely cards and letters.

Tuesday 28 May
More cards, flowers, letters. Dad was so highly thought of.

What It Feels Like For a Girl

Mum and I planned his service with the Rector today. I think it will be really beautiful. We're having a piper and Simon and Iain will carry Dad in too. Ordered the flowers. Tonight helped Mum move the dining room back to normal. To top it all, we learnt that Simon's Granny died <u>tonight.</u>

Thursday 30 May
Jubilee picnic at school. It seems so unreal that life etc is just carrying on. The picnic was a rainy fiasco and all the time I'm thinking my Dad has died and I'm picnicking on the school field! James really enjoyed it though. Bought my skirt and shoes for Friday. James was talking about Granddad tonight. He said he'll really miss him and he wants to talk to him. He explained about Pixie Lane, pixies and the chocolate button tree. I hope Dad that you know how many people you've influenced. I hope you are happy now.

Monday 3 June
Jubilee holiday. Half term. Collected Mum and took her to Liz's for the street party. Bit chilly. Street was decorated with flags and bunting. Had BBQ. I missed Dad being there. It felt weird just having Mum. Sophie and James enjoyed themselves. Left at midnight. Sophie is making a scrapbook of the Jubilee. She dressed up as a princess; James went as Bob the Builder.

Wednesday 5 June
Sophie and I had our nails done for Dad's funeral. Sophie wrote a beautiful card for the flowers. 'Dear Granddad, We love you. Thank you for the chocolate button tree. We miss you very much'. James signed his name on it too. Went to see Mum. Julie and Steve arrived at 5pm. Julie bought the Indian meal. Steve seems very nice. They go well together.

Thursday 6 June
Collected my photos today. It was a film that sat in my old camera for two years. My Dad was on that film. God I'm dreading tomorrow. I can't believe I'll be saying my final goodbye to my Dad. Julie and Steve left this morning for London. I went and bought some food bits for the funeral. Julie G came with a shepherd's pie – bless. Helped Mum sort the house for tomorrow. She's had 189 cards and letters.

Friday 7 June
~~Chemo 5.~~ Dad's funeral. Went to Mum's at 12.00pm. Iain and Keith looked fantastic in their kilts. Ann and the others arrived at 1pm. Dad and the cars came and we left at 1.50pm. The church was packed. The service was just as Dad would have wanted it. The piper *(playing the same lament that Fi chose for her own funeral)*, the hymns, the tributes. Sophie was very upset! When we left to go to the crematorium was the hardest. Saying a final goodbye was awful. I now have to believe he is really gone. Back at Mum's, the house was packed. We stayed with Mum until midnight. Iain, Keith and Lisa did too. Today we said goodbye to a very special man.

> *My Dad.*
>
> *How can I begin to say what he means to me? He was generous with his time and his advice, never judgemental and always supportive of what I did. Dad was a real family man. The family was everything to him especially our history and who we are. He wanted us to be proud of our roots. He hated change but he was happy to embrace computers and the Internet!*
>
> *He was always there for me. A phone call, the daily visits of him just popping by is what I will*

miss most. When I had my daughter Emily he spent hours with me at her bedside. He loved his grandchildren and was so proud of them. He loved being with them and has had a profound impact on their lives. James will miss their chats and trips into Harpenden to do 'jobs' with Granddad. Sophie will miss walking in the woods with Granddad looking for the chocolate button tree. They will miss Granddad's dinners, treats and the sweetie tin. To me he was simply the most wonderful dad a daughter could have. He was open and honest and always gave it to you straight as he saw it. He always wanted the best for you. Simon will miss him for his phone calls at work asking how to sort out a problem on his computer and the phone call asking him down the Old Bell for a quick pint that never was!

My Dad never knew how highly people thought of him and we are all the richer for knowing him and my family are the luckiest because he was my Dad, Granddad John and James' mate.

Sunday 9 June
Cooked lunch for Mum today. We all went to the church service at 4pm. We laid a wreath for Dad and Emily in the Garden of Remembrance. We talked about Mum's house and tried to find a way for us to buy it but I don't think it's a realistic thing, which is really gutting.

Tuesday 11 June
Sophie's school trip. Had a good day. Feel really tired now. I went in my own car. Bekonscot was really nice. The kids had fun looking for all the places and things. It was nice to be able

to do something normal. Although I've done lots of trips, I felt a bit protective of Sophie going. Came back to find a rose plant on the doorstep from Liz B.

Thursday 13 June
Emily's birthday. Bloods. Solicitor 10am. Borderline bloods. Need re-testing tomorrow. Went to solicitors. Iain has done loads re: Dad's estate. I feel useless really. Took our flowers down for Emily's birthday. I can't believe it's eight years now. No one really remembers except grandparents and us. Went to Amanda's for curry. Do I hope for chemo? I guess I should really.

Friday 14 June
Chemo 5. Had bloods re-checked. Got chemo about 11.30am. Felt really sick as I sat there. Psychological I guess. Emma took me and had to drive my car as hers kept conking out. Came home and just vegged on the sofa. Kids went to Liz's. Guess I feel crap as I am approaching the last chemo. I know I dread feeling so awful. It's the sickly feeling I hate.

Tuesday 18 June
Hils and I went to St Albans. Walked around Verulamium Park and fed the ducks with Spencer. Hit McDonald's and the shops! Had a nice day being normal! Mind you, then I feel guilty about moving on without Dad. I know I haven't accepted that he is dead. To me it is as if he is just somewhere else. Emma phoned and has booked a cottage for us all at New Year.

Wednesday 19 June
Pilates with Maureen. Didn't do Pilates but ended up sitting in the sun on her hammock having a drink. Felt really bloated today. Went to doctors.

Thursday 20 June
Sports Day. Yellows won. Sophie did well and was pleased. James was in the red team. Liz and Mum came to watch. Guess what – Sue rang tonight! We actually had a decent chat. I told her about Dad and she was shocked.

Monday 24 June
Lovely weather. Went to Tom's in the afternoon. Tom and James played in the paddling pool. Had a parcel from Sue. Some smelly stuff and a letter. Had reflexology on feet, as did Mum. I slept really well tonight after that.

Thursday 27 June
Had a phone call from Mr P *(surgeon)*. He said no point in going private, as I'll only be there 48 hours. He doesn't do reconstruction at that time because radiotherapy causes scar tissue and therefore they recommend it later. I was very upset as I just want my body back. BAD DAY. I got upset about Dad a lot too. Decided to take charge and book a holiday. One week at Eurodisney. Plus we're going to stay in the posh Disney hotel and hang the expense. Really crap day.

Friday 28 June
Spoke to Margaret M who had done her last chemo plus she had reconstruction after the mastectomy. I may get away with a lumpectomy. Helped out with PTA sorting. Liz took kids to the zoo tonight. Simon and I went to the Chinese restaurant. Really great food. Had a good chat. Decided to book Disney but not tell the kids.

Sunday 30 June
Sophie's Rainbow Trip, Woburn. Mum came for lunch. Sophie had a lovely time at Woburn. She even bought a pressie

for James too. They talked about holidays and decided they wanted to go to Heaven to chat to Granddad and Emily.

Tuesday 2 July
Had a haircut! Clare and Hils came round. Hils thought my hair had grown! Clare cut all the long bits off then did a No. 6 clipper job! It looks much better all one length. It resembles a No. 1 all over!! Hopefully by the time we go to Eurodisney it will have got to a decent length for me to wear.

Friday 5 July
Dreading this. Chemo 6. Had chat with Dr M *(oncologist)*. Booked mammogram for 18 July 2.30pm. Chemo OK. Didn't feel as sick. I had student nurse giving chemo. Got home, felt OK until 3pm, then felt crap. Liz took Sophie for haircut. They stayed over at theirs. Managed pizza for tea. James had his stilts for being good. Sophie got her roller blades.

Sunday 7 July
Lunch at Mum's. Went wigless and everyone was OK with that. Had lovely lunch. Still weird without Dad not being there. Mum talks about feeling lonely, missing the company. Felt OK healthwise today.

Monday 8 July
Last pills today. No more steroids. OK weight, drop off please, this is not good. Did ironing and had coffee with Maureen all before collecting James at 11.30am! Maureen showed me her reconstruction and it looks fabulous. Went out with Hils, James was at Mum's. Booked nail appointment for Hils and me for Friday. Watched Sophie's ballet this afternoon. Felt tired but NOT SICK! Spoke to Helen tonight.

Saturday 13 July
School Ball. Fantastic weather today. Everyone looked brilliant. Lovely to see Claire again. Food was good but dancing could have gone on longer. Went to Paul and Julie's after until 3am!! Drank lots of champagne.

Monday 15 July
Had lunch with Hils and Shirley at the Old Bell. Sorted out currency for holiday. Maureen had her chemo today so she is now through it too. It is such a relief to know now that it is over and done with.

Thursday 18 July
No one at school knew about my job! Neither Judith nor I got a mention in assembly, not a thank you, nothing. I was really cross. Alex and Linda got their farewell assembly. Went to Sally's Virgin Vie party. Had a makeover – went wigless!! Spent too much.

Friday 19 July
End of term 2pm. Still no mention in final assembly today. I am really pissed off. I feel really undervalued for everything I have done in the last two years. Judith had a card and vouchers from the Infant staff last Friday but .... Oh well, life is a bag of shite as I should know by now. Went to Iain and Em's tonight, had pizza and watched Tim get evicted from the Big Brother house.

Sunday 21 July
Disneyland Paris, 9.30am. Got to Waterloo at 8.30am. Kids had no idea. Sophie finally twigged as we took suitcases from the car. *"Why have we got suitcases for a day in London?"* It was great to see their faces. Got to Disney at 1.45pm. Hotel is

amazing, weather hot. Checked in and went to the park. First stop Autopia, then It's a Small World. Watched electrical light parade and fireworks. Got to bed at midnight.

Thursday 25 July
Back to Disneyland. Up at 7am and in the park by 9am. Went on Peter Pans' flight twice, Dumbo, Casey Jnr then actually got the kids back on Pirates and onto BIG THUNDER MOUNTAIN! Sophie was fine but James wasn't. Bribe was a cowboy gun!! Sophie actually went back on it again. Had a family photo with Mickey. Went into Disney Studios and saw Sully. Went to Cinemagic and sat near the actor who went into the screen. Came back into Disney and went on It's a Small World, Alice's Maze and the Autopia cars. Finished with a character tea at Café Mickey. Fantastic way to end the week.

Friday 26 July
Had a lie in. Did tons of washing. Saw Mum. Dropped the kids into Emma's. Went to the hospital. Yes, it is a mastectomy! I'm booked in for 8 August for two days and no reconstruction until October 2003. Why is life such a bastard to me? I know at least with a mastectomy it will all be gone but Fuck It, I'm 34 years old. This isn't fair. I've been through so much this year. Kate won Big Brother!

Saturday 27 July
Feeling totally SHIT. Really sorry for myself. Cried a lot. Shouted a lot. Iain and Emma came over tonight. My Mum has popped in too.

Tuesday 30 July
Tricia had my two today whilst I was at L&D. They ended up staying all day and for their tea. Jan C, the breast care nurse

was very matter of fact. I took Mum with me too. I saw lots of photos and a fake boob. It really doesn't appeal and I still can't believe it's happening to me. I look at my poor boob and realise in a week I'll be saying goodbye after 34 years. Got some bra and swimwear catalogues.

Saturday 3 August
My bruv couldn't babysit, anyway Richard offered and so we were able to go into London with Iain and Emma. Had hoped to see a show but ended up having a few drinks and a meal. Very expensive evening though. Got back at 1.30am. Felt awful as Richard had sat from 7.30pm. Simon had drunk so much he went off in a strop whilst we waited for a taxi. Nice to know he'd just abandon me at that time in the morning!

Tuesday 6 August
Spoke to Rachel on the phone today in Oz. She's doing well. Went out on my bike for a ride this morning. Went to the hospital for a check up. Found out I have a heart murmur! It's not serious and I had an ECG this afternoon too and <u>more</u> bloods. Went into Cobham and they may well have a bed for me on Thursday. Took kids swimming and I went in too. Did twenty lengths. Spoke to Sarah L tonight.

Thursday 8 August
Got up at 7am. Had my light breakfast. I've managed to get an amenity bed so that's a relief. Feeling numb really. I can't believe this is really happening. I wanted to speak to my Dad today. I really want him to look out for me today. Can't believe I'm losing my breast today. We got to the hospital at 11am. Got a room in Cobham Clinic. Mr P *(surgeon)* came at 12.30 and drew on me. Then it all became real. Boy did I cry. Going to theatre at 3pm.

Friday 9 August

Writing in retrospect. Don't remember a lot about yesterday. Very sore, very sick, very down. Back from surgery 5.30pm. Slept a lot. Mum and Si came to see me. Three drains in. Felt really awful. Sweated a lot and was very sick. Friday am, slept on and off for most of night every 20 minutes. Couldn't get out of bed and go to the toilet. Needed a commode and a lot of help.

Saturday 10 August

Nurse got me up and washed me. Can lift my arm about 90 degrees. Mr P came, pleased with operation. Drain out today. Lots of visitors. Very tired. Can't believe how flat I am on my right side. Physio came. Really painful. Like red hot needles in armpit/chest. Drains removed. Nearly died of pain. Felt much better when they're out. Mum came in, Si and the kids too, Hils and Shirley. No one came after 2.30pm. Very lonely, very down, very sore.

Sunday 11 August

Going home today. Slept most of night. Doctors came and checked me over. Got home 1.30pm. Had lunch at Mum's. Drain leaking at the side. Very tired and a bit sore. Can get arm above head now.

Monday 12 August

James' football school 10am – 3pm. Site still leaking. Mum changed dressing. District nurse arrived about 4pm. Changed whole dressing. Not ready for that and saw scar. Not pretty. She changed all dressings and re-dressed round drain. Very tired. Hils popped in. Em phoned. Mum came by too. Claire D phoned. Had a nice chat. Got period today. SO LIFE REALLY IS A BITCH.

What It Feels Like For a Girl

Tuesday 13 August
Had two lovely bouquets today. Had a better day today. Mum came and took me to her house for a while. Sophie went swimming and Si to the gym. James is really enjoying his footie camp. Drain not leaking which is better. Mum changed the bag for me. 100ml since Sunday. Feeling tired, achy and pissed off.

Wednesday 14 August
Tired today. No one came by. Helped Sophie with her project and she's doing well. Liz came and cleaned the house. Arm exercises easier. District nurse came and changed the dressings. A couple of people called. No one understands. They all think I'll be up and busy. My life is shit. I've lost a boob, not a toenail. So many people expect you to be 'fine'. God help them if it happened to them. Even had stupid things like 'does it still hurt?' and 'you're OK now eh?'!

Friday 16 August
Had a lazy morning, saw Mum briefly. Went to LSD *(nickname for L&D)*. Mr P *(surgeon)* seemed in a hurry. He came in, had a look, said 'remove drain', then went on to say the tumour was larger than anticipated, he may have even said there were two of them. He removed eight of the sixteen lymphs as they had cancer in them too. Referred me to Dr M *(oncologist)*. He said three weeks of radiotherapy, start Tamoxifen for five years and the tumour was hormone positive so need to blast ovaries by injection for two years or by removal. Therefore now referred to a gynaecologist for that. Feel totally low – everything female has let me down. I am so scared I'm going to get this back and it will kill me. Went to pick kids up. Stayed at Iain and Em's until 11pm. Cried a lot tonight.

Saturday 17 August
Went to Mum's today. She said she had been really upset last night too. More tears for both of us today. Took Tamoxifen this morning. Strange vapour in throat? Sat in garden and did nothing really. Si did the shopping and cooked us a special tea. I do love him.

Monday 19 August
Mum took me to LSD *(nickname for hospital)*. Physio lady was very good. Said my muscle was very tight but I just had to keep working on it. Really hurt doing all the exercises. Got Mum to fix boob in place. Exercised arm tonight.

Tuesday 20 August
Went to Lou B's. Had coffee and the kids played. Then came back for lunch. Went to see Maureen. Had a good chat. Then onto Linda's. Amanda was there too. Got on the Breast Cancer support online quiz. It was a good laugh. The 'online girls' were fun. Working hard on arm.

Wednesday 21 August
Liz came and took the kids out for the day. Maggie took me down town. Had lunch in Slug and Lettuce, Maggie's treat. Arm doing well. Mum was impressed. Got on the Breast Cancer conference in Brighton on 5-6 October. Kids had tea at Tricia's. Got more flowers from Claire D, Jacquie and from Simon's work!

Saturday 24 August
Dad's Internment. Went into Harpenden to get some flowers. Got Mum a heather plant and cut some off to give to Dad. I'd promised heather for his funeral. It was very simple but really hard as it was really saying goodbye to Dad. It's so weird to think he is now lying in St Nicholas' churchyard with Emily.

What It Feels Like For a Girl

Sunday 25 August
Decided to make a cake with plums from Hils. Jezza phoned and we ended up having the kids for lunch whilst Hils was working. Left for Nottingham at 3.45pm. Lovely to see Jon, Hels, Jack and George. George is smiley and the spit of Jon!

Tuesday 27 August
Left Jon and Hel's at 9.30am. Went to Shirley's. Had a lovely chat and kids were super. They enjoyed playing in her beautiful garden. Left there at 11.15am and headed for Wales. Clear roads and got to Julie's about 4.30pm. Julie has a fab ring. Massive solitaire diamond!! Looking at four bedroom detached houses for £150,000!! Crazy.

Wednesday 28 August
Went to Barry Island. Kids had lots of fun making sandcastles and the weather was fantastic. Saw Avril, Julie's mum and Steve tonight. Left Julie's at 10.30pm. Got home about 12.45am! Did lots of exercises.

Thursday 29 August
At 9am Jan BC *(breast cancer)* nurse came over. She explained my tumour was stage 3 of 1-3! It was 4cm big and partially ductal but the rest was invasive with eight infected nodes, sixteen removed, so rather a lot, and a serious tumour so good job I did go to the doctor. She explained after radiotherapy I get six monthly checks. Felt low today and tired. I guess it's because it all came back again when we talked about it. Went up to school to see all the changes. Went out for lunch with Si and the kids. Si went out tonight. I watched TV and did some ironing. I wish I had a magic wish to make this all right.

Monday 2 September

Hassled radiotherapy appointment. Had a mega clear out of clothes in wardrobe. Very satisfying. Penny came over for the day as Tricia starts work today. Kids played nicely. James and I went to take Hils and Co to fetch Jezza's car from WGC *(Welwyn Garden City)*. Then we went to hers for tea.

Tuesday 3 September

SCHOOL. Got kids up and they were so excited! Sophie loved her first day in Y2. James ran straight into Nursery. Went to St Albans and got some clothes for the kids. Hils was in Watford and got me a bra! Went to park after school. Sorted out eyelashes/brows with Penny.

Wednesday 4 September

Handed out invitations for THE PARTY! Found a stringy cord going down my right side. Painful to stretch. Maureen got my pansies and I planted them out in the tubs and the borders and it looks pretty. Nice sunny day today.

Friday 6 September

Seeing Mr P *(surgeon)* 3.20pm today. Well, I saw the Registrar instead. I had to wait one and a half hours for a three minute appointment. He had a look and didn't say much. Mentioned ovaries again and well, we'll throw all we have at it at your age, as there was still cancer in the lymphs after chemo! How reassuring. Decided now that if I have ovaries out then no danger of ovarian cancer. So bonus point.

Saturday 7 September

Got period today, 28 days exact! Went to doctors for Tamoxifen. Had a good chat with Liz L. Saw Liz B and Cath

P in town. Took Sophie to Tap. She enjoyed it but I thought the lesson was shambolic. Kathryn stayed the night.

Sunday 8 September
Well, correction. Have period pain but not much occurring. Tamoxifen? Mum came for lunch today. Took Kathryn back to Iain and Emma's. Si went to gym. I watched our wedding video so I could see my Dad again.

Tuesday 10 September
Period arrived for real. Really painful. Tamoxifen is making it worse. I just wish they'd stop now. I hope the appointment with Mr O *(gynaecologist)* comes soon. Planned lessons for tomorrow.

Wednesday 11 September
Teaching today. Got in at 8am. Had a busy day. Rather hectic but I enjoyed it. Everyone was happy to see me, including the parents, which was nice. Rushed this evening. Sophie's ballet at 5.45pm so collected her from Katie N's.

Thursday 12 September
Taught 1C today for half the day. Took James to McDonald's for lunch and did party shop at Tesco's. Sophie went to Rainbows and curry for me at Suneela's with the girlies. Had a good laugh tonight. Got home about 11.30pm.

Saturday 14 September
Took Sophie to get her rabbit today. A lovely mini lop in white with grey smudges. Dad would have loved him. He's called Smudge and we get him on Monday.

Sunday 15 September
Went to Poplars Nursery at Toddington to get the double decker hutch. Sophie loved her party. They all had a good time. Ann L made a fantastic cake. Sophie had lots of super pressies.

Monday 16 September
Back to normal please God, or at least a future to hope for. Amen. Picked up Smudge at 10.30am with Hils. He was OK and seemed to like his hutch. Sophie was so excited to see him. Did Pilates tonight. Easing up slowly. Tamoxifen is giving me abdominal pain.

Tuesday 17 September
Radiotherapy mapping 4pm. Well, got a call to come at 2pm instead. It was very uncomfortable lying on the bench and holding my arm up. It was cold and undignified. Finally got away at 3.30pm and home by 4.30pm. My appointments will be 3.30pm which is crap as it will mean I can't do Pilates, collect Sophie, do clubs etc. Nightmare. So pissed off. Why do I get such a hard time? I've had a bucketful so far this year. Smudge came out for a play in the house. Sophie loved having her cuddle.

Wednesday 18 September
Boob fitting 10am. Went with Mum. Got a full boob and two new bras. Had two pockets put into old bras and looked at swimsuits but didn't find one I liked. Mum bought me the bras and swimming prosthesis. Sophie tended to Smudge. She loves cuddling him. Let him hop round the house. Pleased with bouncing boobie.

Thursday 19 September
School trip to Whipsnade. Great trip. Sophie had a super time. Lots of walking and sketching. Weather great. Got home and

Smudge not well. He hasn't eaten or drunk all day. Very listless. Ended up phoning the vet. Hils popped in and stayed with the kids whilst I took Smudge to the vet. He's dehydrated and has a food mass in his stomach. Given medications to help him pass it. Tried to get him to drink and eat tonight. Very worried he won't make it. Poor Smudge and poor Sophie. Got radiotherapy appointment changed to 11.50am.

Monday 23 September
What a crap day. Got to school and MW told me Margaret M had died yesterday in hospital *(from cancer)*. Talk about a slap of your own mortality. Then Mount Vernon hospital phoned and wanted me back to re-correct some areas of the mapping. Like I have nothing else to do. So I went off there with Julie G and then by the time I got back I had to shoot up to school to get Sophie. Hils made my day by cheering me up with a jacket she bought me from Per Una. Lovely blue cord.

Tuesday 24 September
Dad's birthday. Tough day. Went with Mum to the churchyard. We both laid our flowers and put cards there. Went and had a coffee and a piece of birthday cake together. Cleaned out Smudge and he seems happier. Hopefully he's getting better. Went for tea at Hils. When we got back we released the kids' balloons to Dad. It was quite emotional. I do find it so hard to believe he has gone.

Wednesday 25 September
Got woken up at 1am today by James covered in sick. He carried on being sick. I had to arrange to get Sophie collected to and from school. Poor James just kept retching. He eventually could keep water down by 4pm. He went to sleep at 5pm.

Thursday 26 September
First radiotherapy. Kept James at home today. Left home at 11am to Mount Vernon, got there by 11.35am. Parking wait of five minutes. Treatment wait of one hour! It was uncomfortable but actual blasts only last three minutes total. Got home 1.35pm. Went to park with James. Got Sophie. Cleaned out Smudge who seems MUCH better.

Friday 27 September
Second radiotherapy. Waited 35 minutes today. Mind you Julie G took me and we had to go via her college so a long morning. After radiotherapy, we went to Rose and Crown for lunch. Very tired today but I guess that's the strain of the week.

Saturday 28 September
Very tired and out of sorts today. Too much time 'thinking', not a good thing. Kids went to Mum's. We went to Hils and Jez's. Had a great time. Food good. Jez got loads of themed pressies for his 40th. Got to bed at 3am.

Monday 30 September
Yet another wait at Mount Vernon. Left home at 11am with Hils. Managed to make shepherd's pie for tea, sort out washing and nip into shops beforehand. Got to Mount Vernon at 11.25am. Bummer as we were 25 minutes early. Then had to wait for 50 minutes. My appointment takes 20 minutes. Got home at 1.45pm. Missed Margaret M's funeral. Went to the Fox for a late lunch. Went to Pilates and then got home at 5.30pm to do tea and bed routine.

Tuesday 1 October
Well, I popped into Sarah's for coffee. Iced Sophie's cake and then set off with Liz B to Mount Vernon. RECORD…

2 hour wait. Dr M *(oncologist)* wanted to view the set up or something so I ended up waiting on his arrival after he'd had lunch etc. I was livid. Got home at 2.50pm. I was so angry I'd had to make lots of adjustments to childcare etc. They have no consideration and no one apologised or came to explain. Went bowling with staff tonight from school. Really good fun. I won three games!! And got three strikes.

Wednesday 2 October
Sophie's 7th birthday. Sophie woke up at 6.10am!! She loved all her pressies. Simon had the day off. Paula took me to Mount Vernon. Waited 60 minutes today. Home by 1.30pm. Got food for party tea. Collected Katie N from school with Sophie. They had a good party tea. Penny, Alex and Odette came too. We made badges, bead pictures and had treasure hunts. Went to Governors Meeting tonight. Sophie loved her cake and all her pressies too. I hope she had a lovely day.

Thursday 3 October
Today Sally drove me to Mount Vernon hospital. We got there 10 minutes early. I still had to wait an hour. So far I have waited nearly 7 hours. Maureen had had 14 treatments in the waiting time I have had. Still, they set me up and zapped me in 10 minutes so that was quicker. Simon was off today too. I think I am getting hot flushes these days. Not doing much other than going to Mount Vernon every day.

Friday 4 October
Pat collected me for Mount Vernon. We left at 11.10am and as we got in at 11.50am I was shown in after 5 minutes!!! I was out by 12.05pm. The traffic was crap so we were back by 12.45pm.

Saturday 5 October
Brighton Conference. Left home at 7am. Got 7.15am train. Had to pay excess fare as ticket was wrong! Busy day. Very interesting talks. Met a nice girl called Billie and saw Lesa from chat room. Very interesting talk from an oncologist. Dairy issue not solved. If on Tamoxifen it may be counter productive to cut out dairy and do extra soya. Must ask Dr M. Also must ask about bone density scan as I will be entering early menopause. Must also ask about the urgency of ovarian ablation. Aromatherapy was interesting... did some on our BC *(breast cancer)* partner. Lots of people at different stages, some in chemo, some in radiotherapy, some newly diagnosed. Glad I came.

Sunday 6 October
I had to give a presentation feedback. After conference went for a walk along the seafront with Billie, Caz and Jo. Billie gave me a lift to the station. Got home knackered about 4pm.

Monday 7 October
Very tired today. Saw Dr M at Mount Vernon. Asked lots of questions and actually had a good chat. Waited for an hour for radiotherapy today. Went to Pilates. Practically asleep by 7.30pm these days.

Tuesday 8 October
Managed to jump queue to get seen early so I could get back to school for 1.30pm Harvest Festival. Sophie did very well and the assembly was lovely. Managed to get back into tight black jeans!!

Wednesday 9 October
Radiotherapy was only 20 minutes today. Paula and I had lunch in Café Blue Dog as we were back by 1pm.

Thursday 10 October
Got to radiotherapy for 10.45am and was seen on time as it was a training day. Came home by 11.30am and went to bed. Very tired. Liz took James. After school, Sophie had Rainbows. I had an early night. Head feels like it's full of cotton wool. Can't think straight.

Friday 11 October
Emma took me to radiotherapy. Again seen on time and home early. Stopped off at St Albans McDonald's! Tricia collected Sophie from school. Kids went there for tea so I had a rest. Early night again.

Monday 14 October
Mount Vernon – three left. Got in, 20 minutes wait today. Hils and I came back and went to The Bell. Went up to school and spent £53 on uniform! James was so excited to be in uniform. Did Pilates. Simon was late home. He had been on a course and wine tasting. Not too tired today.

Tuesday 15 October
Mount Vernon – two left. Shirley took me today. I waited half an hour and home by 1.30pm. Parents Evening tomorrow. I had Katie and Spencer tonight while Hils and Jez went up to school tonight.

Wednesday 16 October
Last radiotherapy today. Paula arrived with champagne and party poppers. Waited 50 minutes today. Then that's it.... weird feeling of 'what now?' Went to Harvester with Paula for lunch. Parents Evening tonight. Sophie had a brill report. She's on target for level 3 in her SAT's and has worked really hard. James is.... a boy. He can be silly but on the whole, bright.

Thursday 17 October
Freedom Day! Cleaned out Smudge. Went out for lunch with Hils. It was a surprise she'd organised. Linda, Sally and Julie G came too. It was a nice way to celebrate. Bought Sophie a pressie for doing so well at school and a bribe for James! Hils told school I was available for work now! CF apparently shot off to the office and informed them!

Wednesday 23 October
Met Helen and Katie L, Dagmar and Anne at Activity World. Had a good old gossip and catch up. Dagmar is leaving to move to Ireland in January. Helen seems happy enough. Chilled out in afternoon and Mum came to babysit so we could go out for a meal tonight with Maureen and Colin. Went to Café Blue Dog. Food was excellent and I drank too much wine.

Thursday 24 October
Felt a bit hungover! Went into school to photocopy all the emails for Maureen. Then picked kids up from Tricia and had everyone back for lunch. Went to Hils at 3pm. Kids had tea, Hils and I had too much wine! Got home at 8pm, very drunk!

Saturday 26 October
James not well. He has a temperature and croaky voice. Got a cough too. Didn't go to Harry's party. We did take him bowling but he was very sorry for himself. He got a strike, Sophie enjoyed herself. Paul and Julie came round for drinks with Elliot. Elliot stayed the night.

Sunday 27 October
James very hot – 39°. Rather concerned. Sophie went to London to do the Stride For Life and raised £117. James has croup and was admitted to QE2 A&E for five hours today.

Breathing shallow and heart rate up. Given Dexamethasone and Calpol for high temperature. Very scary. Very nasty cough. Saw Pauline – Emily's health visitor.

Monday 28 October
What a weekend! James slept in our room last night. So much better. I was really scared yesterday that he might have to be ventilated as his heart was working so hard, as were his lungs. No school for him today. He was rather grumpy and not himself. Simon worked from home as the gales had upset all the trains. Did nothing today really. Very tired and lacked incentive.

Tuesday 29 October
I kept James off again today. He is still coughing but not as noisy as he was. I had my hair cut for the first time in eight months! £30!! God, prices have gone up and I didn't have much cut! Feeling a bit low and neglected really. I need some me-time. I need to get back to the gym.

Wednesday 30 October
Great. Period again. Well, now I know why I had backache! Helped Helen with the Christmas boxes. Cleaned house and had PTA meeting tonight. Went out with Hils, Shirley, Suneela and Helen afterwards. Hils and I drank a bottle of red each! Very drunk and got in at midnight.

Thursday 31 October
Oh... not well... threw up this morning and had to get Tricia to take the kids to school. Shirley was sick too. Finally felt better about lunchtime! Didn't do a lot today. Sophie went to Katie N's Halloween party. I took James, Sophie and Penny trick or treating afterwards. Hils was out with Jez in a pub!! God she has stamina. Jez was text flirting!

Friday 1 November
Better today. Helped out in school. Rosie had me do the spelling test! Cheeky. Did readers for her and other errands! Sophie went to Felix's party after school. James went to Spencer's for tea. Hils and I had white wine spritzers!

Monday 4 November
Went to the gym today! Did a workout – felt knackered. Didn't realise how unfit I was now! Had a swim too! Then had lunch with Hils, Shirl and Helen at the gym. Went to Asda and got some Xmas pressies. Went to Pilates today too! School was broken into yesterday. They had police helicopter, dogs and four squad cars! Caught some Y10 boys from the secondary school. Went out to Cathy's for a drink tonight to cheer Shirl up.

Tuesday 5 November
Really achy today! Having coffee with Lyn W. We went up to school to get James after and had a chat with Gilly. It was nice to catch up with Lyn and hear her news. Had Elliot home after school for tea. We did sparklers. Watched a programme on Sex Tips!!!! Had some fun sex after!

Thursday 7 November
Spoke to Sue on the phone last night. Did the usual boring domestic stuff. Ladies' night up at school was good fun. I got some chrimbo pressies sorted. Went for a drink after with Hils and Claire.

Friday 8 November
Helped out in Rosie's class this morning. I was supposed to be teaching Nursery this afternoon but it was cancelled. Got a letter from Mr O *(gynaecologist)* – apparently I had an

appointment but didn't show! Funny as I never got a letter in the first place.

Saturday 9 November
Went to gym with Hils this afternoon. Disaster! My swim boobie is punctured! What a waste of £40. Had tea with the Sinnotts. Had a fun evening of chat and booze.

Thursday 14 November
Thought about going to the gym but instead decided to clean out the kitchen cupboards! Cleared out loads of rubbish. Taught the Nursery class this afternoon again and did large apparatus and painting etc. Booked tickets for Harry Potter movie on Saturday. Phoned Mum and asked if she wanted to come.

Sunday 17 November
Helena's christening was lovely. Rev'd 'JR' did it. Had food and drink at Glen Eagles after. Tricia and Richard went a bit OTT.

Tuesday 19 November
James' school induction. Spent morning cleaning and ironing. Went to school meeting this afternoon. MW spent more time talking about school buildings and status than on routine for Reception children. I even got her to mention reading but ended up having to explain it myself! James had a super time in CF's class.

Thursday 21 November
Went to gym with Emma. Did good workout. Collected James and then we wrote his Xmas cards and played games this afternoon. Took Sophie to Rainbow's. Then it was off

to the Big Night Out! Met up with Hils, Shirl, Sally, Pat and Manda!! Si came along later. Si went and sorted my personal trainer and got kids toys from Toys R Us! Kids had their faces painted: Santa for James and as a reindeer for Sophie!

Friday 22 November
Worked in Reception today. Student was very laid back and critical of the school! Seems odd for a student. Easy day really. I heard readers and did an art activity. I hope James gets on OK in Reception. He seems as if he is ahead of some of them in reading and he hasn't started yet. Odette stayed for tea. Si went for a beer with Steve, Sailesh and Co.

Sunday 24 November
Went to Daz and Sarah's today. Matthew is very like Charlotte. Had a lovely day at the christening. Daz and Sarah haven't changed. The kids all had lots of fun dancing at the disco. Got home at 4.30pm. Sorted Sophie's room out for decorating.

Tuesday 26 November
Busy day. John arrived and finished Sophie's room today. It is a really bright blue colour. She's happy. Danny came and finished doing the fence with his mate. I went to the gym this morning. Had an hour's workout. Grabbed an OJ then collected James to have his school lunch. He was really good and ate it all.

Wednesday 27 November
Weird day. Got to L&D at 9am. Was seen early by Mr O *(gynaecologist)* to discuss having my ovaries out. He was rather curt and blunt. He said I would need vitamin D and calcium supplements now until I was fifty. This wouldn't guarantee it wouldn't come back either. I will go in on 14

January overnight and hopefully come out on 15 January. Oh well, won't be able to start my personal trainer until February now. James and I had a nice walk in the woods this afternoon. Took my broken boobie back. Had Virgin Vie party. Got £52 in commission!

Thursday 28 November
Went to solicitors to sign over all the probate things for Dad. It was really odd and stirred it all up again for me. Felt really low this afternoon. James had induction afternoon. Went out bowling with Y2 mums. Chatted a lot to Deb R. All my crew weren't there. Got home about 11.30pm.

Friday 29 November
Must go to bed early. Went to gym with Hils. Came home and took it easy really. At home, James and I chilled out and tidied this afternoon. Hils popped in for a coffee after lunch. Went to Hoddesdon after school for Aine's party. Nice to see them all again. Mum retired today. It was all very emotional for her without my Dad being there. Watched Celebrity Big Brother. Mark Owen won.

Sunday 1 December
Mum's 61st birthday. Cooked lunch for Mum, Iain and Lisa. It was strange again without Dad. His not being here is really hard again. I think Mum had a nice day. Did a cake etc.

Thursday 5 December
Working in 1C. Busy day, my playground duty and I helped choreograph dances at lunchtime! So now it's rest for me. Went out tonight with Hils, Shirley, Linda, Amanda and Suneela. Had Greek food then onto the George.

Friday 6 December
Supply teaching in the Nursery. Had a nice day in Nursery today. Enjoyed taking it easy and less fast paced. Bloody cold day mind you. Went out and met Simon at the Old Bell as the kids were with Liz and Rog tonight. Met up with Paul and Julie too. Went for coffee, home 1.30am!

Wednesday 11 December
Working pm, 1S. Wasn't sure if I was working the morning too but as I wasn't I went and got my swim boob and did a bit of shopping. Went into work in the afternoon. Play rehearsal and Literacy Hour. The student was in. Had Chinese at Shirley's with MEAT!

Tuesday 17 December
Busy day. I went up to school eight times today. Dropped kids off. Went to B&Q and got singing Santas. Went to school to watch the play. Came home, took Simon to station then to Dunstable to get Sophie's curtains, more Xmas lights and a McD's. Then dropped James into school for play production. Got him at 2.40pm and went back to get Sophie later. Mum came to put up Sophie's curtains. Went for tea at Hils. Stayed until 8pm. NATIVITY VERY GOOD. Kids were great and sang well. Simon in Croydon at Xmas party.

Wednesday 18 December
Got an appointment for post radiotherapy at 14 weeks! Eight weeks overdue and I had to chase them. Not very good really. I get so angry that I have to chase them up all the time. Made mince pies this morning.

Friday 20 December
James' last day at Nursery. It was really weird knowing he

isn't going back there after chrimbo. Took kids to St Mary's for party. Simon was very good as Santa. Sophie and James were both fooled but Sophie then guessed. Had a drink back at Jez's. Si went out for a beer with Steve and Ian.

Saturday 21 December
Emily's 8th Anniversary. Weird day. Took Emily and Dad some flowers. Very emotional. Mum had found a gift tag from Dad to her in the Xmas wrapping paper box and that set her and me off. Did some last minute card delivering and roast lamb for tea. Si went to the gym.

Sunday 22 December
Simon's birthday. Mum came and took kids to church. Then we all went to Liz's for lunch. Stephanie had a baby girl tonight. Went to Helen and Mark's for drinks. Swapped pressies with the Sinnotts. Didn't go out for Si's birthday, felt bad I hadn't made a cake or anything.

Monday 23 December
Four and a half weeks since last period and I had hoped that was it. Four months on Tamoxifen hasn't stopped them. Well here's hoping this is the last one! It should be as in three weeks I'll be ovary-less! Went to panto with the girls and all the kids this afternoon. Babysat for Hils tonight as it was her birthday. Told kids we are going to London tomorrow.

Tuesday 24 December
Must pick up turkey. Going to London for the London Eye at 11am then on for lunch and then the Lion King at the theatre. We're going with all the grandparents. Sophie and James had no idea about what we were going to see. James threw a wobbly at the London Eye and didn't want to go on

it. Eventually we got him on and had a capsule to ourselves because of his fuss! We had a great view and then we went to lunch in Covent Garden. We walked into the Lion King and Sophie twigged, James didn't. It was excellent. Great costumes etc. Really amazing scenery. Got back 6pm and went to Hils for drinks then back to prepare for Xmas.

Wednesday 25 December
James was up at 5.45am but actually didn't open his stocking, he came into us. Sophie got up at 6.45am and it was then all excitement. We opened pressies and the massive mountain was gone by 10am! Liz, Roger and Alister came, then Iain and Lisa. We swapped pressies. Iain and Lisa had been to see Dad's grave. Mum arrived at 12.30pm. We had lunch then more pressies. We played the games. I had lots of DVD's, CD's, jewellery and clothes. It sounds ungrateful but despite all that it didn't feel like Christmas... my Dad was missing.

Saturday 28 December
Got up at 7.30am and on the road by 9.30am. Met up with the Sinnotts at 11.30am near Bristol. Both cars bulging with stuff. Got to house in Devon at 2.30pm. Very nice. It is huge. There was a massive hamper of goodies for us all too, with chocs etc in it. Kids all went swimming. Lit a real fire and ate and chatted.

Monday 30 December
Panto today. Up late. Went swimming, had lunch, went to Plymouth to the panto. It was very good. The kids enjoyed it. Very different to St Albans Arena!! Got back, more swimming, sauna, the boys cooked tea. Emma said that they were going to see Chicago in January. Iain had planned the perfect day: breakfast in bed, nails, hair, show, dinner and stay in posh

London hotel! Sometimes I feel like I really got clobbered with the life-doesn't-care-about-you vibe.

Tuesday 31 December
Em even thinks having my ovaries out isn't such a big deal as I didn't want more kids now but... it's another piece of shit in my life. Simon keeps telling me how brave I am and how proud he is and that I act as if nothing is different but he doesn't get it. I think he forgets what I have been through. I am not asking for special treatment but sometimes it would be nice to be pampered. I can't wait to stick two fingers up to the end of this BASTARD YEAR. Did fireworks. We went swimming, sauna etc and played games. The kids had a party tea and watched a DVD whilst we had our steaks later. At midnight it felt like a weight off my shoulders. I phoned Mum and left a message on her machine. We let the kids go swimming briefly at 12.00am. Then they went off to bed. We stayed up until 4am.

Wednesday 1 January
Got up at 10.30am feeling OK. No hangover and not too tired. Sophie still not 100%. Started the year with a bacon sarni! Went to Bude beach and it was lovely being blown about. Kids played on the beach and then we came back. They swam, I read. Sometimes I can't be bothered with the constant entertaining and doing something.

Thursday 2 January
Iain and Emma are off to Jane's for the day. We all had a swim and sauna. We left for Plymouth about 12ish. We went to the Aquarium which was good. Trouble is, once you've seen Sydney's it's not the same! Had lunch, did a bit of shopping and got back around 6pm. Had our tea and the Sinnotts got

back about 6.30pm. Swim and sauna again... gave myself a sauna headache. Had a long chat to Iain in the sauna about life in general. I don't think he would have dealt with this if it had been Emma. Log fire and a chat until 2am.

Friday 3 January
Breakfast in bed! Today is the last day here. Lazy day and mad packing! Iain took Matt out to play Jedi on some hill.

Saturday 4 January
Home to washing, ironing etc. James went to Rory's party this afternoon. Went to see Mum. Sophie gave her the wind chime to say thanks for looking after Smudge. Life back to 'normal' hopefully now.

In celebration of the life of Fiona Crompton

Young Guns

Fi, Head Girl at sixth form, seated fourth from the right, with her usual beaming smile.

Me at sixth form, seated far right on a bench where the cushions have been ripped up and positioned far left.

Me, Fi and an Elmer Fudpucker.

Flirty Fi

A 'playful' fallen angel.

Fi 'engaging' with me and a giant birthday cookie.

Fi being 'enticing', not quite naked in my bed.

Fi looking 'coy', with that famous smile.

From the top:

Fi and Nina Barough, founder of Walk the Walk.

Fi with Sally Gunnell.

Full Mooning with cousin Debs.

Tired and emotional with best friend Emma.

Walk On:

With Norma and her daughter Steph, Hlls and Sophie.

A welcome post-MoonWalk treat.

Iain and Debs' gang doing it for Fi in 2010.

Sophie and fellow Moon-ers in 2010.

On this page:

Emily Bean.

Sophie and James in my laundry basket. Underneath is a photo of Fiona with her brother Iain in a similar pose minus the laundry basket. I love the resemblance between mother and daughter.

From the top:

The WNTW 'after' shot.

Fab Fi in WNTW dress and funky boots.

Fi's 39th birthday, renewing her wedding vows.

My Beautiful Friend:

Full of love and fizz, the day after a chemotherapy session.

Fi with Schnauzer puppy Mac, named after her dad.

Foxy chick with foxy red hair.

8

Positivity

As mentioned in Fi's diary entry for 24 October 2002, throughout the year she had been emailing her friend Maureen and had made copies for each other to put in a file. Fi had three brightly coloured, smiley-faced files full of this correspondence and they were extremely important to her in order to keep her spirits high and her will strong. Maureen also was going through the same experience of a breast cancer diagnosis and treatment. The files contain lots of funny, rude photos, jokes and stories that are readily available via the Internet, as well as their own conversations. It was their own little support unit to keep each other positive.

Maureen was also a teacher at the same school as Fi. At the same time, breast cancer had affected another teacher, Jackie, and also a member of the school office staff, Margaret. Sadly Margaret lost her battle with cancer in September 2002, as noted in Fi's diary. These four amazing women became known between Fi and Maureen as the 'Giant Four',

Maureen's nickname based on Fe, Fi, Fo, Fum: the oft-repeated phrase from the fairytale with that famous giant, well known by infant teachers, parents and children alike.

The Giant Four as created by Maureen

I've come up with a good name for us four – but this needs working on. How about Fe, Fi, Fo, Fum?

Fe – is for you. My best friend at college was called Fiona and her nickname was Fe-Fe or Fe for short.

Fi – is for Jackie. She has **defied** all odds and come through her op and keymo with a positive attitude and been very successful.

I'm not too sure about the last two, but could be:

Fo – for me as I am going to extirpate the **foe** - to understand this you need to have listened to Mendelssohn's Elijah recently.

Fum – I need some help here, as I can't think of a connection between Margaret and Fum, so Fiona thinking cap on...

Fiona replies, thinking cap securely in place:

Fe, Fi, Fo, Fum is good. I was always Fi for short (Fe will do phonetically it's the infant teacher in me) and as for Margaret she always has her finger or if need be Fum on the pulse at school!! Fum, get it! Again infant spelling allowed. Work with me here.

POSITIVITY

Make Fun
Nicknames often feature throughout their correspondence. Oncologists and consultants were given titles such as Grand Master, The Cure Facilitator, Plastics Man, The Creator, The Butcher and The Barber.

FE: Actually Lump has had a name from the start as I refused to have a tumour. So TREVOR was named. Why Trevor? Well, every Trevor I have come across has been a bastard. So that's his name and I didn't want him to stay so I picked a name I didn't like.

FO: Ermintrude!! What do you think – a good name for a boob or what? You can always have Ermintrude II. It looks like a real udder at the moment but I am assured that the swelling will subside.

FE: Love the name Ermintrude, yes, definitely a good choice. The udder connection is a hoot, in fact one could say 'udderly ridiculous!' Did they mention to you the sense of humour side effects to all this? Apparently if you didn't have a warped sense of one you will do!!

Through Sick and Sin
The files are full of positive, supportive and funny messages sent in order to help each other through all the treatments they had to endure. Here are some of their accounts during chemotherapy:

FO: Oops... must have taken the pill too late! Three mighty heaves ensured that I re-examined my lunch but I do feel better now! At least I have a genuine excuse for not eating now and I've nearly downed my last of my two litres of water. Must go and nurse my Tupperware container now.

FE: Get them to give you a Werthers sweet to suck; it totally takes the sick feeling away from the Cyclo drug. Hey, it's only taken six goes to find that out!

FE: I am glad you agree what a strange effect keymo has on everything! I don't think we will ever be the same again. I know that I won't ever want to eat any more chewing gum after this! Nor will I get totally plastered again as the effect is so like keymo without the fun beforehand!

FO: SHEEP TICKS ARE ATTRACTED TO KEYMO CHEMICALS. Would you believe this, but sometime over the last few days I picked up a sheep tick from Orienteering. My first priority was to get to the surgery and have this persistent thing removed from my leg. Persistent in that all attempts to remove it (with tweezers), kill it (with salt, perfume, eye drops and anything else in my toilet bag), suffocate it (with a smear of Nivea and a plaster and then Vaseline) had failed and of course it would have to be day seven post keymo, the beginning of my lowest white cell count. Well, the local emergency doctor felt she couldn't tackle it so guess where I spent three hours yesterday evening – the A&E department. The offending animal was about 1.5cm long, well bedded in and removed by a surgeon under local anaesthetic. I now have about five stitches in my leg and another course of antibiotics to take! I hope the above account has managed to lighten your day for a moment.

FE: I feel OK today which has surprised me. I took my anti-sick pills as instructed. I don't feel nauseous and maybe it's positive thinking but I never had morning sickness and don't often puke so maybe that is why? You probably didn't want all that info but hey we will know each other well through all this now!!

Positivity

The wee is still a bit red but that is the drug and should fade today/tomorrow. God the things we talk about!

FE: Get the flags out this time tomorrow I may feel crap but I will be a KEYMO graduate!!!

Hair Today
On wig wearing as an antidote to the awful, dreaded and disheartening loss of hair, Fi comments:

Hope your night out was as terrific as mine! I walked into a packed room head held high with my husband and best friend Emma and her husband by my side! OK, a bit self-conscious at first, but then I thought 'sod it' I intend to have a good time and anyone who stares is just jealous of my fantastic new hairstyle! In fact some people's looked dodgier than mine! I had some lovely comments from people saying how good it was to see me. Some of the guys there were balding so the ones I know best I jokingly asked for scalp care tips and they said well done for being so up about it!

Tomorrow we are off to dinner with friends. Another outing for a wig! Long or short? The only downer is one of the wives going is the one who couldn't stop staring at my hair, then went on to corner me as to how you look for a lump and how would she know etc, never a thought for how I was feeling. I came really close to punching her!! I am not a violent person but some people take the biscuit!

Question: Does a wig go frizzy in the rain? Answer: No, apparently not! Nor does the rain drip off it as if it were Teflon coated!

Can Do Attitude
Promoting their positive thinking, Maureen and Fi sent each other lists of the day and messages of encouragement:

FO: My achievements today include:

- Arm going right back on the third exercise and I mean flat back, none of that cheaty how far back can you stretch your thumb nonsense to make it seem that you are touching the floor. Brilliant.
- I was able to lie on my left side for a short while in bed last night – first time since the op and it was hardly uncomfortable at all.
- Ermintrude didn't object to me doing the repetitive ironing this morning – oh dear does this mean that vacuuming is going to be back on the agenda soon?

Positive points for the day:

- Get an imaginary ride on a rollercoaster…. This is how I decided to view my keymo treatment… just scream my way through them and get off at the end thinking how brilliant it was. How far round the world did you get last Wednesday? Have you got to plan another journey yet? Or did you miss the flight?
- Get rid of masses of unwanted visitors in my blood.
- Get to read my book for two hours.
- Get to chew gum, drink ginger beer and don't cook any meals.
- Get to snooze more than the cat.
- My hair is dropping out because the keymo is working.

POSITIVITY

FE: My achievements so far today are:

- Got kids up and out without a fight!
- Sophie did her comprehension this morning in one go!
- James ate breakfast, cleaned his own teeth and ate his vitamin without complaint.
- I washed my hair in HOT water; still got A LOT left and blow-dried it on HIGH!!!
- Thought 'sod it', I refused to be dictated to by a lump.
- Took my enormous house-sized vitamin.
- Emailed my friend before 8.45am (that's you by the way).

My positives are:

- The sun is shining.
- I have slept tons and bags under eyes are going!
- Planting sunflowers later.
- Have lovely friend who posts surprises through my letterbox!
- I did two crosswords that have no clues just missing letters!
- Ate whole packet of Jaffa cakes but still got into size 10 trousers this morning! (Bridget Jones or what!!!)

FO: I actually woke up this morning with a smile on my face. Strange but rather lovely feeling. Possible reasons for my smile:

- I have a brilliant floppy hat that makes me feel special.
- I have a brilliant friend called Fe.
- The sun was shining.
- I don't feel icky, headachy or bloated.
- I just feel HAPPY.

- Jo phoned to ask if I'd like to walk her dog with her this afternoon. I had to say no because of a visitor but it was a very kind thought of Jo.
- Colin *(Maureen's husband)* came home at lunchtime – he had also come home at 9.30am so I could use the car for the doctors. I love Colin.

Maureen writes to Fi:

I've decided that every third Wednesday I'm going to think about something really fantastic to do (in my head). Haven't quite decided what but the idea is going to be so brilliant and positive that it is going to carry me through. I am not going to enter that room gagging... The Barber told me that some people sail through keymo – well I AM going to be one of the sailors – not a sinker and SO ARE YOU.

Wonder whether you have been watching any of the Marathon? What fantastic athletes they all appear to be. Well, we are facing and achieving a Marathon of our own... and managing a pretty good job of it too.

I'm so sorry you have had this news about your Dad. I'm not going to use those awful words that have made you want to eventually burn your cards – but I am really hurting for you. Please try and remain strong – this is important for everyone concerned. Come and share your anger with me – we are in this together.

Rest is your friend – be comfortable with lots of rest – rest and sleep are gifts, not a waste of time. Speak seriously to those white cells Fe. Have the best day possible.

Positivity

Your body rebuilds when you relax: meditate and think on a precious childhood memory, favourite smells (do this today before keymo kicks in!), let your mind run to several happy thoughts. Do what you can and feel good about things you ARE able to accomplish today.

Have a friend over for coffee. Push through feeling physically bad and be with people.

Think of a rainbow. It's not the pot of gold you're after – just the sunshine after the storm.

I hope you are feeling well rested and have the yucky feeling under control... did I tell you how dry crackers worked for me, instead of the sicky pills? I still think you have done amazingly well not to be delayed this time – after all you have been through in the past three weeks. This illustrates your amazing abilities and strengths – and I'm not just saying that.

Have a good day, keep taking the pills and so what about the extra weight. We can and will cope with such minor inconveniences and we will be trim with full heads of hair again one day – and maybe even able to visit the chiller section of the supermarket without experiencing withdrawal symptoms.

Celebration. Wisdom reminds you to celebrate and honour all things large or small in your life. Find something to celebrate NOW.

Good old Grand Master. He does try hard with his bedside manner! I am really sorry that you have to undergo more female removals, but we must find a bright side to this.

You must not lose track of the fact that your ovaries too have already served a wonderful function and you have your lovely children to prove it.

Think positive about what you CAN wear for Christmas – you know you will look fabulous in on or off the shoulder, because you are you and your personality will carry any kind of dress. I mean this Fe.

Sleep well, oh hot flushy one.

I am devising a new award scheme for you. You are awarded:

- **GOLD:** If you are more than one hour late in for your appointment, and manage to keep calm and positive.
- **SILVER:** If you are between 30-59 minutes late in and are still calm and relaxed, maybe ten pages of your book to be read.
- **BRONZE:** If you are between 0-29 minutes late in… and manage to enter without a sarcastic comment either verbally or in your head.

Fiona says to Maureen:

You have done really well. I am very impressed with ALL your achievements. Please don't overdo it with the tap dancing. Great news with the bra.

Thank you for your poems. We shall have to compile an anthology between us and call it something like "Keeping Abreast of Boredom".

Positivity

"Dear Fo, it is Fe
I was so pleased to read
You are now feeling in control,
No longer reaching for that bowl.
You will soon be dancing again and strutting your stuff
Just take it easy and Ermintrude will not puff.
The Plastics Man with his needle will give you relief,
Just make sure you see him to spare yourself grief!
Another weekend has arrived once again
Let us hope it brings sunshine not rain!
Let others pay court to your every need
Just remember you're a very special person indeed.
Take it easy my friend and remember to smile
And together we'll kick this and show them in style!"

I say two fingers up to our unwelcome intruder and bring on back normal life. We CAN and WILL do this and thank God we are tough cookies, Fo.

Keep smiling and remember we are FANTASTIC!!

Have been thinking about you all day in between my rushing about. Hope you are feeling as well as possible in this phase. Your mentor's orders today are:

- Keep taking the tablets.
- Keep drinking the beer (ginger variety only).
- Chew lots of gum.
- Rest and be pampered.
- Sleep longer than the cat.
- Go nowhere near reports.

- Smile lots as it makes people wonder what you're up to!
- Read mentor's emails.
- Remember to press send!

I make you laugh! Hey it's mutual Mrs W. I think it really helps to have a fellow sufferer – no strike that – a fellow fighter to go through the battle with.

Thank you for the yoghurt, it was lovely to have ginger in another form other than a biscuit or a beer. I will never question the healing power of ginger again!

I loved your 'e male' yesterday. I thought it was so spooky that you sent me a piccie of Jaffa cakes as I had eaten a whole packet of them that afternoon! Did you know that they contain less calories than the average biccie?

All rest and no play makes FANTASTIC WHITE CELLS!

Congratulations to you and just think, in three weeks this will all be a bad stomach dream!

HUMOUR is the key word and a POSITIVE MENTAL ATTITUDE.

Thank you. I really needed your ego boosting email. It means a lot to me as you have been there and had those thoughts and come through it this far.

Oh my Angel Card today was great. I was wondering about what I should do, where I should be heading and dealing with all the things, and the card came up with 'Choices'. It basically

Positivity

told me that worrying is simply my head trying to control my life. I should make decisions from my heart, from my deep, inner stillness and then I'll stop worrying.

I have been amazed at the kaleidoscope of emotions that we went through in the last seven months. I am glad we have it all in print. Life WILL improve for us from now on... Positive thoughts and aims must be the way forward.

I had some lovely flowers from school yesterday. It was a nice surprise. I also had a note asking me to do some supply teaching!

Had my six month MOT and passed without incident! I think I would have been shocked if they had said there was a problem, as I hadn't prepared myself for one. That is the effect of being a positive thinker!

The Best Medicine
Humour was paramount. As well as sending each other a constant stream of jokes and funny pictures from the Internet, their messages contain several witticisms and puns.

FO: Thanks for the males. What's it like to be active in the radio variety??

www.farmergiles.co.uk Have you tried the frozen pea packet remedy? Only the softest of cushions for you my girl. Keep thinking positives...

How long will my pizza be? We don't do long ones sir. Only round ones.

FE: I don't work here, I'm a consultant.

Right, must go and catch up on Eastenders. I do like seeing something that makes my life look good!!

Girl Talk
There is much talk about boobs, of course.

FO: Must finish my tap practice now so I am ready for my lesson tomorrow. I have no problem with the jumps now and feel Ermintrude has totally healed. So just think Fe, one month down the line and you'll have a nice pert right boob that feels totally at home – no problem. And the morphine is bliss.

What an absolute pain to have such a long wait yesterday. I don't know any other profession that would do it – teachers, lawyers, bankers etc. All that for four minutes and a grope.

I know that feeling about saying goodbye to your boob… and yes, yours has not been around as long as mine had – now Fe, just think of the positives here. It has served its purpose admirably and fed your delightful children. You are not only parting company from your boob, but more importantly Trevor and the Cancer as well…. This is GOOD NEWS. Your eventual replacement will be pert at all times and stand proud for all to see your wonderful profile. With a carefully chosen name you will be able to introduce her to everyone and cause endless wonder from your friends. Come on – just think how much amusement Ermintrude has created! I will not entertain the idea of 'blancmange' or 'doomed chicken fillets'.

FE: Thank you for all your advice. I found it really helpful. I had read somewhere about taking arnica and thought I would

POSITIVITY

try it, so if you don't want those pills I will have them. Do you still have Jackie's bras? If not I was going to ring her anyway. I do have some crop tops that they suggest because I won't have anything to support until I get my fake boob fitted. By the way I would never call Ermintrude a chicken fillet or blancmange. She is far superior. That is what my replacement will look like until I have my reconstruction next October or thereabout. I have decided to call it Marjory after the first chicken in Big Brother.

Read that there was a very interesting article in Hello magazine about Koo Stark who has recently had a mastectomy so I feel that the rich and the beautiful aren't exempt from this. She, like me, can't have a reconstruction yet so I got a strange sense of comfort knowing others have to go through this too. Does that sound strange?

That aqueous cream is very good. I am rubbing it into my shark bite! Yes, my son thinks it is like having an action man for a Mum! He has an action man shark attack so hence his vivid imagination.

I have finally found a bra that stops my boob roaming around… it is an M&S front fastener, which is suitable for walking, golf and yoga!!! Didn't know that boobs could play golf etc!!!

LUXACOMFORT: Adheres directly to the chest wall so you can stick it on and go. I couldn't face another op *(reconstruction)* so Meryl suggested I chat with Jan about a contact prosthesis. Well, I saw Jan and rushed straight to the prosthetic department to catch them before closing. I saw a lovely lady and she said the one I had was excellent and I would only get a contact one if mine was damaged!! Well I know what she means but I couldn't knowingly destroy this boob so I am going to buy one. Now these contact ones are even more realistic and as the name suggests you actually stick it onto your skin so you can wear normal bras again, not worry about swimming and changing and also it behaves even more realistically, moving properly and feels less firm and it also lies flat when you do. You wear it all the time and can even do so at night. You can wear strapless tops and go bra-less if the need arose. So I feel quite excited, as this is the gold medal boob of all boobs that are false. So watch this chest!!

Yes, I can sleep with the boob on!! It is settling in well and I often forget it is stuck on. It is much lighter than the other as it is attached and not weighing down a bra. I haven't tried swimming with it yet but have worked out in the gym. I went for a six mile walk this morning before teaching Chris' class this afternoon. What a beautiful day it has been. I was only thinking the other day about plug alerts and wearing a hat... funny how twelve months can change a person. Thank God that is all a distant memory.

I love the sunshine but oh boy I think keymo alters your heat tolerance. I have no desire to sunbathe now! I am glad of the stick on boobie so I can wear strappy tops again but the heat makes for an interesting test of adhesion!

This is Your Life
Fi reflects on her life with the 'Beast'.

I have done the biz at the LSD, only two more to go, hurrah! I too saw the Grand Master himself, no free coffee, plenty of parking spaces and he threw in a joke for James. He gave me the punch line first so thankfully he is a consultant, not a comedian. Here it is: Why was Tigger looking down the

Positivity

toilet? Because he was looking for Pooh. I too got a big booty bag. A huge bottle of Gaviscon. Steroids are back on the menu, and a new regime of three days of anti-sick pills, not one. Shake, rattle and roll. They have reduced my dose of FEC *(type of chemotherapy)* as it took so long for my white cells to bounce back. Last night another friend who is an excellent cook made a fabulous chicken curry for me. We are so lucky to have all these people who care and help us. Off for a snooze, let the keymo tell Trevor to FEC off!!

When people ask if I am ok, I say yes, and then they say 'are you really because you always say yes?' Next time I shall say 'oh no, I have a rash and a temperature!' Honestly you can't win. I know they mean well, but I have begun to hate that question now.

I am so relieved that we are in 2003. I wish you the very best of health and happiness to us both as we truly deserve it. I'm back!! It all went well and I had it all laproscopically and incisions in the belly button and the right hand side so you won't know they're there, but my left ovary was larger so it needed a bigger cut so I am rather tender on that side. Strangely enough it's not the stitches that hurt but all the trapped air I have had pumped in and now have to absorb. I look about three months pregnant! I am on slight painkillers as the third day is apparently the worst as everything comes back to life. Last night I went to an Ann Summers party, which was at a friend's house and had to try hard not to laugh at anything! I think it was a tad early to have done that, as I feel a bit rough this morning. I feel OK now that I have eaten and popped a few pills!

Well I have to say, as a NHS patient, I was really annoyed this morning. I turned up at my second home... the LSD, and was informed as I checked in to see the Grand Master he wasn't there today. I did actually utter "Shit, I don't believe this as I have lots of questions for him... that's just great. How long have you known he wasn't going to be here?" Clerk: "since last Wednesday". James got a star for being the best-behaved boy in assembly today. Then it was a bit of a Crompton double act as Sophie had asked earlier in the week to play them out on piano. I have so many GREAT things to celebrate in my life, how can I not be positive?

Time is flying and I sometimes forget that it was so serious and still could be again but that is at the back of my mind now rather that at the front so that's progress.

I can't believe the Beast has claimed another conquest, poor Mrs X (mum of someone in Sophie's class). It is so awful that so many people can get affected; the sooner they discover a cure the better. At least on the anniversary of the banishment of Trevor I will be drinking French wine in the Vendee and nowhere near the LSD.

Really Useful Information
Maureen and Fiona created their personal guide to coping with chemotherapy, designed to enlighten and empower.

FE and FO's Alternative Keymo Leaflet

- ♥ Having a POSITIVE MENTAL ATTITUDE is of paramount importance. Try to write down four positive points every day and if possible share them with a friend.

- ♥ Don't even try to pronounce or remember medical words of more than twelve letters!

Positivity

- ♥ Work hard on getting the correct amount of Sennas taken on the days immediately following your treatment, as the alternative bloated consequences are most unpleasant. Do not take any of the ghastly liquids offered, just more Sennas.

- ♥ Make a careful study of any blood clots as they progress up the legs. Endeavour to make sure that they don't make it into the body, where they can become fatal. Superficial clots are the desired kind, if you have to have any at all. Clots that get stuck in the hands can also be a bit of a nuisance, as can swollen hands, feet and other body parts. Avoid social functions that require you to clap your hands e.g. concerts and sports days, as this activity can be painful.

- ♥ Don't desire to experience the 'feeling down there' when having your drugs – it's not a pleasant one!

- ♥ It would appear that sheep ticks are partial to keymo chemicals so avoid orienteering in sand dunes frequented by sheep, especially just after your treatment.

- ♥ Never go to a hospital appointment without a good book!

- ♥ Take your horse pills regularly.

- ♥ Take care what you wear when visiting the keymo unit for treatment. You will probably have a burning desire to throw these clothes away.

- ♥ Don't worry about not being able to expose your skin to the sun. Apart from a couple of days immediately following treatment, your skin will assume a healthy tanned look that will be remarked on enviously by friends who work indoors.

- ♥ Generally speaking, this is an anxious time for you. Make good use of the five minute emergency appointments if they are available at your surgery. Always precede any conversation with the receptionist with the fact that you are having keymo, as this will ensure you get an immediate appointment.

- ♥ Spot park rather than queue and pay to use the official hospital visitor's car park. Use the money saved to buy magazines, sandwiches or other comfort items from the hospital shop.

- ♥ You need to decide whether or not to use the cold cap. Do you wish to sacrifice your hair to regain hours of your life away from hospital? Whilst highly effective you need to be aware of the side effects. You may experience nausea on passing through the freezer or chiller section of the supermarket. You may be unable to use your own freezer.

- ♥ Should you decide not to use the said cap, you need to purchase a very stunning wig that, if you time it right, your friends and most likely your husband/partner will fail to notice isn't your real hair!

- ♥ Body hair will be affected regardless of whether or not you use the cold cap. The positive side to this is that you'll be the envy of all your friends

- as you are freed from the chore of waxing these areas!! You can also bare your legs without worry. Steer clear of using mascara to save your lashes.

♥ To ward off the inevitable sickie feeling, you will need to buy ginger beer, ginger biscuits and crackers. These will henceforth become basic store cupboard essentials.

♥ You will need to acquire a chewing gum habit to rid yourself of the oh-so-pleasant metal taste. Fear not, this becomes a distant memory by keymo three when it just disappears.

♥ Sleep. Oh yes, you will do a lot of this and so you will need to buy/steal a hammock or comfortable sofa upon which to doze and rest in comfort. If you have a cat, set yourself up in competition with it to see who can sleep the longest.

♥ Plan a Grand Party to celebrate the end of your treatment and thank all the friends who have supported you through this unique period of your life. Alternatively/ in addition, celebrate your survival by going on an expensive holiday.

♥ Finally – email. You must find a like-minded friend with a similar sense of humour who you shall email daily to lift your spirits and make you rock with laughter. This above all else is the most important piece of survival.

Notable Afterthoughts:

♥ Don't underrate the value of retail therapy, be it from shops or catalogues.

- ♥ Make use of being in to get all those little jobs done by workmen e.g. new kitchens, kitchen floors, fitted bedrooms etc.
- ♥ Suck a Werthers when having keymo, it helps keep the sickie feeling away.
- ♥ Keep anyone who is shopping for you up-to-date with your fads!

Glossary:
- ♥ Sennas – constipation pills.
- ♥ Horse pills – the largest, most expensive vitamin pills on the market purchased, after a lengthy discussion from your local Health Store.
- ♥ Keymo – the friendly way of spelling Chemotherapy.

You Are Beautiful
One of the last messages in their files of positivity was the water bearer story, found on the Internet, sent by Fi to Maureen. Whatever our flaws and imperfections we are all unique and worthy in our own right.

A water bearer in China had two large pots, each hung on the ends of a pole, which he carried across his neck. One of the pots had a crack in it, while the other pot was perfect and always delivered a full portion of water. At the end of a long walk from the stream to the house, the cracked pot arrived only half full. After two years of what it perceived to be a bitter failure, it spoke to the water bearer one day by the stream. "I am ashamed of myself, because this crack in my side causes water to leak out all the way back to your house."

Positivity

The bearer replied "Did you notice that there were flowers only on your side of the path, but not on the other pot's side? That's because I have always known about your flaw, and I planted flower seeds on your side of the path, and every day while we walk back, you've watered them. For two years I have been able to pick these beautiful flowers to decorate the table. Without you being just the way you are, there would not be this beauty to grace the house."

9

Kids

This traumatic time had gone on without me knowing. I hadn't got in touch or visited Fi that year until the usual time for contacting old friends came round at Christmas. Fi's Christmas newsletter in her card to us summarised the previous year of horrible events as described in her diary. I felt a million miles away from her when I read about her ordeal and wished it were possible to send hugs through the post, as this was my immediate reaction. The second reaction was to sit down on the stairs in disbelief and shock. In July 2003 I finally got to hug her after she had had her operation and when it was convenient for her to have a visitor staying.

On my visit, she was her usual, remarkable, upbeat self when telling me all about her nightmare year and how it had put her off blackcurrant drinks for life - all told with her usual honesty and humour. On the day of the diagnosis, she told me how she had returned home in shock to find Hils, her neighbour and friend, with a box of tissues, a big bar of chocolate and a bottle of vodka to ease the trauma. She explained how she felt without going into too much detail and having to relive it all. I got a sense that it was now something consigned to the past, and she was ready for a fresh start and a chance to enjoy getting back to normal with work, life, Simon and the kids. She had a great way with children, be they her own, those in school or the little ones at Toddler Time, a group she ran at St Nicholas' church in Harpenden for two years up until 2000.

Fi was in her element being a mum and organising family life. Sophie and James were being brought up in a happy, down-to-earth, loving environment, encouraging independence and self-confidence. Of course, there was always lots of fun and laughter. Her children were the most precious things in the world to her (and Simon) but they were never precious, impolite or attention-seeking. Sophie loved coming home from school to find her mum singing, dancing and whistling away in the kitchen. Whistling really irritated her, she says, but not when her mum did it. She remembers all the sayings her mum would tell her as she was growing up - words of wisdom (or silliness!) to help her through life. A particular favourite was something Fi would say to Sophie and James every morning when trying to get them to leave for school *"C'mon groovers! Let's rock!"* The children would reply, *"Mum, groovers don't rock, they groove!"* During the final months of Fi's illness, Sophie compiled a list of her favourite 'Sayings To Make You Smile' one night when she couldn't sleep. After it was complete, with smiley faces and angel wings adorning the text, she put it in her mum's room for her to find when she woke the next morning.

"Mates last a while. True friends and the memories last forever.

When today ends, there's always tomorrow.

Live for the moment, before you know it the moment's gone!

Those who care are always there.

Good friend + good cry/laugh + good chocolate = all your problems solved (for a while anyway!!)

Keep talking about someone and they never die."

At school there was nothing Fi enjoyed more than having a class of children to teach. We had many a discussion about the limitations of the National Curriculum and over-assessment. Our B.Ed (Hons) course had been a very child-centred degree examining in detail how children learn, motivation and teaching strategies, developing children's confidence and self-esteem, with the emphasis on encouraging enjoyment of learning and fulfilling every child's potential. Nurturing enjoyment and curiosity in learning was at the centre of Fi's (and my own) approach to primary classroom life, rather than teaching children how to cope with questions on a SAT's paper (SAT's are the stressful and time-consuming standardised tests and tasks used to measure progress in the National Curriculum). Fi brought fun to her teaching with her sidekick Nibbles, a glove puppet mouse used to encourage learning. She was able to put the politics of teaching to one side and focus on what really mattered in school – the children. She treasured every card and picture that any child made her, and it was the gifts made by children that she really loved.

The fresh start required, due to the previous year from hell, came in the form of a house move. Just after my visit in July 2003, their house was sold and an offer accepted on a house round the corner for them to move to. It was bigger and just what they needed, but it was also situated perfectly for the children to walk to school easily. An additional important factor to Simon and Fi, was that it was surrounded by a network of friends and neighbours ready to help should anything happen in the future, as well as friends for the children to play with. In other words they knew there would always be plenty of people close at hand. They were being completely practical and sensible, as well as their usual sociable selves.

A few months earlier in May, Fi had completed her first of many MoonWalks: walking the Half Moon of 13.1 miles with her mum and close friends, in their bras, at night, through the streets of London to raise money for Walk the Walk, a charity raising money for breast cancer projects. It was to be the start of something that she would become extremely passionate about. But more of that later.

For now the future was bright and Fi was teaching back at her local primary school and, as always, her usual bubbly, happy self. Initially, she taught on a supply basis, when Sophie and James were still quite young, but then eventually found herself working full time. Sophie and James would enjoy setting up her classroom with her before school started, as they all went in early together. Her colleague Chris Fellows, who worked with her in the Foundation Stage, remembers the time when they both had to sort out the Early Years Unit in preparation for Ofsted (the name given to the team that inspects schools).

> *"Both of us had/have daughters called Emily who had health problems, and had lost other loved ones. I remember Fi, when dealing with challenges at work which were seen as 'enormous' by others involved, would hug me and say 'in the great scheme of things...' She knew what was really important. Going back to*

that Ofsted, where Fi's talent and humour kept us calm (ish) – our unit had corners and you couldn't always see if an inspector was approaching, however meerkat-like we became. So using an infant reading scheme book title as code, 'The Magic Key' as in 'I've found the Magic Key!', 'Have you seen the Magic Key?' we managed to alert each other as to who was entering the unit whilst talking (with teacher's articulation) to our puzzled pupils!"

Norma, the school secretary since 2001, always knew when Fi was in the building because *"a cloud lifted and lots of laughter was heard."* Into the school office Fi would stroll, *"this beautiful lady with her whiter than white teeth sparkling as she smiled, swinging her latest Radley bag."*

On one of my visits, I joined Fi in the classroom. The children adored her; she had a great relationship with them, full of banter, kindness and fun. I assisted with work on the art table, hearing readers and helping with maths and writing tasks. Everyone was very welcoming and I loved teaching by her side. The day flew by – if only we could have taught like that all the time!!

Later in 2003, Fi met up with Caroline, one of the other ex-S Block girls, and me, for a weekend in Nottingham. We had a meal out with Hels who had now settled down in West Bridgford with Jon (the 'Darlings' of Fi's diary). Before we left for home, we drove onto the campus to check out our old accommodation. S Block had been renamed Serlby for some reason, perhaps to make it sound less like a prison. We all posed for photographs outside our respective rooms, unable to peek inside due to the vertical blinds at every window (not like that in our day!). There were now banks, newsagents, cash points, a gym, a pizza place and a travel agent on site like some little student village. All we'd had was a shop and a laundry where your clothes sometimes came out dirtier than when they went in, unless they were stolen in which case they didn't come out at all. The infamous student union bar had been refurbished (inevitable, given the state I remember it) and was now called 'The Point'. *'What's the point of that?'* we all cried sarcastically. Clifton Building, home to all those education lectures, was now sold off and a private dwelling. We sneaked through the gate for a photograph. Fi later sent me a newspaper clipping reporting that the new owner had been forced to move out of his million pound residence on account of the ghosts. We had never had such spooky experiences during our time there, but I don't think an apparition wailing and dragging their feet through a room would have been particularly out of place or seen as unusual amongst the students. Next came a quick pit stop in town, noting how the TBI seemed far less sophisticated and how so many pubs had changed names. It made us realise that we weren't actually twenty anymore, despite how we felt and behaved. The place we thought used to be The Malthouse pub had now changed radically. Fi and I had lunch there. Now renamed the Pit and Pendulum, it had been transformed to look like the set of an old horror movie complete with bubbling mad-scientist equipment, torture apparatus, toilets behind a bookcase door and cocktails named after the seven sins. Even the plates we ate off had spiders painted on them. We thought it was brilliant and we allowed ourselves to feel twenty again. After a quick wave at the much-loved Irish Club, off down the motorway we sped, back to our separate lives.

For the next few years we got together at times that school and family holidays would allow. Simon and Fi drove up for a weekend with us in the freezing north, where we counteracted the cold by treating them to a well-deserved spa day at Seaham

Hall. Playing 'name an 80's band in alphabetical order' in an outdoor hot tub amongst the frosty trees will always be a great memory. We always appreciated Fi's incredible courage at having gone through such an awful time with such a positive outlook, and admired them both for their strength and love of life.

Due to another job relocation, my husband and I moved to Belgium in April 2006. In the same month, Fi's wonderful positivity partner and friend Maureen, passed away. The loss hit her hard. She had always mentioned Maureen whenever I was visiting, either with a funny story or things that reminded her of the person who kept her going through that awful time in her life. Fi really missed her. Later, when I saw the folders of all their correspondence during their treatment, I understood just how much Maureen meant to her.

Somehow, being in a different country made me email Fi more than when I had been in the UK, and ironically it was easier to get to her from Brussels than from our previous place up north. Within weeks of our move, Fi told me about an amazing opportunity that had come her way. If anyone deserved spoiling and being pampered it was her, and this was the ultimate indulgence and most massive of treats. Something amazing was about to happen in her life. She kept me informed every step of the way by telephone and email, and I felt as excited as her about the whole thing.

10

I Never Felt Like This Before

This is Fi's account of the whole amazing experience, step by glorious, behind-the-scenes step, written a few years later in a Photobook that she dedicated to her mum, Simon, Sophie and James with the words: "You make me strong and you are the most precious things in my life."

What Not To Wear Part One: Interview Day.
I have heard through Amoena magazine that they are doing a programme on What Not To Wear about mastectomies and are looking for people to go on and have the restyle. They really want to focus on women who are looking to adapt their wardrobe following breast surgery, rather than women who need a complete fashion re-think! I'm in two minds about it, as I don't want to be ridiculed, humiliated and made to look stupid. What would my friend Maureen say? *"Go for it! Apply! What have you got to lose? Once in a lifetime and £2000 of free clothes!"*

It is 13 April 2006 and so I fill in the application. I get a call from a researcher called Sarah Allen who wants me to do a phone interview with her. Then she asks me to do a video entry for them! Oh my God.

> "Basically, it's your chance to tell us why you want to go on WHAT NOT TO WEAR. Definitely get any family or friends involved if they are up for the idea, talking about why they would like you to go on the show and how they feel you would benefit from it. In addition, we need to see your body shape so could you model a few outfits – we need head to toe shots. Any problems call – but don't hold back because the more we get to see your character, the better it is. When you are modelling your clothes – talk us through how you would describe your style and how your style has changed since the mastectomy and the problems you now face style wise and also emotionally and physically. Basically, the video is designed to give us a visual and verbal representation of your story and why you need our help. Try and vary the locations... so maybe do the head to toe modelling shots in the bedroom (or somewhere different at school if you are going to do your video there) and then the 'Why you want to go on WNTW' piece in a separate room. When you talk about why you would like to go on WHAT NOT TO WEAR, just tell us a bit about you and your story – how recently you had the mastectomy etc, what you hope to get out of appearing on the programme – you don't have to go into too much detail, just so that my executives and the presenters get a feel for you and your character."

This I do and find it really hard to think of how best to present my case. I use the kids, Simon, Emma and Han and

Han from school. I send it off and wait.

June
It must have worked. I get a call from the BBC inviting me down to London for a show day. We will be filmed with the new presenters Lisa Butcher (model) and Mica Paris (singer) and interviewed on camera. We are going to a house in Holborn.

Sunday 18 June – Father's Day!
I leave Simon with the kids and head into London. Feeling very nervous. I arrive at a hall in Red Lion Square. We are seen by a researcher and a psychologist. Over 85 women are there of which they will pick five for the show, then the final two. The day begins at 9am. We are all filmed walking to the house at 18 John Street, Holborn. We are supposed to be at a party hosted by Lisa and Mica. Mica is chatty but Lisa is more aloof. They split the group into two rooms, one with Mica and the other with Lisa. I am in Lisa's room. They chat to us, serve drinks and then after many takes we are set free for lunch at 3pm! I have been on camera with Lisa so whatever happens I will have a one second shot on TV. Then we come home.

21 June
Just had a phone call from Sarah to say I am in the final five! I have just screamed her ear off down the phone. We have to go back, the five of us, to the house on 30 June.

30 June
It is another early start with lots of waiting about! Back to John Street and meet the others. Lisa Jane – double mastectomy, Diane – never wears her prosthesis, Christine – lymph oedema and Sarah – single mastectomy at 29 years old.

I remember LJ, Christine and Sarah but not Diane. We are all nervous but we get on chatting about our lives, experiences and families. We have to do the therapy couch. We take it in turns to talk to Lisa or Mica about our experiences and why we want to be on the show. It is very emotional and draining. I feel quite unnerved, as I want to get on the show but at what cost? As we bond as a group I begin to think that the others deserve it more than me. I try to second guess the show, as to who will be picked. Who will make the best TV? I thought Christine or Sarah. I then realise that Christine and I have been interviewed by Lisa, the others by Mica. So it is her or me in our group. After lunch we have to do the line-up take a couple of times and the room keeps getting hotter and hotter. We are looking more and more fed up and none of us are thinking that we want it anymore!

Finally they make a decision. We are called back into the room again. They call out Diane's name, then mine... *'You two are about to find out What Not To Wear!'* The others are asked to leave the room. Diane and I are stunned. They film the two of us and our reactions. Then the champagne comes out. Diane and I are given our camcorders to do our video diaries. They give the others a Moulton Brown gift box of goodies and then send us off in taxis. It is 8.30pm by the time I am home, exhausted and still in shock.

Sarah rings the next day and goes through the requirements of filming. They want to film a day in my life at school. It becomes a huge nightmare from here on in to juggle dates and people. The BBC wants to start to film 'A Day in the Life of Me' on Thursday 13 July! They were wondering if the curry club would be up for a visit from Lisa the presenter? They send Lisa to me. She has to come to the house, get the kids up and do the school run. Then she has to teach in class. They do the wardrobe then too. I have removed my firm favourites from my wardrobe in advance in case they take stuff away and I have nothing to wear that I like!

My shopping days aren't until 2 and 4 August so it is a way off yet. Lots of my mates feel a little stressed at the questions they are being asked, especially Emma. Don't blame her either. I had a real go at Sarah Allen on Thursday and threatened to pull out! *(In the end, Emma decided not to take part in the show.)* I said that I was fed up with them prying into my relationship with Simon and trying to find 'funny things' that had happened with the prosthesis. Also got very cross about it being referred to as a falsie. I have a real issue with that as they said the British public wouldn't know what it was, as the term prosthetic can mean a limb. Hello?! It's a programme about women who have had breast cancer – what do they think we wear? A false leg?

I do hope that they are kind to us and I suppose this is the worse bit: 'creating' the image of us that they want to 'transform' so they can be responsible for saving and evolving us. Must remember to do the video diary the night before!

> *Dear Lisa*
>
> *Welcome to my life! I am a primary school teacher and I teach Reception children who are four and five years old. I hope you have a great day and enjoy meeting my family, friends and colleagues. Here is what you need to do.*
>
> *Get Sophie and James up for school. They need to be dressed before they have breakfast. School clothes are laid out.*
>
> *Give them breakfast. Sort out their packed lunches and bags for school.*
>
> *You need to be at school for 8am so you can get my classroom ready. Sophie and James come with*

you. School starts at 8.50am.

You will need to set up the classroom and I have left a lesson timetable for you at school. My classroom assistant Denise will help you. The class is really lovely and excited about your visit.

At lunchtime go food shopping with Simon. Meet him at Sainsbury's at noon in Harpenden.

Meet the girls for Pimms and nibbles at Sarah's house about 5pm.

Have a lovely day, Fiona.

Lisa arrives at 7am with the film crew. She sits in the car until they are ready to film. I have got the kids up but they are good sports and pretend to be in bed asleep so Lisa can get them up. They eat a second breakfast and have a chat to Lisa on camera, then they go off with her to school. We are running late. It is 9am.

They film the kids going into school, then Lisa in my class with Hannah as chaperone. They get the kids to do some paintings of me and have a chat to them. Then they break for lunch and get ready to send Lisa to Sainsbury's with Simon! (This part is cut from the final show). They do the shopping, then head home to unpack it and have a chat about me. It's the wardrobe next, then off to meet the curry club in Sarah's garden for Pimms. The girls are in for a grilling.

Friday 14 July
Feel violated. Not much left from my wardrobe and feel terrible. Next stop – the 360° mirror. Dreading that. Have to go back up to London with Diane. She has to fly from Edinburgh so at least I get to go home every time I film.

Wednesday 19 July
Have all my film dates now and they are all in the holidays.

I Never Felt Like This Before

Wednesday 26 July

The 360° mirror day and rules. I have just finished the worst bit of the WNTW experience. The 360° mirror. That bastard takes no prisoners! I had to get to 'the house' in Holborn at 9.30am. I was then asked to change into my worst looking school outfit – combats and a t-shirt (which up until now I had thought was OK!! Worrying!) Then Diane and me were filmed walking up the street to the house and knocking to be let in. Diane had her 'watch what the friends say' bit and sees Mica living her life on video. I meanwhile was sat in a room at the top of this four-storey mansion house sweating my stick-on tit off! About an hour and a half later it is my turn. Mica Paris is very chatty and friendly. I go in and sit on the sofa next to Mica. I look like shite as I have not been made up nor cooled down. They however look stunning and have minions to spray them and mop their faces! The 'day in the life of' was funny and my mum comes across very well. However, she was on a cancer crusade and pointed out that I am very brave as who knows how long I have to live!!!!!! On National TV Mother! Then she said how I am stuck in the size 12 mindset but the menopause has blown me up to a realistic 14 but I won't accept it! Simon made a crack about how I feel less sexy and my mates said that as I had had cancer they didn't feel they could really say my style sucked! I had to laugh as I could see that all their comments have been heavily sound bitten. So I made some comment that no one with two boobs could possibly understand why I dress more functional and less noticeable and that really I felt a lot of love from the video as they do care and are just chuffed I am alive! Then we broke for lunch.

After lunch it was a few video diary bits, then I waited two hours whilst Diane did the mirror. It is now 4.30pm and I am getting hacked off and in the 90° heat, looking less than glam. At 5pm it is my turn. They asked me to bring three outfits then only used one! Mind you, the one that I had chosen I later learned followed the rules they had set so that was why they didn't use it! The mirror was horrid. In my clothes I didn't feel too bad plus I had lost 4lb so felt slightly better. My arse looked quite pert! Then we were asked to do it in underwear! I said no way, but had brought a sports bra and sports shorts so they had to lump it. I hated standing there in those. I felt really vulnerable, especially with a skinny, gorgeous model telling me my 'problem areas' – like I didn't know already!

Anyway, after that was THE RULES. No trousers featured anywhere! I was to blossom from the garage forecourt flowers I am, into a beautiful orchid – expensive, sophisticated and elegant. They had a long flowing skirt number with a very expensive Monsoon top and hideous cardigan for work! Did love the purple boots though – suede wedges, but not with the lime green skirt.

Evening wear was an empire line, sexy blue dress with a vest top under with a brown sparkly shrug. They teamed it with champagne open-toe, four-inch heels and a clutch purse. I think the shopping will be a challenge. Not sure where we are going but fancied the Kings Road rather than Oxford Street. I think Monsoon is one of their shop choices and possibly Principles and, I hope, Hobbs. Still, I will see. Shopping days are next Wednesday and Friday.

2 August. What Not To Wear Shopping Day One

A car came for me at 7am! I dropped the kids into Hilary's and set off with Kevin to Oxford Street. He proceeded to tell me who he had driven for and how he worked for Ronnie Wood of the Rolling Stones! Anyway after being talked to all the way into London, I was dropped off in Oxford Street. Liz met me and took me to Starbucks for coffee and I met up with Hazel, the stylist, and Sarah, Ceri and Sarah the camera lady (she had worked on Pop Idol!) We set off for French Connection first. The shop had been closed for us and so I was filmed wandering about looking at the clothes and talking about what I thought I should buy and what the rules were. I picked out some stuff and didn't really take much notice of the prices as it wasn't my cash! The stylist had also been round and got some stuff too. Amazingly my stuff and some of hers were the same. I picked all size 14's – or age 14 as I renamed it!

I was then filmed trying and modelling some of the clothes. I had picked a dress and it was following the rules. Yes - it had an empire neckline and, yes - it was a crossover and yes - it was calf length. They teamed it with boots and it looked amazing. I felt so good that when I had gone back into the changing room I cried! They then filmed that bit too. I was amazed at the way I felt dressed in a dress, and I never thought I would cry like that. So I then gained some faith in them, and me, and tried on lots of bits. Strangely I stayed away from the trousers and although I picked a pair of jeans was reluctant to try them, but they looked fantastic! Low slung and NO muffin top! Got two dresses, a pair of boots, jeans, a jumper, a top and a fantastic jacket. Left the shop at 10.30am and a mass of cast off clothes in the changing room. I actually didn't want to put my own clothes back on.

We went off to East in a taxi. It was in Covent Garden. I was so not used to shopping this way. I would never have jumped in a taxi, I would have gone by Tube and certainly wouldn't have jumped from Oxford Street to Covent Garden and then back again! Anyway, East was lovely. Very ethnic and chic. I tried on a fantastic suit but the jacket was too big and they didn't have my size in the skirt. I had begun to realise that the size label is becoming irrelevant if you look good in it as who sees the label? Oh my God, Mica! Am I learning What To Wear? I got a great top, necklace, wrap over top and a skirt.

Then we walked to Pizza Express and had lunch. Then it was back in a taxi and off to Laura Ashley! Now, I'm not a fan of them as I had images of flowers and sofas! It was much harder shopping in there. I felt really uncomfortable and didn't find much that I wanted to try. I did however end up with a fantastic black cocktail dress that is so Marilyn Monroe, and a wrap over jumper and camisole.

We wrapped filming at 5pm with me walking down the street and having a piece to camera sitting drinking a latte in a back street café. I felt a million dollars as people kept looking at me and wondering if I was famous!

I said goodbye to Sarah (camera), Ceri and Liz, then went off with Sarah and Hazel to John Lewis to bra shop. I got measured as 34B so I was already two inches smaller! I had amazingly lost 4lb these two weeks also. Got two vest tops for under 'V' clothes, two posh bras (black and the other white). Then I got a Lejaby bra and knicker set for £88!!! It was gorgeous but more than I would spend on an outfit!

After that we went to a bar for a well-earned glass of wine, courtesy of the Beeb! So happy and excited with my choices but not allowed to bring them home until they have been scrutinised by Lisa and Mica. Bring on Day Two!!

4 August. What Not To Wear Shopping Day Two.

Car picks me up at 7.05am. Journey in was OK, got to go to Carluccios in the Market Place just two minutes walk from Oxford Street. Had the usual breakfast and coffee on offer. Mica and Lisa arrived and ordered their breakfast on the Beeb of course. Poached eggs or scrambled eggs on toast. Poor Lisa! She is suffering from a cold so is sneezing and coughing and doing a good impression of a poorly person! The whole crew is there: Liz, Sarah, Ceri and the infamous Tracy *(infamous because she is a real character!)*, the series producer.

I Never Felt Like This Before

We started with Mica and Lisa going through what I had bought on Wednesday. It was good to refresh my mind on what I had got. Well, they hated the jacket and top from FCUK and also a dress from Laura Ashley. I wanted the jacket but I wasn't fussed about the other things. A runner was dispatched to return the items and came back and said FCUK hadn't charged us in the first place for the jacket so I could have it for free! Louise the stylist was amazed at how much stuff I got, as I seemed to have got great discounts from the stores! In fact, when I had finished both days I was the contributor who had got the most stuff from the whole series. I was amazed by this as Diane, my co-contributor, had got lots of free stuff like swimsuits and bras from the Anita shop, plus two prostheses. Anyway...

We walked to Oxford Street and went to Debenhams and the nightmare began. Tracy was really bothered by Lisa so was trying to think of a way to send her home but still do the shoot. Mica and Lisa are supposed to help me to shop on Day Two so they were coming with me. We filmed going in, then going out of the shop, with lots of faked-up shopping. Then we filmed the end sequence when they said goodbye and how well I had done. We then filmed a stupid sequence when I was supposed to ignore the rules and get a size 12 dress and look wrong! Then Mica says to Lisa we need to have a chat about size. "Leave this to me Lisa, we'll see you soon." This meant Lisa could be put into a car to go home.

We broke for lunch at, guess where, Pizza Express, and it was now 2pm. Had a break for an hour then we went back to Debenhams. Mica and I then went round looking at all the dresses and this silly 12/14 scenario. I was getting so pissed off by all of this. I got really cross with Tracy and explained that I was a bright person and a teacher to boot, so why would I do something so stupid? She said it was good for TV as many women in the UK were falsely squeezing into a 12 when they are really a 14. It would be an eye-opener for them! CRAP. I was made to look stupid so I moaned to Sarah and said I was NOT HAPPY about being shown this way. After three hours of this, we wrapped! Louise the stylist had gone round Coast, Phase 8 and Debenhams getting clothes for me to try on unfilmed so I could decide what to buy as I had bought nothing all day. We ended up with three dresses, two were £80 and one was £130, linen trousers and cardigans at £55 each! Got some stuff from Wallis and then Tracy said to go and spend the rest before the shops close! So we went to Jigsaw and Hobbs and spent the rest. So in 90 minutes I managed to spend £800. Not bad for dresses, skirts and some shoes.

Felt really unwell, as I hadn't been able to drink anything and so felt light headed and dehydrated. Got in a car home and was almost sick. Got home at 9pm and was really angry. I felt the day had been about making TV, not my shopping day. Felt used and manipulated by it all.

Thank God I'm not with the BBC for a few days. Ceri phoned on Sunday to apologise for Tracy and to promise me that as she made the programme and did the edits, I wasn't going to be shown looking like a plank. Felt a bit more reassured but still did a massive video diary venting my anger at Tracy!

8 August

Hair Day. Wow, was I ready for this! I got the train to London, then a car took me to 166 Brompton Road, Knightsbridge! It was Paul Edmonds hair salon. He trained Richard Ward and works a lot on TV. His client list includes Natalie Imbruglia and Emma Thompson amongst others. My appointment was at 2pm and Liz was there to meet me. It was amazing. Paul came to look at my hair and he said he wanted to shape it but didn't know where he was going with it yet. He trimmed it a lot then sent me to the colour department to have it lightened and lifted. His top colourist Simon came along and they spent ages discussing the look they wanted. Diane then arrived with Sarah. There is a mini-restaurant at the salon and so we ordered freshly squeezed juice cocktails: a Love Potion (pineapple, orange and passion fruit) and a Spring Clean (apple, kiwi and mint). £4 a go but all on the BBC. Later on, after we had been there three hours, out came this wine and then some toasted sandwiches and humous and pittas. It really would be easy to get used to this. I felt very like Julia Roberts in Pretty Woman. Whilst my colour was developing, I had my eyebrows dyed. Then Paul did the final cut. He left it casual, as he didn't want me to see the final look. I love it. It really frames my face but is short enough to give the impression of length too. It is a really sexy haircut even if I say so myself, and it can also be very chic! So very versatile but a cut out of my price range. I left the salon at 7pm and got a train home. The kids loved the new hair but James said he had never seen me with shorter hair, but I guess he doesn't remember four years ago. Can't believe I have been given a cut by a world-class hairdresser for free. Now I am so excited about the modelling day and the makeover. I am loving this TV stuff.

9 August

Modelling Day. Well the day started off badly. Poor Mum arrived at my house at 7am as my car was supposed to be there at 7.15am. I had been up since 6.30am. The driver phones at 7.30am to say he is coming off the M1. I think he is lost. When he eventually arrives he is very chatty and tells me he got lost but no problem he knows how to get to London even though he has left his Sat Nav at home! Great.

We arrive at 9am at the house in John Street. Breakfast is set in the kitchen. I am surprised they aren't all overweight as there are so many pastries and cooked stuff. Anyway, Starbucks delivers lattes and all is well with the world. I get lots of 'wow!' and 'you look fab!' from the crew and then Mica gives me a great big hug as she walks in and says how amazing I look. True praise? Well I took it that way. Paul is back to finish the hair.

Diane and I chat about how we are looking forward to the day and sad that this is nearly over, especially as this is the nice bit. I have my hair redone by Paul. A bit more cut off and then it is styled. The make-up artist comes to do Diane, and Lisa and Mica come and sneak a look. Diane has new glasses and they look amazing and with her hair done she looks ten years younger. Her make-up looks fabulous, then she is off to get her first outfit on. I am not allowed to see her from now on. Next it is my turn with Sarah the make-up artist. Every reflective surface is covered so we can't see ourselves. It is really weird, as I know that my eyelashes have been changed with eyelash extensions. Well it takes about an hour but everyone just keeps saying how beautiful and amazing I look. I so want to see it too. Liz keeps me entertained with her love-life stories whilst I wait for my turn to see my look with Mica and Lisa. After a 90 minute wait, I eventually get to go put my first outfit on. They choose the green floaty dress and I am set with shoes, earrings and ready to go when they break for lunch! After half an hour a BBC press photographer comes and Diane and I do press release shots with the presenters. After lunch it is FINALLY my moment.

I have to walk down the stairs and into the room. I stand in front of the covered mirror and talk to Lisa and Mica. Then they take the cover off.

It sounds so stupid but I really did take my own breath away and I cried!

I was stunned at how different I looked. I then did the trouser and dress top outfit, then the posh frock outfit. After all that, Diane is brought in and we are finally allowed to see each other and react. Then Lisa shows me how to walk in heels and we have a laugh. Then it is a wrap and we have to rush off to a warehouse loft to do our modelling shots.

That was huge fun. We get three other outfits and we just have a laugh modelling in them. It was so much fun and really amazing. I couldn't believe how fast the time went. Soon it was 7.15pm and we had to go. I was allowed to keep my make-up on but I wasn't allowed to take any clothes yet as my 'New Life' day isn't for another week. Diane and the crew were dashing to the airport to fly to Scotland to film her New Life Day. I was driven home and the look on the kids' faces and Simon's was amazing. Mum and Liz and Roger, plus Iain and Lisa came over to see too. I didn't want to take this make-up off. The eyelash extensions were incredible. Still have to pinch myself that I have done all this. What an amazing experience. I know it has been really bad in places but the last few days have more than made up for it. Before they left, Tracy admitted to me that I was her favourite What Not To Wear contributor. (A fact I was to learn she really meant from the heart when I was ill again later.)

Next week is the last event. My New Life reveal to family and friends. I can't wait for the programme to be shown and I hope it is going to be great.

17 August

New Life Reveal. I get a train at 9am to Kings Cross and a car takes me to Whitechapel to a small photographic studio. I am told that Simon, Mum and the kids are coming to meet me here and we are going to have a family photo session. Kate (Molly's mum) is going to take the photos so I am really excited. My hair is done by a freelance hairdresser called Paul (are they ever called anything else?!) and I have a lady called

Amanda to be my make-up artist. My look is recreated and I get into my outfit: the red floaty tunic and beige linen trousers and red shoes from Jigsaw. Kate arrives and sets up the studio. Simon and Co arrive and he comes in first. He is so nervous and they catch his reactions on camera. He has a huge grin on his face and says really lovely things. I am in tears and he says I look as beautiful as when he married me! Young, sexy and so beautiful. That is just what I wanted! Mum and the kids come in next. They are afraid to touch me. James is speechless and Mum cries and hugs me. We start the photo shoot and it is excellent. We spend an hour getting some fantastic photos of the family group, and me and Mum and the kids and various poses and groupings. I am very pleased and Kate is ecstatic about getting her name on the BBC and hope it will lead to more. I am hoping we will get a good discount as the photos are incredible!

We then hightail it home and the journey takes forever. Simon is driving and the crew follow later. We come home and do sandwiches and await their arrival. At 4pm it is make-up refresh and the next outfit to go to school. I wear the French Connection dress and the wicked boots. I go up to school and I am SOOOOO nervous. In the staffroom are Han B, Elaine, Denise, Maggie, Mo and G. They let out screams of delight and are so complimentary. I am so embarrassed but they love the new me. I feel alive and so amazing.

Next it's back home and another outfit. Green silk dress and new shoes (thanks to my stylist Louise) and off to Café Jeera to see the curry clubbers. Before we go, quick piece to camera about ditching my old clothes now in bin bags and off we go. Harpenden is so funny. People stop and stare at me and Simon as we walk down the road to the curry house. We are greeted by a man on the door wearing ceremonial dress! He invites us in and the staff are so excited. Pat and Simon,

Rodger and Suneela are there. The reactions from the guys are amazing. Rodger keeps saying how beautiful and amazing my eyes are and Simon D is so sweet and says how sexy I look.

Suneela, Pashmina and Pat are great and compliments and jokes about my legs are flying everywhere. The headwaiter brings out a bouquet of flowers and two complimentary bottles of Moet! The BBC has given us £100 towards the meal. They film for a while then it is time for them to go. I will really miss Sarah, Ceri and Co. Even Sophie has a soft spot for Tom the Runner. Fabio and Dave, the camera and sound men were so great today. I do a piece to camera for the last time saying how I have felt and how I have changed and can't help but thank Lisa and Mica for all this.

Then Ceri lets me do a message about breast cancer and how I feel now as this has helped to revitalise me. I said how it was hard to deal with the idea and then the reality of having a mastectomy, but all this has shown me how to dress and have the confidence in myself to be sexy and confident and start to peel back the last four years of pain and learn to relive my life, to make the most of it and love myself again. They leave and we stay to eat. The curry house treat us like royalty. Free starters, fantastic service and great food. They are taking lots of photos and video on their mobile phones!! Feel like a celebrity. This new look could be so easy to get used to especially as I went and bought the eyelash curlers, lid liner and eye shadows!

Look out Harpenden. Fi is back! Carpe diem!

Harpenden did indeed look out. The day the programme was aired, an article appeared in the local press telling how Fi's femininity had been 'hijacked' by the mastectomy and the WNTW experience had taught her how to be stylish and

> *practical. A few weeks later, the Radio Times mentions the programme in their letters page. Women coming to terms with a mastectomy and a change in body shape really benefited from the programme. A shopping trip and a confidence boost can start to make a difference in helping women to feel better about themselves.*

Fi herself had made an impact on those she met during the WNTW experience. Co-contributor Diane Devlin told me:

> *"Fiona was a very special person and even though I met her within a short space of time, it was pretty concentrated and full on! She lent me her stretchy shorts to wear when we were in the mirror and I really needed that! She was also such a loving and proud mum and committed teacher. She spoke of her kids and Simon often and she was so HAPPY to be having all the pampering and new clothes! So grateful for the experience. I remember her texting and phoning Simon, calling him babe and looking forward to showing him the lovely way she looked."*

What Not To Wear After A Mastectomy producer and director Ceri Rowlands remembers:

> *"When it came to selecting our Ladies, Fiona stood out. She was lovely, bubbly and unflinchingly honest. Couldn't have found a better person to get the message out to women that you can recover your self-confidence. She was also very patient with the Production Team, though I'm sure she was swearing under her breath a lot of the time. On our last*

I Never Felt Like This Before

filming visit, her husband asked me what we thought of the colour pink. I guessed this was her favourite hue, but had to trot out the style guideline that no one out of nappies had any business wearing it. Anyway, I laughed out loud when I read the request that everyone at her funeral wear pink! Good for you Fiona."

Sarah Allen, part of the WNTW production team, remembers Fi well.

"In my job, I have met hundreds of contributors, but Fiona still stands out to me. When I first started researching breast cancer and started talking to possible contributors about their own personal story, it became very clear early on just how strong these women were, even though they had been through a traumatic experience and one which I couldn't begin to imagine, their dignity and positivity was humbling. Fiona was such a person. On the filming front, Fiona was amazing, if she was tired she didn't show it, she didn't complain about the long hours, the early starts, the trudging around the shops and being constantly on camera, she just embraced the whole experience and smiled. My strongest memory was the 'day in the life of' filming when I followed Fiona's life with our presenter Lisa Butcher. Fiona's life and everybody in it were amazing, kind-hearted, down-to-earth and completely genuine. It really opened my eyes to how loved and well-respected Fiona was. From her beautiful happy family – Simon, Sophie and James - to the children in her class and her colleagues, to her mum and close knit

circle of friends, it was clear that Fiona was very much loved by all; people just wanted to be around her. Fiona was a pleasure to spend time with – I don't normally sneak to the pub for a glass of wine after a long day of filming with contributors, but Fiona felt more like a friend and was refreshing to be with. Her positivity shone through and I thoroughly enjoyed the time we spent together. I came away from the whole experience envying Fiona and wishing I could step into her shoes and really live her life, if only for a day."

Researcher Liz Hotchin considers her a true inspiration to women:

"The one thing I will always remember and treasure about Fi was that she was one of the girls and made you feel like you were part of her club. From the first moment I met Fiona at the house in John Street, I knew that she was just right for WNTW. Not because of the way she dressed necessarily but her attitude toward life and what she had been going through meant she was just going to enjoy every single moment and that really came across on camera. It was a new job for me and I really couldn't have second-guessed who was going to go through on the day, but when Fi was picked I was so happy because I knew we were in for a laugh. Phone calls and organising of filming days ensued and it was so hard not to tell Fiona everything that we were planning despite her constant asking and second-guessing!

I really felt that I met a friend in Fiona, we'd often text and Facebook and I remember taking her along after filming to see Paul Edmonds again to get her hair done (courtesy of the infamous Tracy) for a ball she and Simon were attending. We went for lunch afterwards. The wine flowed and we had a jolly old time. I loved hearing all about her stories of Simon and the kids and I'm sure I bored her to tears with my constant tales of my sham of a love life, although if I did, she never showed it!"

When I contacted Tracy Jeune, the 'infamous' series producer, she was happy to tell me how Fi had been a perfect contributor for the show.

"How could I ever forget Fiona? As I read her account of her What Not to Wear journey it was as if a switch was turned on in my head and I was back in John Street, watching five women waiting to hear which ones would learn What Not to Wear. It was a very, very difficult decision. How do you make such a choice? Breast cancer is no longer a taboo subject. It is openly discussed. For the women who have had it, each has had to find her own way of coming to terms with it. But for a woman in that position to choose to put herself forward to undergo the tough treatment for which What Not to Wear became known, required a particular sort of personality. She would have to have strength of character, an ability to remain authentic to herself whatever was thrown at her, a strong will, stamina, vulnerability, a sense of humour and, importantly, be prepared to take a risk. Fiona fitted the job description perfectly. It was wonderful to see her shock and pleasure at being chosen. And she went on to display all of

those character points throughout a tight shooting schedule during a very hot and often uncomfortable summer as she went on the What Not to Wear journey. We all liked her. I was probably as nervous as she was on the 'reveal' day. What if, after all that effort, the risk she had taken had it not been worth it? She had put her faith in us, after all. I watched her very happy reaction to her new image with relief!

Once the filming was over, we kept in touch via email. Hearing about her fundraising activities, I realised just what a tour de force Fiona was, and how privileged we were that, in applying for What Not to Wear, she had sort of chosen us, not the other way around. Surely she must have known we could not possibly have turned her down?"

The Fi effect had been in action again.

11

Change

Following the life-affirming experience of the WNTW makeover, Fi settled down to celebrate Simon's 40th birthday and Christmas with her family. She had had the brilliant idea of giving Simon forty fun-filled presents, ranging from slippers to a Kylie calendar, 'Old Peculiar' beer to a book on the 1966 England World Cup victory. Friends and family celebrated with him at a birthday party at a local golf club.

A few months later, in February 2007 and a week after her five-year check up, the niggling ache in her chest and her 'Christmas cough' prompted a visit to her GP as she was worried she had somehow broken a rib. An X-ray showed a shadow on her rib and her oncologist confirmed that her cancer had returned and spread to her bones.

> *To all my wonderful friends*
> *Please excuse the blanket email but I didn't want to do this over and over.*
> *Today I was told my cancer has come back. I have it in parts of my spine, pelvis and ribs. That*

would account for my funny walk!!

Needless to say we are all in shock and the kids are taking it well. Please be sensitive around them when you see them at school.

I am due to start chemo again in a few weeks and well, let's face it, my roots were coming through anyway so I needed a trim.

What I want from you all is your love and support and jokes to keep me going. No cards or sympathy I can't bear it.

I will be in touch when the dust settles.

Love you all, Fi

That email was sent a day before my husband's 40th birthday. His own worries about getting old, reaching forty and hitting a mid-life crisis were now totally put into perspective. It quickly put an end to him mourning the loss of his thirties and he launched himself into the next decade with a new enthusiasm. We realised that growing old should be seen as a privilege and not something to dread.

On 2 March 2007, James' 9th birthday, Fi kept us informed on what was happening.

Good morning everyone.

Thought I would drop you a <u>line</u> or two now that my Hickman line is in!! Ha ha.

I have called it Maurice after a school friend of my dad's called Morris Hicky .

Well, yesterday was a VERY long day. I arrived at Mount Vernon as instructed at 10.30am and had to wait until 3pm till my line went in. 'Try to not be anxious' they said!! Waiting is great, especially

Change

sitting in a ward having read a whole book, run down the charge on my MP3 player and not being allowed to eat.

At 3pm they finally came and gave me a chill pill, a Pethadine injection in my bum (ouch) and a charming gown and then a lovely old porter (bless him) wheeled me on a trolley across the car park in the drizzle to the minor injuries unit for the line insertion. This took about 45 minutes and wasn't as bad as I thought as the doctor pumped me full of local painkiller and did his thing.

Then back to the ward at almost 5pm for the chemo and bone strength drugs. Having the line in was great as I felt nothing and so two and a half hours came and went. Finally got home at 10pm, after a brief stop off at a drive-thru McD's to satisfy my strange craving for a quarter pounder with cheese! Told you chemo alters your brain! So far, touch wood, I haven't felt sick yet. Mind you I have got a drug cupboard to be proud of and a list of when to take them! So far this morning I have popped seven pills already: anti-puke, steroids, anti-inflammatory, pain and indigestion relief. Just to let you know too that they say my down days for infection risk will be 15-19 March so coughs, colds and poorly folk are to be avoided!

Thank you all so much for all the lovely texts and messages yesterday; they were a real boost to me.

Much love to all, have a nice day.

Fi and Maurice!! (The new addition to my chest!)

The following day, on her 39th birthday, Simon and Fi renewed their wedding vows in St Nicholas' Church in Harpenden. She wore a fabulous WNTW outfit and a silver heart necklace from Tiffany & Co. The sun shone. It was a beautiful day. As Fi said later in a Valentine book she made for Simon "Thank you for marrying me twice. I love you."

And afterwards, the chemotherapy began.

Hello Fi Fans!

Update for you all. Chemo number 2 went ahead after a slightly dodgy blood result! Luckily I had taken my steroids so brought my cell count up. Must remember to try not to be super woman the day before my blood test and take it easy instead. I am thinking of doing a time wasting audit for the NHS. I arrived at Mount Vernon hospital at 9.30am and wasn't seen until 10am, then had to see the consultant in clinic about 10.30am, then do a repeat blood test ...wait for the results and at about 12ish they gave me the bone strengthener drugs in the drip (1.5 hrs) whilst chemo was ordered. Along came chemo at 1.30pm and that takes an hour, then they flush Maurice and get you a little party bag of drugs to take home and before you know it, it is 4pm and you are free to go. Hair cut is hanging in there but best not to brush or touch it too often!! Otherwise feeling OK. Thanks for all the texts and emails, you guys are stars.

Lots of love Fi xxx

Fi continued to tell her fans what was happening.

Change

Hi there, Fi Fans!

Thought I'd keep you guys posted. I hope you are all well and rested after Easter. Have felt OK so far. I had a long wait on Monday - it seems silly that they get you there so early, then they have to order the chemo and it didn't help that they had forgotten I was coming! The chemo takes 2.5 hours to drip through but I did get a complimentary aromatherapy foot massage as I was waiting! Even the nurses asked how I had managed to keep my hair and wouldn't believe it was a wig! When I went up to London to the Kylie exhibition with Sophie, my mate Emma and my god daughter, we also went to a posh wig shop in Notting Hill and they helped me choose a real hair wig which is so much cooler and I can wash and style it too. I decided brunette is the way forward now! Fancied a change anyway after my mate Hils shaved my head. Not quite brave enough to do the scary lady skinhead look, but at least now there is no worry of leaving my hair DNA all over the house!

Tuesday I had a resting day although I did have to resort to playing on the Nintendo Wii station and lost the tennis and bowling game against my mate. I blame the chemo!

I managed to do the school run today and have been out with a friend to walk her dog. I think the fact that I read the medication package this week helped as I think I took too many pills last time.

I think the sunshine is helping too. It's nice to be at home when it's like this and not at work! Gotta have some bonus.

I am due my half way scan to see how I am responding so hopefully news will be good.

Anyway, off to sit in the garden now with a book.

Lots of love Fi xx

In April 2007, Fi's cousin Debs' husband, Peter, ran the London Marathon, just after his 56th birthday, with sponsorship money going to Walk the Walk. In May, Debs walked the 26.2 mile MoonWalk for Fi. It was their way of doing something to support her through her treatments. The chemotherapy continued until June.

Hi there, Fi Fans!
Had another long day at Mount Vernon Hospital. Don't know why they ask you to get there for 9am when nothing happens until at least 11am if you are lucky.

First problem was they didn't have me booked in for chemo! Then they hadn't got results of the half way scan, as they hadn't been processed for reporting yet! Love the NHS! Hey, found someone worse at communication than the education system. If we kept parents waiting all day for parents' evening think of the uproar! And this is life-saving treatment!

Waited four hours to get chemo as after the doctor examined me, he forgot to order it! So finally got home at 7.30pm. I take a packed lunch with me but am thinking I need to sort out my tea too.

Well that was chemo 4, two more to go. I am feeling tired today but not sick. I think all the hanging about drains you so have spent a chilled out day in my own bed finishing a trashy novel (thanks to Liz!).

Thanks to everyone who has sponsored my cousin for The MoonWalk. We walked the 26

Change

miles together last year and it is an amazing night. Hoping to be up and about tomorrow.

Love Fi

As a system of sending hugs by post had still not been invented, smiley faces and funny pictures would have to do instead. Fi was regularly boosted with supportive messages and emails. Her honesty meant that we could all try to understand a little about what she was going through and offer, not sympathy, but some cheerful contact and support.

Hi All

Chemo number 5 is done and only one left to endure. I had my scan results and they indicate that I am responding to the chemo, which is a great relief. With bones it is hard to monitor change but the scan has shown that the tumours haven't grown, so that is brilliant news. I will be monitored after the chemo ends and will also continue with the bone strengthening drugs for a few more months as they also seem to be helping.

For a change I was in the chemo suite at the hospital, which seems to run a tighter and faster ship, so yesterday wasn't as arduous as it is on the ward.

Feeling much more with it today but maybe that was the extra week I had off the chemo due to the half term holiday and the relaxing time we had on the canal boat last week despite the trauma of James falling in and needing to be rescued! I don't know who was more scared - him or us! Luckily we pulled him out and he didn't swallow any of the brown and murky water. We had a great time and saw lots of beautiful scenery and would recommend it to anyone.

Love Fi

Fi and I sent each other funny emails and You Tubes, and I made a spoof of the movie 'Trainspotting' from photographs of that canal boat holiday in Wales, entitled 'Boatspotting'. Choosing life, as in the song from that great movie, was certainly something Fi and Simon were doing.

Dear Fi Fans!
Hurrah I'm finished with chemo!!!!!!
Yesterday was the day I was half looking forward to and half dreading as although the chemo is over I have a week of feeling rubbish due to the after effects of chemo before I will feel like I am able to celebrate being free and me again...look out! In eight weeks I should have my own hair and God only knows what colour that will be! A surprise no doubt.
It was a long day although we were lulled into a false sense of security as I was seen by the consultant (who was very pleased with how it was all going), had my blood test on time and my bone strength drugs on time... BUT... the blood test machine was playing up so they had to retest by sending off to Watford General and that takes at least an hour, then they have to order the chemo again ... another two hours, so the afternoon dragged on and I was able to be set free at 4.30pm.
However the M1 and M25 were both stuffed due to a tanker spill and so instead of a 40 minute

Change

journey home it was two hours!

Still, I had the compulsory McD's quarter pounder with cheese to soak up the after chemo effects and no, I don't know why that works or why you crave one (probably will never want one again!) before I got home.

So I just want to say a huge thank you to all of you for the texts, emails and love and support you have given to me, Simon and the kids especially. I am so proud of how they have dealt with this.

Love to you all, Fi

In the summer of 2007, Fi and her family went to Disneyland Paris followed by a relaxing stay at cousin Debs' house in France. Then the new school term arrived and it was back to work for Fi and a first day at secondary school for Sophie. I was doing some supply work at the time, which was proving a bit of a shock to my system after a few years out of teaching.

Hiya honey

I too think I am allergic to teaching, I have been back three days and already I am stressed! 'Why do we do it?' I ask, and why are there 30 kids in my class? I think I need to go private and have 12 in a class. I even have a Mandarin speaker who speaks no English!! And no assistance for her. I do, thank God, have a FANTASTIC Teaching Assistant who is a real lifesaver.

Thank you too for being part of my life. I agree with all that you said too - how mushy are we! I have realised how lucky I am to have great mates and those who pop back into your life and want to

stay are just as special, if not more so.
Planning awaits deep joy!
Love to you in choccie land. Can't believe it is the big 40 for us both,

Love Fi

Christmas 2007 brought a once in a lifetime safari trip to South Africa where Fi, Simon and the children stayed in a beautiful apartment, bringing back amazing photographs of the wildlife and fabulous family memories. Fi was determined to do amazing things, have adventures and make the most out of life. She told me her theory on time wasting and people who brought negativity or caused upset in her life. If they were a hassle, she didn't waste her (now precious) time on them. If she came across as abrupt with someone because of it, then so what, she had cancer and was never going to hear the words 'all clear'. She could pick and choose whom she wanted in her life and 'sod the rest'. I was therefore quite honoured that she included me, and by doing so she made me feel quite special that I was part of her life. I figured her theory was quite a good policy to stick to and for anyone to follow. Why waste time when you'll never get that time back? Make every moment one worth having.

Friendship emails and messages about strong women (thank you Maya Angelou) continued through to 2008. March 2008 was to be her 40th birthday and Simon had contacted everyone to surprise her with a party at the golf club. I couldn't wait to see her and decided to get her forty presents all related to Belgium and labelled by way of explanation, stealing her idea from Simon's 40th. This was another little 'project' that I did for Fi under the remit of 'Time On Your Hands Productions', so called because of my now self-induced state of retirement in Belgium. Her surprise birthday party had absolutely blown her away. She had no idea of what was planned until the car pulled up to the door of the venue. She had been moaning at her friends about Simon's apparent lack of interest in her birthday who had merely said something about having a nice curry, preferring some quiet time together after the previous year's treatments and heartache.

The tea lights forming the shape of the number forty, the 'Sexiest Girl in the City' cake complete with Manolo Blahnik style diamante stiletto and a thong, hundreds of pounds worth of John Lewis vouchers, flowers, spa vouchers, her friend's band playing all her favourite music, the crowds of people who kept silent as she walked through the door before shouting 'Surprise!' were all testimony to how much people cared about her. What followed was something rarely witnessed by any of us, and certainly something never experienced by her children. Fi was speechless. I don't mean that in the usual use of the phrase. She actually did not speak for about five minutes (Sophie was timing it). The impossible had become possible!

That night she felt 'truly spoilt', duly apologised to Simon and ate her 'humble pie', saying she was a lucky lady to have such a wonderful hubby. She danced the night away, found time for everyone and was beaming all night. In an emotional speech Fi thanked everyone and tearfully reminded us that she hadn't thought she might make it to her 40th birthday. If one day she wasn't going to be here anymore then it surely would be ages away? She seemed unstoppable as I watched her dance with Simon, her kids and her godson Sam, Debs' son. Chatting to everyone, laughing and smiling endlessly, I really thought she was going to beat this again. The chemotherapy was obviously keeping the tumour from spreading and she looked so well. Sometimes medical science can be surprised by the unexpected. Maybe the impossible can become possible for this too? I honestly thought she would just keep on going. I just couldn't imagine anything else other than her being here.

Afterwards Fi sent me a big thank you email: *"Tell you what, this forty lark is great!"* That was true for me too, as in June, as part of my own 40th celebrations, I went to see Fi for a girly time. Actually I had a great time with all the family. We all watched Doctor Who in the dark, sipping champagne, with James and me giggling behind a cushion whilst watching Dalek Caan's wavy tentacles. We danced along to music DVD's of Duran Duran, The Cure, The Smiths and Lloyd Cole. We listened to the nostalgic Ashes To Ashes TV Soundtrack, watched Gavin and Stacey episodes back to back and belted out karaoke songs. For my birthday she had bought me a goody bag of girly things with the main present being a DVD box set of Brat Pack movies including the infamous 'About Last Night'. OMG!!! Cue girly screams!!! Brilliant!!! Fi and I spent a day in London, shopping for James and my husband in the Arsenal shop at the Emirates Stadium before getting more serious retail therapy underway at Portobello Market. Fi posed with the military jackets reminiscent of Adam and the Ants, (there's always an 80's reference in everything we do!), we drank smoothies whilst ogling glorious cupcakes, bought groovy clothes, arty prints and a school bag for Sophie. Gossiping and giggling, we had a great time. The day finished with champagne at the bar at St Pancras station, and I took a photo of my beautiful friend.

When we had left the house that morning, and after all the busy crowds of London, the walking and shopping in the heat of the city and the underground, I had completely forgotten that we had spent the previous day in a hospital ward. I hope she had too. She never gave any indication of feeling ill or tired, her mood was always upbeat and we never stopped talking. Fi had warned me that my visit was going to coincide with a 'keymo' day which wouldn't have normally been on that date but had been changed (not an unusual occurrence). She had been concerned that I shouldn't feel obliged to accompany her in case I was squeamish of needles. She had even thought of alternative plans for me. This was out of the question. I didn't mind at all, in fact I had hoped she didn't mind me tagging along since I knew how much waiting would be involved and I figured she would need the company. We arrived at the car park and found a spot. Whilst driving in she was telling me about a parent at school who had been upsetting one of her colleagues. This, in turn, was upsetting her as it was unfair and without justification. She explained how she sometimes saw this parent in the same social circles and how she felt uncomfortable about it. I reminded her about her own theory on 'Timewasters' – why didn't she come out and say how she felt? Who was going to argue with her? It says a lot that Fi, given her intentions, found it difficult to put up with such trivial hassles on top of her health situation. It brought it home to me that at times she wasn't quite as strong as she made out. This, of course, is obvious, as no one can maintain a consistent state of vitality, no matter what their intentions or how effortless they made it appear to others. Fi truly did make it look effortless. It looked like she was taking all this in her stride, unpleasant and unfair as it was, she just got on with it all. Most of the time, she made you forget she had cancer (even when we were at a hospital appointment for chemotherapy treatment). In the end, she didn't react to the person in question, she ignored. More important to her was the planning of adventures and good times: she had swum with dolphins in Jamaica, travelled to Singapore and Australia, seen the Great Barrier Reef, held crocodiles in Darwin, surprised her kids with numerous trips to Disneyland, had a romantic anniversary in Venice, was going to go to fly in a hot air balloon (when weather conditions were right, and she would have to wait another year until that happened), been on safari in South Africa, renewed her wedding vows, reached her 40th, and was soon to be whisked off for a weekend in New York as a romantic present from Simon. As long as she had time left, she was determined to fill it with happy memories and new adventures.

We checked into the chemotherapy department and Fi was seated straight away. Then came the anticipation of the needle insertion. Fi was making jokes about the procedure but also let slip how this was the worst bit as she really didn't have many veins left that allowed the needle to go in. It was always painful she admitted, and looked away, as the nurse found a vein on the second wincing attempt, with my foot resting against hers in support (unable to hold her hand, it was the only thing I could make contact with from my position). After that, we drank our tea, chatted and watched the contents of the drip disappear. She said she didn't feel a thing. Next, we walked to a neighbouring waiting area to see the consultant. We waited for half and hour. Then an hour. She commented on how it amazed her that she had been first in for chemotherapy that morning, they would know how long that would take so why wasn't the consultant ready for her? Running late is one thing, but over an hour? We speculated on what might cause the delay. For us, teacher-trained, highly organised and efficient planners, the whole system seemed unbelievable, unless they were in the habit of overbooking appointments, except that it didn't look that busy at all. The lack of urgency and communication was noticeable. Of course, waiting wasn't too bad as we were chatting, but it was starting to get ridiculous once lunchtime was looming and we were getting a bit peckish. Finally, Fi went in to see the consultant alone. She didn't give me details except to say that as long as there was no change it's fine. After only a

Change

few minutes, she emerged and then it was off to the pharmacy for her prescription. Again, we waited for over an hour and again, Fi made the comment that since she was a 'regular' and had a repeat prescription how difficult could it be? We joked and chatted and the time went by soon enough, especially after a sugar intake from a chocolate bar. But I really felt for Fi having to put up with this time after time, waiting and waiting when time was so precious. It really was not conducive to positive thinking and living life to the full. We pigged out on a KFC before going home. Fi, to my amazement, didn't want to rest afterwards despite my offering her a 'little lie down' and almost immediately opened a bottle of champagne. We got stuck in and chilled out on some Gok Wan. Now there's a boy who can recharge a girl's positivity batteries.

I left that brilliant weekend, armed with a CD of hundreds of photos from all her good times, memories and adventures. My next project for Time On Your Hands Productions was to create a selection of movies comprising of family holidays, the kids, Simon's 40th, Fi's 40th, the renewal of their wedding vows and the life story of Smudge, Sophie's beloved rabbit who had died recently aged six. Considering her diary entry of 19 September 2002 when Fi didn't think "Poor Smudge" would make it, that rabbit had obviously been taught a great survival technique. It must have been all of James and Sophie's cuddles that did it.

That was the last time I got to see Fi.

But I watch those movies whenever I want to see her again.

Through the rest of the year and onto 2009, we kept in touch via the gift of Facebook and Skype. Fi seemed to be constantly doing something or going somewhere. Her energy seemed to know no bounds. She and the family attended her godson Sam's passing out parade. Sam would call her 'GMFC', meaning 'Godmother Fiona Crompton', which she loved. They would chat endlessly and had a very close relationship. She was so proud of him.

There were visits to New York, several trips to Debs' house in France, a theatre trip to see 'Calendar Girls' and meet the original ladies themselves (which she found very exciting!), a holiday in Wales and a Norfolk boating holiday, not to mention her finding time, energy and strength to do The Half MoonWalk with Sophie. We were all kept informed by photographs of every event. Fi was very generous about sharing her good times!

And all of this went on at the same time as her chemotherapy treatment.

Mindful, from first hand experience now, of the amount of waiting time and how demoralizing it can be, I sent Fi a parcel of envelopes containing various messages (another little project from Time On Your Hands Productions). The intention was that she took one envelope along to each chemotherapy session to give her something to do. There was a booklet of funny pictures, facts about Fridays (the usual keymo day), blissfully idyllic beach pictures with a hypnotic message to induce a relaxed state, as well as cute pictures of our new rescue pup Billie, chewing her foot. The only requirement was that this one should be opened first:

Dear Fi

Well, you're sat there waiting YET AGAIN for apparently no reason other than the 'consultant's running late' which leaves a mental image of some white-coated medic, stethoscope flailing in the wind, papers flying out from the files tucked under their arm as they race down the corridors, skidding round corners, rushing to their next waiting patient, ready to respond, reassure or reveal. Then cynically, the image transforms into the same white-coated medic, feet up

Change

on a desk, dipping a biscuit into a cup of tea....

Time is ticking by – fast for some, but painfully slow for others. I'm here thinking about you waiting (and that time I waited with you), and I bet you're just sitting there thinking what other stuff you could be doing and wondering what that woman opposite is here for. Do you remember "You've Got A Friend" by the Housemartins? (They always remind me of you for a variety of reasons not least our fruitless but fun-filled afternoon trying to record Caravan of Love). Try not to weep at the sentimental lyrics – but they are true, from me to you, and it's a lovely tune, which you can keep in your head after you've finished this letter and imagine me belting it out in my Belgian living room as if I'm there karaoke-ing with you... In fact imagine me now, walking towards you from down that corridor there, hairbrush as a microphone, singing to you as I move forward into the seating area. People turn and look to seek the source of the beauty of my angelic voice; a baby stops crying; senior citizens awake from their slumber; the receptionist lets the phone dangle loosely. More amazing is when the original members of the Housemartins follow on behind, singing backing vocals and encouraging all to wave their arms and sway in time. Those unable to raise their arms, lift crutches, stumps or tattered magazines – anything just to be part of the moment...

Remember the 'oop oops' at the end of the song? I love how they sing that bit. Those oop oop's are very important.

So are you. So are lots of things. You know what matters to you.

So after you've been seen to, after you've waited

and the time has passed by at last – get out there and have a KFC for me.

Forever, Bobs x

I was happy that I made her happy.

Hey you,

Wow, you are such a fab mate. I love my parcel and have opened Envelope One so far and yes, shed a tear at the Housemartin's song but had prior to that laughed out loud at the vision of you (more lyrics there, can't remember the singer – girly I think) singing hairbrush aloft and proud down that corridor!! Will keep me smiling that is for such. Gifts like that mean so much as they are from the heart and have been thought about and crafted in the genius of Babs G. You should develop a business for this in your Time On Your Hands Productions. Teaching was a mere inconvenience to you!! Seriously babe, thank you and you know without getting too mushy and blaming the early onset of drugs, I am really blessed with great mates. Off to imagine you and that brush again!!!

Love you, your mate, Fio xx
(I used to called her Fio as in Duran Duran's Rio as she had the same smile as the album cover graphic.)

She told me how she chuckled at the rude envelope I sent which emphasised the boredom factor (involving a man with an over-developed forearm if you get my meaning) and the need to keep smiling, particularly since a chemotherapy session in February had prompted Fi to write a letter of complaint when after a four hour wait she discovered they had not even ordered in her chemotherapy and it put her five days out of sync. Nothing came of that complaint other than a letter of apology. When, in March 2009, the family had a new addition to the household in the form of a Mini Schnauzer named Mac (after Fi's dad), John Hegley's poem entitled 'Love Poem By My Dog' also made her smile.

She thanked me for *"having time on your hands for me"*. The feeling was mutual.

Fi's next news in July 2009 was that she had been approached to appear in a Cancer Research UK TV advertising campaign. At this rate, she'd be qualifying for an Equity Card! We all waited in anticipation on the launch date and when it was aired, caught the fleeting glimpse of Fi saying one word "Breast".

Poignant.

We were proud, and a little disappointed that she wasn't on for longer (she'd had her own TV show for goodness sake!). I emailed to tell her so and she sent me the link to an interview she had done for the advert. She tells the researcher:

> *"I was 34 years old when I was diagnosed with breast cancer and subsequently I've had three doses of chemotherapy over the last seven years and I've lost my hair three times which isn't easy at all, especially when you've got young children.*
>
> *My children, when I was first diagnosed, were four and six, and now they're eleven and thirteen, and my breast cancer has progressed to be secondary in my bones now. But I'm still having chemotherapy and responding well, so that keeps you going, it's a positive thought.*

> *The worst part for me was telling my children because I don't know if I'm going to be there to see them grow up. I don't know if I'm going to see my daughter walk down the aisle, if I'm going to meet my grandchildren. And those are the bits that really tear you apart because you've got no control of it, and I think the worst bit is not being in control, and you don't know what is around the corner and you don't know how it is going to affect you and the best thing you can do is stay positive for the people that you love and that's why you fight.*
>
> *Basically I want to raise more money for Cancer Research UK because recently I found out how expensive chemotherapy treatment is, and for every treatment whether it's £1000 or £3000 a session or more for a course of treatment – I can't give anything back other than... I don't know how else to say thank you for the fact that I'm still here for my children, for my husband and if this helps to raise money then that's my way of saying thank you for keeping me here."*

The researcher who did the interview was none other than WNTW buddy Liz Hotchin.

> "*The power of mobile phones and social media allowed us to keep in touch and we kept threatening to meet up but one thing or another got in our way and it was only when I had got a job on the Cancer Research UK advert in 2009 and I was responsible for finding real life contributors that I knew that there was no one more real than Fiona and we were eventually going to be able to meet up.*

Change

I immediately got in touch and asked her if she would be up for getting involved... from what I can remember it was an immediate 'Yes!'

I did question at the time whether or not it was sad that the only time we could get together was because of cancer... but then I realised that everything that Fi was doing to promote awareness was such a positive thing and I felt proud to be part of that.

I drove up to Harpenden to interview Fiona about her story, even though I knew it, and by the end of it we were both in tears – I was trying to hold the camera and put on my 'serious' TV hat but she had plied me with white wine and so the heavens opened! I remember at that time she was 'off' wine but I could have sat there for hours catching up with her!

I got back to the office and showed my Director Fiona's tape and everyone fell in love with her all over again. I was so happy that everyone else saw what I did. The filming of the advert itself went pretty quickly and I was here, there and everywhere but Fiona's filming was on an estate in South East London – she kept laughing the whole way through – I was on my back holding up a light reflector and she kept staring at me and laughing (not sure how impressed the camera man was but hey ho!) but she nailed her lines – like a true pro!!

I knew she was back on the chemo and that she was wearing a wig but to the untrained eye you'd never have known. We hung out in Cafe Rouge for what seemed like an eternity and ate and drank for hours... and again I bored Fiona with my tales of boys and my love life and she again spoke so highly of Simon and the kids. Sophie was in training for doing her first MoonWalk with Fi – she was so incredibly proud of her and I just kept thinking that Sophie and James had the best mum ever.

After the advert finished, Fi went off in the car and again we said we'd catch up. We spoke on the phone and texted when the advert went out and then I got another job that again meant I was everywhere and nowhere. It was then that I got the news. Simon had emailed. I was so upset. Fi had been full of beans when I'd seen her and any sort of bad news she may have been harbouring she never let on. I said a prayer for her on the day of her funeral as I was unable to attend and still now I often think about her. She truly was a gem, an inspiration for all women... you go girl!"

Soon after the advert, Fi was sporting her own hair again, dyed a deliciously foxy red. She looked gorgeous and I told her so, as did many other Facebook friends.

My thoughts whispered to me that since her hair is growing back then chemotherapy must be stopped for now, and is that good? But a month later, a knot began to tighten in my stomach when I read a posting on her Facebook wall at the end of August:

"Fiona Crompton is very proud of her two incredibly brave children. They are amazing and we had a big love in tonight."

I emailed her on 1 September, asking about how James was feeling about his impending attendance to secondary school. There was no immediate reply, which was unusual. Hours later, at around 11pm, an email arrives.

Change

Dear Everyone

Sorry for the blanket email but we can't face all the phone calls. This is to update you on Fiona's condition which I am sorry to say has suddenly deteriorated. The cancer has spread from her bones to her liver and despite aggressive chemotherapy the liver is unable to fight it any longer. We have been told by her oncologist that it is likely to be a matter of weeks.

Fiona has decided to stop the chemotherapy and is now relying on painkillers and other medication to keep her comfortable. We know this will come as a shock to many of you because it has also come as one to us too. We have had a family discussion and the children are fully in the picture, they have been so brave and so strong, we are incredibly proud of them. They are our central focus now and we want what is best for them, and decided that being open and honest with them was the best way forward.

We are so grateful for everyone's love and support and ask that you please treat us as normally as possible during this time. Please don't send flowers but words of support and help will always be well received. You'll understand that Fiona will be tired a lot of the time so text or email contact may be best, and if you wish to visit please let us know first as she may not be up to it at certain times.

Best wishes to you all
Love Fiona, Simon, Sophie and James

The following day sees Fi's Facebook wall full of messages offering hugs and love, and of how people are inspired by the strength and courage of the whole family. There is a steady stream of visitors to the house and a steady stream of Facebook messages. On 3 September, Fi posts photographs of James' first day at secondary school. She is a proud mum standing next to her 'baby boy' who is now taller than her. Her smile is still beaming. She is extraordinarily amazing.

12

Walk On

One thing that truly demonstrated Fi's fierce determination was her participation in The MoonWalk: an annual event that raises money for a charity known as Walk the Walk (and nothing to do with a certain Mr Jackson). Most of us, me included, never get up off the couch and do something involving exercise, let alone training and raising money for worthy causes. It really is usually a case of 'talking the talk' but never actually, and literally in this case, 'walking the walk'. The world is full of people with good intentions that never come to fruition.

But not Fi.

And not Nina Barough, who decided one day that it would be fun to power walk the 1996 New York City Marathon in decorated bras and fundraise at the same time. Joined by her friends, they raised £25,000 and donated it to Breakthrough Breast Cancer. Although many people wanted to continue this 'one-off' fun fundraiser, Nina doubted it would happen again due to her busy life and work schedule. But when she was diagnosed with breast cancer in 1997 and had to give up running her own production company, the support of women wanting to power walk the London Marathon for her kept her positive through her surgery, radiotherapy and drug treatments. The women raised in excess of £25,000. The following year, another team entered the London Marathon to repeat such success. Twenty-five women were unable to get a place, so Nina created a special marathon starting at midnight in London. Intended as another 'one-off', word was spreading so fast at this annual charity event that Nina had to find sponsors and set up an official charity. Walk the Walk was born!

Like most inspired decisions, Fi's decision to MoonWalk was made as a result of a drunken night out. But it wasn't Fi that the alcohol stimulated, but the secretary at the school where she worked, Norma. In December 2002, Norma was out with friends on her birthday. During a very boozy session, her sister persuaded her that it would be a great idea to do The MoonWalk.

When her head stopped banging the next day, she realised that training for the full 26.2 miles with her two small children and a full-time job was rather ambitious. Not one for going back on her word, she discovered and decided upon The Half Moon option (half the distance), which meant she wouldn't be on the same route as her sister in The Full Moon and would have to walk on her own. At this point she thought of Fi, recovering from breast cancer and desperate to get involved in helping the cause. Fi agreed, and Norma had a walking partner.

So in 2003, a year after her diagnosis, Fi walked the 13.1 miles Half Moon, around London with her team entitled 'Breast Foot Forward', which included Norma, who brought along two friends from her aerobics class, Sue and Angela, as well as her mum Jean and close friends Emma and Hils. Fi was impressed with her mum joining her at the age of 61, but actually, anyone who knows Jean knows she is an extremely active lady! It was all a new experience and rather decadent to be out and about in your bra in the middle of the night with only a plastic mac to keep you warm and dry. She was extremely proud to have been able to meet none other than Nina Barough herself whom she considered amazing. Years later Fi would never know that Nina would share the same sentiment towards her. After reading Fi's story Nina remarked *"I am just blown away by this amazing woman, she has clearly left such a footprint on your hearts it is lovely to see. Fiona represents everything that Walk the Walk stands for: courage, strength, compassion, energy, optimism, determination and fun."*

Fi was very proud too, of herself and her team, for finishing in the early hours of the morning. Her local press reported on their fundraising with an article along with a photograph of Fi's beaming face. They raised £1300 that night, in memory of Margaret, otherwise known as 'Fum' of the 'Giant Four' who had lost her battle with cancer the previous year. From then on, despite Norma initiating the whole thing, The MoonWalk was considered by all as 'Fi's baby'.

The following year, Fi signed up again for The Half Moon. Again accompanied by Emma, Hils and Norma, they were also joined by Hannah, another teacher from school, along with Dave, Hannah's dad. On the night she found herself walking alongside Sally Gunnell and couldn't resist a photo. Fi always had a knack of meeting famous people!

Taking 2005 off, 2006 was a big challenge as Fi decided to do The Full Moon of 26.2 miles in tribute to her positivity partner, Maureen, who had died that year when her breast cancer had returned. Fi considered Maureen as someone who had *"potentially saved my life"*. A new bra was needed and fashioned with musical notes reflecting Maureen's love of music, as was Fi's nail art. After some serious training (up to five hours at a time as the date approached), Team Crompo included Emma, who was also walking The Full Moon for the first time, and Fi's cousin Debs who was no stranger to The Full Moon Marathon. Debs' husband Peter had given Fi lots of training tips for walking the distance and she was totally motivated and ready. The Big Tent was buzzing with women and men, all with their own reasons for walking. Waiting was the worst bit according to Fi, but finally they set off through London at night, passing the sights of Big Ben which struck 1am as they walked by, then Tower Bridge and Buckingham Palace at 23 miles.

Just stop for a second and think about what a distance 26.2 miles actually is. Measure it out. Think of driving somewhere, to a shopping centre or town that is 26.2 miles (42 kilometres) away. Now think about walking it, in the dark and through the night. If you were anything like Fi, you would have been so excited that you would have been awake all day, just eagerly waiting to walk for about eight hours, without stopping or taking a break if you can help it as it spoils the rhythm. This isn't just about doing exercise, keeping fit or doing something healthy. This is a challenge. For someone in Fi's condition, to push herself and motivate herself to finish this marathon was truly an incredible achievement.

Fi set off, with her closest and best friends Debs and Emma, in the last group. Debs recalls that incredible night.

> *"We got a good jolly-on and things were going really well, until an unexpected hold-up during the walk. This slowed us down considerably and it really pissed Fi off, because she was so up for it that night. At the 13 mile mark, the point where Fi had previously finished for The Half Moon, the reality of The Full Moon kicked in for her, because the distance she'd just walked, she'd have to walk again to finish! But*

she wanted that medal real bad! I was so proud of her, and Emma, it was a new challenge for both of them. I knew how hard it was, it's a mental challenge as well as a physical one. A bit like cancer in that respect – Fi said that to me a couple of times. At roughly 14 miles in Battersea Park, Fiona was really sick. I was worried about her, and she was worried about the distance in front still to go. But after a little break and a gathering of thoughts, we started off again at a different pace and a determination to finish that couldn't be matched. On through the night we walked: talking, laughing and generally spurring each other on. I think when we saw the signs for the last few miles Fiona almost got a second wind, but she was suffering. I knew it, Emma knew it, and Fiona knew we knew. It was one of the most courageous things I've ever seen. The big smiles as we crossed the line together were just the most amazing thing. We hugged and cried and Fi kissed that medal so many times. What a night!"

At the finish line to meet and cheer them home were Simon, Emma's husband Iain and Debs' husband Peter. A very emotional event, as it often is, but considerably more so on this occasion, Fi was tired and proud at the end of it all and had a good cry with Emma and a big hug with everyone.

Unable to walk The MoonWalk in 2007, because of her secondary diagnosis, Fi was undergoing treatment and so her cousin Debs took up the 26.2 mile challenge on her behalf. Debs felt this occasion even more significant than usual. She felt she simply had to walk The MoonWalk as a way of doing something at this difficult time, inspired by Fi's courage. She wore a t-shirt with the message 'This one's for you Fiona!

KEEP FIGHTING, STAY STRONG' and was utterly surprised to be met by Fi at the finish line who stated adamantly *"There was no way I could let Debs finish on her own"*. The special bond that these two cousins shared can be articulated far more eloquently by Debs, in her own words.

> *"I did the walk on my own because my husband Peter had to work that night, which is why he ran the London Marathon instead in April. I trained mostly alone that year and I travelled to the event alone as well. I knew well in advance that no one would be waiting at the finish line for me this year but that's not what it was about in 2007. I did the whole thing alone, sat waiting in the pink 'gin palace' as we called it, thinking about why I was there. Fiona was back in treatment, having found out 'it' was back again. I really was doing it for her. What else could I do?*
>
> *Throughout the early night I got a good few texts from Fi, asking how I was getting on. Being on my own, I was walking a great pace, and to be honest, I just wanted to get finished, and get home. I got a call from Fiona around four in the morning " Hi cuz, how you doing? Where are you now?" she asked. " I just got up for a pee because of the bloody drugs I'm on. Thought I'd call you."*
>
> *I laughed. I'd just been thinking about her. "I've just passed 19 miles," I said. I knew she'd be impressed as that was good going. "Fucking hell!" was the reply, "Are you running?" We shared a bit more banter, then she rang off. Unbeknown to me at this time, Fiona had planned to travel to London that morning*

and surprise me at the finish. She later told me she literally had to kick Simon and the kids awake, and get them all up and out at four in the morning, or they'd miss me finishing! I got another call a bit later as I passed the 25 mile marker with a similar excuse for her being up. I hadn't suspected a thing.

I passed the 26 mile marker about 15 minutes later. There were other women around me, and the final 200 or so yards are just magical. Bearing in mind I wasn't expecting to see anyone, I'd been up all night and was so pleased it was nearly over; I watched others ahead being greeted by loved ones and supporters. Then I saw in the crowd a woman in a pink coat jumping up and down and waving frantically. I looked behind me to see who this woman was waving at, she was obviously really happy to see someone coming in! I don't quite know at what point I realised that the woman was Fiona, but it was a split second before I twigged, and then the tears started to flow. I ran towards her, and we hugged and embraced like I've never known. "I couldn't let you finish alone Debs." I was crying my eyes out, had a quick hug with Simon and the kids, and then INSISTED that Fiona finish the last few yards with me. She didn't want to, but I forced her. I know she was pleased really, because the year before we'd talked of doing 2007 together. As we crossed the line again together, I told everyone who would listen how proud of her I was, and made the guy give my medal to her. She deserved it more than me. I only had one night of pain, which I knew would pass in a few days. Fiona wasn't so lucky.

I wrote up my account for The MoonWalk 2007 for Walk the Walk and they had it on their site for the next two years. It was good to see it there, and Fiona loved to look at it too. She made my night, and I loved her even more for it.

Fiona kept my medal for 2007 with hers, and when it came to the end of her 'walk of life' I'm so glad I was right by her side to see her out. I miss her so much."

The following year Debs walked again for Fi. This time her husband Pete accompanied her. It was hoped that her son Sam, Fi's godson, would join them for his first MoonWalk but the Royal Navy got to him first. Fi, Simon, Sophie and James all turned up at the finish line to cheer on Debs and Pete who both had completed The MoonWalk in 5 hours 55 minutes.

In 2009, Sophie was old enough to have a turn at the Half Moon. Fi's mum made the bras, which had a cowskin theme, because Fi called Sophie 'Mrs Moo' as a term of endearment. Nails were transformed in pink and black with moons and footprints. Temporary tattoos of The MoonWalk logos completed the look. Fi added an extra accessory in the form of a pink bob wig.

They waited excitedly in the Big Pink Tent, listened to Nina's speech and cried during the minute's silence. Paul O'Grady and Nina started off Team Crompo (and thousands of others) at 11.25pm. Fi walked with Sophie and Hilary, Norma and her daughter Steph. She was also accompanied by a very painful back.

Her courage and good humour were plain to see, walking with the mantra *'Nothing's going to stop me!'* Hils, who walked with her all the way, when the others sometimes, inevitably were ahead, was impressed by her perseverance, knowing she was walking through the pain, resting now and again, taking painkillers, but determined to finish. Fi found her 'hair twin' on route, stopping for a photo with a male spectator who was also kitted out in an identical pink wig. At 12.30am they reached the four mile mark at Big Ben. Still smiling, they posed at the London Eye for another photograph. At the finish, with their medals, Fi was incredibly proud of her daughter for completing the walk. Fi's brother Iain had joined them at the finish for the first time ever, with a big surprise in the form of cousin Debs, who had moved to France and so had not walked that year. Fi loved this! The icing on the cake was exactly that. When they got home they were greeted by a cleverly iced cake in the shape of a buxom chest sporting a cowskin patterned bra, made by Liz B, one of Fi's many supportive friends.

Fi considered 2009 the best ever MoonWalk, because Sophie had walked it with her. Her MoonWalk 'addiction' of three Half Moons and one Full Moon along with medals from Debs' MoonWalks was an amazing achievement. She always printed off and kept everyone's comments from her fundraising pages. She treasured the medals, photographs and walker numbers. She raised thousands of pounds for the Walk the Walk charity in aid of breast cancer projects.

And she had walked the 2009 Half Moon during chemotherapy.

In 2010, the year after Fi lost her battle with cancer, The MoonWalk tradition continued in memory of her. I joined Simon and James at the finish to cheer on Sophie and the many, many people that decided to Walk the Walk as a tribute to Fi, inspired by her courage and brilliance.

The theme was 'Showtime' which led to an array of colourful bra designs. Earlier that day, I had sewn the fringing onto Sophie's bra, made by her Grandma Jean, Fi's mum. I painted her nails pink with ten little purple glitter hearts.

Then I finished off sewing the flowers onto her cap for her and trimmed her grass skirt. The costume was all ready, with a few hours to go. I gave her an assortment of pink sweets to provide a sugar boost on the way round.

MoonWalkers descended upon Harpenden station at 6.40pm ready to catch the train into London. I must admit to feeling slightly unsporting for not participating myself, but then I've always been more of an observer in life. After a goodbye hug from her Dad, Sophie began to well up a little when Simon told her how proud he was of her. I thought back to when I had painted her nails earlier and her comment of me 'being Mumsie'. She had then excitedly shown me Fi's gorgeous pink high-heeled ankle boots telling me how they 'just about fit', forever to be a treasured memory and keepsake of her mum. She had inherited Fi's bravery, as well as her love of divine footwear. If anyone could fill the shoes of Fi, it was her daughter. Her son James was doing that too, although maybe something in a smaller heel.

Sophie walked The Half Moon with her closest school friends and some of their mums, joined by Fi's best friend Emma, cake-maker extraordinaire Liz B and other friends, totalling around twenty people altogether.

Fi's cousin Debs with her daughter Hannah and friend Emma, as well as Fi's brother Iain were to walk The Full Moon route.

Chris Fellows, Fi's colleague from school also walked in memory of her wonderful friend; amongst countless others whom I didn't get to meet or hear about. If you were one of them and you're reading this – well done – you did Fi proud!!

Back at the house, we had a Boys' Night In with kebabs, burgers, chips and beer with a side order of Dr Who and Saturday night TV. We went to bed early at 10.30pm so we had a chance of waking at 2am to get to the finish line in London. I didn't sleep much and dozed slightly in between texting Helen, our Trent Poly ('Darling') mate, who was also doing The MoonWalk. Helen had previously walked two Edinburgh MoonWalks in memory of her mum, whom she had lost to breast cancer when she was aged fifteen, as well as in tribute to Fi who *"continues to inspire others and personifies the importance of all the work Walk the Walk does and the charities it supports"*. Helen deemed Edinburgh 2009 a *"fantastic occasion, made even more so by the brilliant team of volunteers who kept our spirits up when our legs were heavy"*. But 2010 held a special significance, which is why she chose London for her third MoonWalk, as it had always been Fi's preferred location.

It was a bizarre experience to be driving into London with no traffic on the road. We parked up and waited a while at the finish, cheering on the walkers as they passed. Meeting up with Simon's dad and friends of the family, we waited for Sophie and her crowd. Simon's mum, Liz, joined us when she finished her shift as volunteer MoonWalk warden, a task she had undertaken many times before. Helen found us, having finished half an hour earlier. She was grinning but tired, and looking forward to finding an open café to get warm whilst waiting for her train at 9.45am. I gave her and Lorna, her walking partner, a pink bag of pink drinks and goodies to give them some sustenance in the meantime. Sophie and her crowd whizzed past and I barely managed a photograph, as we cheered and clapped. It was beginning to get light now and we all felt the early morning chill as we waited at the exit for Sophie to come through. After congratulations and hugs, we headed off home, with two tired teenagers bickering in the back of the car. London was waking up. It was 5.30am when we got home and we immediately went back to bed. Around this time though, we were aware that Debs, Hannah, Iain and Emma were on their way to finish the full Moonwalk.

Being there in 2010 was the first time I'd been involved (other than donating) in this very important event in Fi's life. She often talked about her achievement and pride at being able to do this challenge and the emotional rollercoaster it took her on. I still hadn't felt the urge to do it myself, which I found quite strange, because I would have done anything for a friend like her. It felt like a 'Fi thing' and not a 'me thing'. I lacked the passion that she so vehemently showed. The thought of walking in memory of her, instead of alongside her supporting her as she walked with enthusiasm, brought me a kind of sadness, not triumph. Rather than MoonWalk, I wrote this book. It's shocking the lengths I will go to in order to avoid exercise.

Fortunately, not everyone felt this way. Sophie raised close to £1500 that night, and all the others walking for Fi, raised thousands more.

On Fi's Facebook page, Sophie's friends Felix and Penny, as well as her brother Iain and cousin Debs kept her updated on the night's events.

> *Felix: We did it Fiona :) We finally did it. It was hard but we completed it :) I thought of you so much, and they played 'I've Had The Time Of My Life' in the tent, it reminded me of you so much!*

> *Penny: MoonWalk was last night, thought of you a lot. Sophie was amazing and so was everyone else! I think you were in everybody's thoughts. We've raised a lot of money! I miss you lots, love you.*

> *Iain: Fi – Debs, Hannah, Emma and I did it. We got round The Full Moon in 7hrs 42mins. I have some nice blisters, but have no idea how you did it on chemo. I had a good cry with Mum at the finish line.*

I know it was your fave charity but I can promise you I will never do it again!

Debs: Hey Fi, how he did it with the blisters he's got I'll never know... he was fantastic to finish it, however the very best bit was your mum dressing them for him on Sunday – now that WAS funny!!! I knew you'd be with us – we all had a tear when they were performing 'I've Had The Time Of My Life' on stage – and how spooky it should be performed when Sophie's group met up with us... We owe it all to you xxxxxx

Fi's brother Iain may have said 'never again' but in fact he signed up to the 2011 MoonWalk in memory of Fi and for a friend who lost her battle with cancer in 2010. He feels it is something he will continue. Whilst walking The MoonWalk, walking the same route as his sister, it is his time with Fi.

Many others will continue to accept the challenge of The MoonWalk, raising money to go to a variety of breast cancer charities and projects, as well as in tribute to such an inspirational, wonderful woman. Fi's influence is encapsulated by the words of Nina Barough, founder of Walk the Walk:

"She also had the very special ability of bringing people together. Her greatest gift is her legacy that is still encouraging people to stand and be counted, to make a difference where it matters and to still take part in The MoonWalk, and of course no one could forget that wonderful smile which still lights the hearts of those that knew her. It was such a privilege to have met Fiona, a truly extraordinary woman!"

The Fi effect continues and will go on for years to come.

13

Angels

From the moment Fi was told about the return of the 'Beast', she began a diary again. She continued writing down her thoughts and feelings right up until her final week of life.

Hi

You all know what I am like for writing diaries, lists and letters – so here is my journal for everyone. Not one I have wanted to write but I feel I need to, to keep me sane (ish!) and leave you something about us all.

For Simon, Sophie, James, Mum, Iain, Lisa, Liz, Roger, Al, Emma and Iain, Hils and Debs (in no order!). Thank you for who you are and all that you do.

Tough times lay ahead but I want you all to know I love you and you make me strong.

Much love always, Fi x

Angels

9 February 2007
Not the best of days today. Woke up feeling half optimistic but should have known better! Put on Emily necklace, Dad's eternity ring and cow socks from Maureen (my Father, Daughter and Holy Spirit – good luck?). Superstitious me eh? Picked Mum up at 9.45am and went with Simon to L&D.

Almost felt sorry for Dr A but should've saved it for me. The words I dreaded and didn't want to hear again... your cancer... has returned. Ribs, pelvis and parts of spine. So that pain had a reason now, just not the kind I wanted.

Mum and Simon – you were fantastic. Me – stunned and in shock but not sure why, as part of me had for the last few days suspected the bastard had returned. A stranger day followed... breaking news to Sophie and James was awful. Kids you are so amazing and I love you sooooooooooooooooooooo much. I'm so proud of you both.

Friends and family have responded to my email and texts with such amazing words and comments. It gives me great strength to know how much I am loved and that people care so much. Why though is this happening to me – to us – all over again? Have I not done my bit before? No one can answer these questions and I need to move over them to stay together and get the strength back to fight again.

I'm so sorry I can't make this better or easier for any of you. I feel I've let you down and I am so sorry. I love you all so very much and I am so utterly terrified.

10 February 2007
I've decided to write my thoughts and feelings down so even if I don't feel like talking, you all will know how I feel. It may not make much sense either and that's before the chemo drugs kick in.

It's raining. I'm lying in bed and life carries on around me. Sophie, you are off to paint stuff at Scouts, and James, you are off to a Quasar party. My fab husband, you are sorting everyone out – making breakfast and just being lovely. Today I just need a bit of adjustment time. Can't always be jolly and bubbly, sorry – now that's another word I need to stop using!

Today I ache – every part of me, but I think it's also psychological. Emails and texts aplenty – wonderful friends.

Out to dinner at Iain and Emma's tonight. It was lovely. Thank you Em for the lovely chicken and broccoli pasta bake – and Iain for being 'normal' to me. Feeling tired but happy. Managed to forget for a few hours and life returned to what it should be.

11 February 2007

Sophie has gone riding with Simon. I am up and dressed today by 10.30am! Had a shower and need to think about a haircut. Can't bear the plughole scenario again.

Made some phone calls. Spoke to Helen and Jon and wandered down to see the neighbours. Iain and Lisa came round and we had a good chat and watched Fawlty Towers. Laughed – good medicine.

Helen W came round for a cuppa tea. Told me on Friday that she, Hils, Jane L and Trisha had all got drunk on my behalf! More texts today and so this has now become public Big-time. Oh well!

Spoke to Mum tonight. Got an email from Judith S – I forgot Andy is a researcher – gave me loads of info about trials and drugs. Still feel like it's happening to someone else. Want my normal life back.

12 February 2007

Went rollerblading with Suneela and kids today. I hate getting up. I could easily be in bed all day. Once I'm up I'm good but Simon has gone to work which is great, he has to be busy, but I miss him. Feel scared to be just me and my thoughts. Kids are fantastic but I know they worry about me and I hate that they have this to deal with at their ages. IT'S NOT FAIR.

Lovely day. Enjoyed Roller City then went for a McDonalds! Liz came and took the ironing bless her. I'm not going to say no and it's such a help. Roger came to fix the garage door and ended up house-sitting whilst I was out as it wouldn't shut again. Ocado man delivered the shopping. Simon cooked tea. The kids were fantastic today. I keep thinking how lucky I am to have all this in my life then it hits again. Never gonna be a grandma. And I am the first Mrs Simon Crompton. I don't want Simon to be lonely; he's got a whole life ahead of him. I must stop thinking like this, it hurts too much. I must enjoy my life, be it a year or five years. I want to enjoy friends and family too. Every day is so special. I owe you all that.

Less pain today but very tired still. I haven't kept a diary for five years...

13 February 2007

Sophie and James went to Greenwich today with Liz and Roger. They had a super day at Docklands Museum, a trip on the Thames and 'heelying' all over the slopes of Greenwich!

Han C and Han B came over to see me. Had a girly gossip and it was lovely to have that 'normal' me back again.

Went and got Si a Valentine's card. I didn't want a jokey one. It had to be right. Saw Emma and got masks for the Round Table Ball in March. Radiotherapy appointment is on Thursday at 11am so Iain is having the kids for me. Sophie went to Penny's for a sleepover.

14 February 2007

Valentine's Day. How weird does today feel? Told Simon I want to renew our wedding vows, not in a desperate way but because I love him. We're thinking about it. Must ask Mum how we do that. Lovely card from Si – "I love you more than all the roses in the world". Mine said "A sense of belonging. Terrific friendship. Love that's for real. Being married to you is a lot of things. And every single one of them makes me happy". Perfect. But that's because we are soulmates. Him and me…. Me and Him. 1984> ?

Something we got right.

I proposed again and suggested renewing our vows. Simon said yes! Had a visit from Jenny the vicar. She thinks it's a lovely idea. Love you Simon. So do the kids. Sophie wants to be bridesmaid!

15 February 2007

What a day of mixed emotions. Going back to Mount Vernon was awful. Thank God for Mum and Simon coming too. I know it's been hard for them too. We waited for ages. We talked a lot. Had a chat with Dr A. She said that the fact I'd almost made five years was good. That I was well (!) was good. That it was 'only' in my bones was good. I asked the questions 'What if?', 'What next?' She seems to think that if chemo works it can delay reoccurrence for months, possibly several, so hopefully I'll see my 40th! Who knows, and that scares the shit out of me. Everyone is being so supportive and positive but it almost makes me feel overwhelmed and I want to run and hide. Had a big angry cry tonight. I am angry. Angry at God, angry for my kids, angry for Simon, angry that my life should be like this.

Sophie and James, I am angry because you need me to be your Mum and I can't promise you I'll be there. As your Mum I'm supposed to fight for you and protect you. I'm sorry, so sorry. All I can do is love you and hope you know I will always love you. From the minute I knew you, I have loved you both so much. You are so precious. The very best of Daddy and me. This shouldn't be happening to us. We should be allowed to stay as our family. Forgive me and don't be scared of what has happened. I'm rambling, my mind is jumping!!

I guess what I want to say is I love you, perhaps that's where Mum was right. My legacy will be love. All the memory boxes, baby albums and holiday albums are made from my love for my family.

This is what I need this to be about, not my diary of treatment but my feelings and hopes and messages.

Yes, that's what it should be.

16 February 2007

Not going to write every day unless I feel like it. Highlight today – bought new CRV! The bloke was funny. We phoned to test drive and he then said was it a car we'd consider buying. We said 'yes, let's sign the deal'. He thought all his Christmases had come at once! Due to arrive mid-March. It's lovely, full spec and a camera to help with reversing!

Chris F popped in today too. Lovely to see her and have a chat. Bought me a cow from Prague. Finding eating a chore! Not sure if radiotherapy has affected my stomach. Chest feels better. I feel tired but it's a vicious cycle: no food, no energy. Sorted wedding with the vicar for 3 March. He's coming to chat on Monday night.

17 February 2007

Went shopping with Emma, Sophie and Kathryn. Got lovely dresses for the girls and a gorgeous suit for James. They will all look fabulous. Had dinner with Jacquie and Chris tonight. Weird, me not drinking. Did eat a roast dinner though. Had a lovely time.

18 February 2007
OK Simon – a list for you.

- ♥ Take the kids on amazing holidays – safari, New Zealand, USA, Disney Florida.
- ♥ Create amazing memories for them.
- ♥ LOVE them for both of us.
- ♥ Be happy (tough call I know).
- ♥ The kids will grow fast so keep checking clothes/shoes!!! (nag, nag, nag) Emma will be only too happy to take Sophie shopping!! Just have the cheque book ready, my baby is loving going shopping and she's only eleven.
- ♥ REMEMBER <u>I LOVE YOU</u> – as long as it's not too painful.

1 March 2007
Life has been good lately... bizarre I know. Almost normal. Everyone has been amazing. So far Liz B has made the wedding cake and James' cake. Marcha has sent money for wedding flowers. Babs and Iain sent two dozen red roses and champagne. And so many people want to come to the church.

School came round. Catherine, Sara at lunchtime. Bless, they clubbed together and got me £60 spa vouchers for my birthday. Tracy from the BBC has offered spa treatments, dinner at a London restaurant or a Paul Edmonds hairdo. People have been so generous to me. Emails, texts and donations to Debs' 26 mile Moonwalk. I can't believe how people see me. I'm overwhelmed by kindness and love.

My mates Hils and Emma have been brilliant. I worry how they are, as they are caring for me. This serenity and calm I feel is so nice but then again I haven't started treatment yet!

I am so looking forward to our vows, James' birthday... all the family things. MY family things.

2 March 2007

James' 9th birthday. Early 6am start by James! James had a great day. I think he was really pleased with all his presents and despite having to go to school, he had a good day. I can't believe my baby is nine. Simon collected him from school as Mum and I had been at Mount Vernon for my pre-chemo checks. Long and stressful three hours! Had migraine this evening. First one in four years.

Had tea at Liz's. She'd gone to so much trouble for James' birthday. Chicken spaghetti and chocolate cheesecake. I felt awful and had no vision! Poor Si had to feed me! But luckily James didn't seem to have minded! Came home and I went to bed early. James and Sophie played and chatted on their DS!

3 March 2007

What a fantastic day. Kids woke me at 7am. Lots of cards and great pressies. Sophie and James got me an MP4 player that does music, video and photos. It's so great, when I figure out how to use it! Si got me the CRV car and a CD! Liz and Rog got me a Radley bag and a personal number plate. Mum got me a gold Egyptian cartouche necklace – beautiful – with my name in hieroglyphics. Had a CD from Iain and Lisa and smellies from Al. Emma, Iain, Matthew and Kathryn gave me a gorgeous top from Monsoon. Hils, Jez, Katie and Spencer got me a Radley bag! Had lots of pressies, champers and smellies from friends.

Elaine came at 9.15am to do our hair. It looked amazing. Kathryn and Sophie looked so beautiful and so alike. James looked adorable. Emma and Kathryn got ready here. Flowers arrived and the posies were perfect. The sun came out and everything was perfect.

Arrived at the church. It was pretty full. Got quite emotional walking down the aisle. Had to laugh as I got my heel stuck in the grate and I said "Shit, my shoe!" in front of the vicar, Christopher! Iain came to my rescue and sorted my shoe out. It broke the emotion and the rest of the service was just perfect. Sophie, Kathryn and James walked behind Si and I. They were all brilliant.

The service was personal but just right. Iain did the reading so well – thank you bro. How like Dad he has become. At the end of the hymns and prayer, Christopher said Si and I should kiss. Everyone clapped.

After we walked down the aisle, we had photos done by Nettie (Hils, thank you so much for arranging that). Lots and lots of photos. So many people came along. The church was full of family, friends and love.

Afterwards, we went to Billy's. Cath and Liz had arranged and decorated the back room for us. Great to catch up with everyone. Tara came with her mum and gave James a birthday pressie and an invite to Luton FC! Everyone said how gorgeous the kids looked. I was just so PROUD. I had been able to stand up in church and let the world know how much I love Simon all over again. Lunch was brilliant at Sazio's. Twenty all in and lots more laughter. I felt normal. Today wasn't about cancer; it was about us – love, family and friends. Normality. How I crave that again.

Mum was brilliant. She, Liz and Rog paid for it all. Too kind and generous but thank you.

Debs and Pete had come a long way too and it made everything good. I've been so amazed by everyone's generosity and support.

My birthday, our renewal of vows has just been a perfect day. This day I will treasure.

Thank you to everyone who helped make it so special.

I have had a fantastic 39th birthday. I renewed my love for you Simon, my soulmate, and had all the people I love share it with me.

4 March 2007
James had a super party despite the rain! It just made the fun rings go down the ski slope even quicker. All the kids had fun and no one complained about being soaked at all. James loved it and wants another party like that! Excellent.

5 March 2007
Walked kids to school. Normal routine! Mum collected me and we went to Mount Vernon. New routine! Got there at 10.30am, was told that Hickman line not going in until 3pm! Sat about all day getting anxious and pissed off. What a waste of time. Had pre-med and injection for relaxing (!!), then off to minor injuries unit for line insertion. Bit uncomfortable having someone poking about in your chest, prodding a line into your vein to your heart. Thought I was having a heart attack it beat so fast. All done in 45 minutes, then back to the ward for chemo.

Wow, what a difference. No needles, no pain, no feeling it going up my arm. One hour chemo, 1.5 hours for bone strength drugs.

Finally got home at <u>10pm</u> after a slight detour to McDonalds for a whopper quarter pounder cheeseburger. I wasn't fed at the hospital between 11am and 3pm, then all I had was an apple and a cake from home. Feel tired, bit drained but otherwise sore but OK.

6 March 2007
No sickness yeah! Taken lots of pills and potions and it's only 8am. Slept OK. Kids were brilliant, as has Mum been after all

that time yesterday. Poor Simon has had a tough time waiting about too.

He went off to work and Em popped in and stayed the day. Very pleased she did. Felt OK, but didn't want to be on my own. Lazy day, just watched a DVD and chatted really. Ate lunch, took pills! Mum came and cleaned dressings – ouch! Yes Mum, it does hurt to have that 'gently' pulled off my chest!

Si came home at 5.30pm and we had a big roast for tea. Yum. Mum stayed for tea. Sophie came back with Liz from the netball tournament, they got to the semis but she was a reserve. Grove won! Sophie then went off to Scouts for Fun Rings at Welwyn Garden City again!

I worry about Simon. He is rather stressed by all this and I can't do much about the kids or around the house to help. I'm glad he's going out with the boys tomorrow night. He needs a break.

14 March 2007

Wow, so much has happened in the last week. Me – I'm feeling human again. More energy, a few pains in my left leg every so often. But anyway...

On Friday I went for lunch at Sarah's and Hils had a surprise up her sleeve! Claire and Sally drove down from Derbyshire to see me. They arrived at lunchtime, then after school all the girls and the kids went to Sarah's for tea. It was such a lovely surprise and I was so touched. Hils had arranged for Claire and Sally to stay over so we all had dinner together. Unfortunately the lamb was too rich for me and I was very sick and had violent stomach cramps and the runs. Came home early.

Rest of the week, not bad. Next surprise was going out for lunch with Mum and walking into the Old Bell on Tuesday 13 March only to find my godfather Uncle David sat in there! Mum had cooked that up with him. He flew in from Atlanta that morning and is staying until Friday. I couldn't believe it! Wow!

We had a great time catching up and I learned all about his football career including playing on the same team as George Best – 'Bestie'. How he played five-a-side with Bestie, Tom Jones and Rod Stewart! He wants to watch James at school footie. James is awestruck by the stories he's heard lately. Sophie thinks he's great too.

15 March 2007
Uncle David came up to school to watch James' football training. Very impressed and gave James some training tips for speed.

16 March 2007
Merit Assembly up at school. How proud I am of both Sophie and James. You have both worked so hard and done so well. It was lovely to be up at school for the assembly and to take Uncle David and Grandma Jean.

We went on to have coffee afterwards before Uncle David had to leave. He surprised me with a big box of flowers too! I'm glad he came over. It was so nice to see him and also for Mum too.

17 March 2007
St Patrick's Day Masked Ball. Went along and had a lovely evening. Iain proposed a toast to 'the Newly Weds'!! Didn't feel like dancing as my hip is hurting and my left leg feels a bit painful. Wore my BBC dress!

18 March 2007
Mother's Day. Went to church with Sophie. We went up with Hils and Katie. Church service was communion too so went

and had a blessing from Jenny.

Simon cooked lunch for Mum, me, Liz and Rog. James made mozzarella, olive and tomato salad (with Liz) and a fresh herb dressing. Really lovely. Si did roast beef and Sophie made cheesecake (with Liz). Really good too.

James printed out and designed the menu. He is SO clever on the computer. Really impressed. Had a fantastic Mother's Day. Got DVD recorder for my Archos MP4!

This week: Wednesday went to lunch with Jane C. Lovely meal. Felt very decadent. Thursday – hair by Pope! Went for the old short fave of yesteryear. Feel ten years younger. Found out my natural colour is dark brown and hoping hair will stop falling out as much. James, I'm glad to say, approves of my new style. Friday had bloods done at LSD! So easy with Hickman line but still had to wait about. Got there 9.30am, home by 10.45am! Went to Paula B's 'Chickens For Africa' coffee morning. Won a huge amount of chocolate and eggs for the kids but did donate for some chickens too.

25 March 2007

Went to riding. Went to Mum's for 40th Wedding Anniversary Remembrance lunch. Got her a card, which I think made her day. Ruby Wedding Day, it said.

26 March 2007

Got to Mount Vernon at 9.30am. Had to go to clinic and found white cells down 1.34, not near 1.5 which is acceptable! Overdoing it and feeling a bit coldy. Need to chill out and stop being superwoman again. Had bloods redone. Dexamet brought results up thank God.

Finally got chemo at 2pm after having Biophos for bones at 12-1.30pm. Got home at 5pm. Made some new bald friends, Anna and Sheila. I'm the only cancer x2 person!

James made me a lovely Easter card at Cubs tonight. He's so thoughtful and said tomorrow he'll be Dr James. Sophie enjoyed going to Penny's too. It's good for her and Penny to catch up. Simon did lots of bits today including sorting out the car which comes tomorrow! VERY EXCITING!

27 March 2007

Chris' leaving do. I still can't believe she'll go at Easter. It's all so wrong. Feel OK today – tired but think adrenalin is kicking in. Got up late and had Han B over to finish off the PowerPoint for Chris. It's excellent. Got loads done but it still needs finishing.

The car is lovely. Kids came back with Simon so we all took it home together.

My hair is falling out Big-time. Managed to go to Chris' do. Terrified that people would touch my hair. Saw lots of folk I hadn't seen in ages. It was a lovely evening. Glad I went, wouldn't have missed it. It's going to seem so strange with no Chris at school.

28 March 2007

Feel shite! A real low today. Tired, sickish and balding. Great. Not planning on doing anything. Can't deal with the constant 'How are you feeling?' 'Do you feel sick?' Don't need it, just want to be me. I ache and am already pissed off now that chemo makes me feel so crap. It's the hair loss that is getting me down. Can't touch, scratch or wash my hair anymore it feels. Next weekend I think its wig time! Great. I've said I don't do feeling sorry for myself but I've snapped at everyone today, even the kids and that's not fair. Fuck cancer. I hate you.

I hate what you are doing to my family, my kids. Sophie and James don't deserve this at all. Poor Sophie has begun to look at life and the life of her friends who have it 'better'.

That's so not what she should have to be dealing with at eleven. I know that my eleventh year was hard with Dad in Scotland, and Mum, Iain and me in Lymington with no space of my own but that was easier than this.

30 March 2007
Our 16th wedding anniversary. Well sixteen years ago we would never have seen this coming. We had no money, a small house, each other, hope and optimism. Then along came life at its cynical best! Bless you Simon for sticking with me through good, bad, sickness and health. You kept your side of the vows for sure.

Well, I managed to get to school today for Chris' final assembly and the immortal PowerPoint.

Tonight Simon and I celebrated with a Chinese take-away which my stomach coped with and didn't repeat back! I am so fed up with feeling yuck. I want normal back.

31 March 2007
Simon and the kids went to Watford v Chelsea. Was a great game but Watford was robbed 1-0 in extra time. My day was low. Reality has dawned again. My hair has all but gone and I feel so low. I am shouting at Si and the kids. I look like shit and I'm angry. I'm so scared too. I'm going through all of this for a second time and my poor kids and family don't need it either. WHY US? WHY ME?

1 April 2007
Irony... April Fools Day and I'm literally tearing my hair out. Tears, more tears, lack of appetite and a dreadful taste in my mouth. Too scared to say how I really feel to Simon. Must keep a brave face on for all of them.

Emma knows. She knows how I'm feeling. What I'm thinking. You made me laugh Em when you talked about

Donna and Tiffanys! I think your birthday will be a nice surprise! *(Fi got Emma a little something from Tiffany & Co.)*

Wearing my short wig now. Found Trevor Sorbie's website about cutting wigs. He does it for free for cancer patients. Think I'll call him and see what he can do. I'm so proud of Sophie. She's been a star helping me deal with loving my hair. We shout a lot but Sophie I do love you so very much. James has dealt so well too with the wig. I was scared you'd hate me and the way I look. Thank you both for accepting it. As for you Simon… just keep telling me you love me.

12 April 2007

It's been a year since Maureen died. I miss her.

We had a great time at Dancing on Ice. Three rows from the front and really close to all the skaters. It was great. The kids loved it. They also loved their Wii. What a great surprise that was. I love seeing their faces.

Went to Brighton on the Bank Holiday. Had a great day wandering about in the sunshine. Went down on the train. Sophie and I went earring shopping in the Lanes. Went to the pier and on the land train and then onto the beach for a stroll. Great day.

Took Sophie to London to the Kylie exhibition at the V&A. Went with Em and Kathryn. Kylie is tiny and I was surprised at the poor quality material used for costumes. Some looked really cheap. Went to a wig shop in Notting Hill and had a laugh trying on new wigs. The girls were very helpful. Emma helped me choose a new one. Real hair! £274! Does look so real and hey, I'm worth it!

8 September 2007

It's been a while… chemo finished in June. Hickman line was fab for all that.

Wig worked well but now I have enough to go natural again. That is just great. Bit more grey but hey, it's all mine.

Summer was lovely. Had a wonderful time at Debs' house in France. Never felt so relaxed and carefree. Yes, I actually forgot that I'm living with cancer.

Funny how you panic over things again. So proud of Sophie going to secondary school and dealing with her new school. She's had a super week. James loves being in Y5 with Mr L too. Went back to work myself on Thursday, only for half a day but it felt good to be normal again.

Have a pain again! When I take deep breaths. I'm hoping it's due to movement or something with the Hickman line as it's on that side of my chest. I mean, I've only just finished chemo, it can't be reacting after only three months surely? Come on, give me a few years of inactivity. Poor J has breast cancer after two years clear of ovarian cancer.

I need to phone L&D really.

23 November 2007

Just re-read that last entry. How cruel life can be. Had a scan two weeks ago, the routine three monthly ones. Went to see Dr A with Mum today. I've had similar pains and breathing problems this last week too. It is painful then after a few days, disappears.

Well, to cut to the chase I was terrified what she was going to say. I now go to these appointments expecting bad news.

The bones, no change, no new tumours, abdomen all clear. Blood test reveals raise in activity levels and now I have an active node growing in my lung! Only 12mm but I had a choice. Treat now or leave and wait and see what it does. NO BRAINER.

So it's 'chemo tablets R Us'.

Apparently I shouldn't lose my hair and I can still work. Two weeks on, and one week off. If I respond well I can do tablets indefinitely so confused about how I feel.

Angels

I wanted scan results to say no change, no growths. I want the Hickman line out and to enjoy South Africa with a clear bill of 'my type' of health. So scared that this is the beginning of the end... the slippery slope into the beyond. Will I ever get to have some good news, some normal life again? I've had to decide not to reveal the whole truth now to my friends, as I can't live with their sympathy and sad looks.

So often I am told I am an inspiration, amazing, courageous woman. Sure don't feel that way right now. So, to a plan. Need a meeting with chemo staff to discuss regime. Blood tests, but getting Hickman line out so I can 'enjoy' my holiday. Will probably start chemo tablets before holiday. God I hope I don't feel shite on them.

I feel so guilty that for most of James and Sophie's lives they have had to live with my cancer. I am so sorry guys, you deserved better than that. But I am so proud of you and the people you have become, despite all of that. I'm trying so hard to be brave for you – you are what makes me fight and carry on when inside I am screaming and crying like a terrified little kid. Again I ask. Why ME? Why US?

Christmas Eve 2007
Went to church today. Doesn't feel like Christmas will be tomorrow as we are going to South Africa on Boxing Day. We have no Christmas food in and no cards up and minimal decorations. Kids are very excited. James has been tracking Santa all day! Sophie is more laid back. James didn't get to sleep until 12.30am! Poor Santa was late to bed tonight.

Christmas Day 2007
Up at 6am! James leapt into our bedroom to welcome Christmas Day. I feel so tired! Had a nice day. Didn't go overboard with presents. Wanted this one to be special for the family, more than

presents. Had lunch with Liz, Roger and Al. Went to Mum's for tea. Iain was there. Kids played on all the DS games – the flight should be quiet tomorrow! Having nerves about packing and making sure we have everything... plus I'm back on chemo tablets tonight! MERRY CHRISTMAS!

Boxing Day 2007
Got a bit maudlin first thing about Christmas and my future. Looked at balloon flights for South Africa safari and as Mum, Liz and Rog gave us money for Christmas think we might blow it on that. As I know so well, you only live once so DO IT WELL, MAKE MEMORIES! Bon voyage – see you next year.

2008
Had an AMAZING holiday. Safari, Garden Route, Cape Town. The animals were incredible and it wasn't a hardship at all getting up at 5am! Missed out on a balloon flight but it was so awesome the whole experience. Cape Town was great. Did Table Mountain and took so many photos. I can tick this box now – Safari done! I'm so glad we went. We saw so much, learnt so much. Did all the tours and saw such contrasts. The Townships we drove past had a real impact on all of us.

1 March 2008
After weeks of thinking that Simon had done nothing I had to eat humble pie! I had a fab time at Sopwell with the girlies and came back to a calm house. No party, I thought. Then Si suggests a 'curry' at a restaurant on the A5 with Hils and Jez! Strange I thought, and Grandma babysitting at short notice. Well, we had a drink at Hils and Jez's and then Jez announces no curry, but a meal in a Whipsnade pub. OK I thought. Definitely no party.

We drive towards the A5, down the lanes and turn into the golf club. *"Don't be cross. Take a deep breath and remember all the people are here because they love you."*

Cue tears. Cue "SURPRISE!" Cue shock at 100+ smiling faces and clapping. I've been got good.

School mates, Uni mates, teachers, mates and Sophie, James, Kathryn and Katie too. Couldn't believe who had come. Tried to get round everyone to say hi. Liz and Cath made an amazing cake á la Sex And The City. Jane did the decorating with Emma. Danced my socks off to Ian K's band and it was perfect. My hubby, my kids, my family (including Hannah and Sam), my mates – my PERFECT party. I remember making my speech, just wanted to thank everyone. Like I said, you make me strong and you make me special. Then off to New York with Si!

24-27 July 2008

Had the most fantastic time. New York was amazing. We packed in so much in four days. It was so nice spending grown up time doing sight seeing, meals and just walking about the city. Did some more off my 'list' – a helicopter flight along the Hudson looking at New York from the air. Amazing. Our hotel was beautiful – we got an upgraded room! Mamma Mia on Broadway was brilliant. The photo tour was excellent but in the heat and after three hours I was shattered. We did the Mets baseball game but left after three hours at the ninth inning as it went onto midnight! Fourteen innings and they still lost. Nice to sample the atmosphere though. Brunch at River Café was fantastic, looking at the Manhattan skyline. It was so pretty. What was weird was seeing sights so familiar from TV and the movies in real life. Went to Ground Zero and felt very humbled and saddened by the museum there. Came home Club Class and that was so brilliant. Slept like a baby all the flight on my flat bed! What a way to travel. A fantastic birthday pressie Simon. Thanks so much babe.

August 2008

Had a fab time in France at Debs' house. Always feel so rested and peaceful there. Pete was fantastic and it was lovely to be able to get to know him more. Sam came over as a surprise as he had leave from the Navy. It was lovely to see him. Two weeks of relaxing and the kids had a great time, swimming, learning how to play cards, doing jigsaws, mowing lawns with tractors etc. James loved doing all of that and Sophie was so content to chat, read and swim. Lovely family time. Missed Debs not being able to be there.

September 2008

Oh dear… got some pain… just want it to go away. Want to bury my head in the sand. Can't though can I? Saw Dr A and arranged a scan. Not so great as I knew it would be. Two new hot spots. On my ribs and mid-spine. So I need some treatment. Had been feeling stiff, had pain in my chest and shoulder.

So pissed off by it all. Feel like it's taking over again. Need some chemo again but can have it in tablet form only. It sounds a bit stronger than the last time. Shouldn't lose my hair but need to take one tablet one week then another a week later, but have to do it in hospital and take anti sick pills! Just got back into work mode again but have taken some time off to get my head together which means NO pay as they won't put me on a contract. Haven't told the kids yet. Let's see how I feel. Hoping I should be OK like last time, a year ago. Just feel so depressed and not in control again. My body is just under attack again and now with every ache, twinge etc. I fear the worst.

Again, why me, us, it's so not fair. I'm only 40. I want to see my kids grow up and see my grandkids but what chance do I have eh? The job of a mum is to be there and protect and love your kids. I feel I'm letting them down and cheating them of an easy childhood. They've had to put up with all this crap since they were little. James was four for God's sake. It's all he's ever known. Sophie is becoming a beautiful young woman and needs her mum to be there.

Need to fight, find strength and channel the anger I have. Chemo tablets start 10 October!

23 October 2008

Chemo tablets OK so far! Got appointment with Dr A on 24 October. Bit worried, as it was my L&D free Friday.

24 October 2008

Waited three hours to see Dr A. I went to St Albans in the morning with Emma to take my mind off it. Si came to L&D with me as mum is in Cyprus. Felt really scared and the wait was awful. Turns out that Dr A is on hols next week so clinic has been condensed into one today! Met a girl who has been on This Morning talking about breast cancer. Discussed our TV experiences! Well, got into Dr A at 2.45pm and was now worried about kids coming home from school. I hate this cancer for taking over my life, for getting in the way of everything. I want NORMAL again. Why is that so much to ask for? I want a break from it. Some OK news not more tests, scans and results. So, the good news was that the scans were CLEAR in the liver and lungs but... and there is always one – the soft tissue area above my left boob is suspect and also they are wanting to X-ray the pelvis and thighs as my right thigh looks weakened. But I said I had no pain there but I do get pain in my lower back and left leg, so next Friday it's X-ray time and I will need to think about getting my limbs pinned if they show real danger of breaks. Fantastic!!

How the fuck am I going to do The MoonWalk now? I SO intend to even if I'm to take six hours. I feel like I'm failing myself... falling apart and having to fight my own body for survival.

25 October 2008

Had a real mother-daughter moment. I need to be here to help. We had a big hug and we both cried! Sophie was so grown up about it all.

6 December 2008

Well, here we are in December! I've had four cycles of Vineralbine but it makes me feel so tired and nauseous. I have lost nearly a stone! Well, that's a bonus I guess. Went to see Dr A and was worried what she would say about the X-ray as my back pain is worse and I have shooting nerve pains in my legs but no! The lump I'd found on my left chest side has grown, which I'd felt for weeks, so Vineralbine is not really helping. Need to have more effective chemo! So having a biopsy to see if the lump is hercep+. If it is, great, but I doubt that very much. So, a biopsy on Monday and the fourth chemo to start 2 January. So, I will be bald by my birthday! Not telling the kids till after Christmas as don't want to ruin it for them. It's so not fair to them. Mum has been a legend and so supportive. Don't know what I'd do without her. I had to wait to tell Simon until he came home. He never says much but I think he doesn't want to think about it too much. Christ knows what I'll do about work! I need sick pay so will work the first week then go off sick! See, it's taking over again. Think I'm having Taxol which can numb your hands and feet (great!). Don't think I'm going to get to MoonWalk with Sophie now. Off to Iain and Emma's tonight. Good friends, good company.

21 December 2008

Emily's anniversary – 14 years ago at 7.45am this morning. Can't believe that it has been that long yet it is all so real in my head. I can still see us running in from the car park to the ward and all the faces just looking at us. Now 14 years on I am scared again that this will be my last Christmas – in Wham's words! I ache and feel so low. I am tired, really tired, and don't know how I am going to get the energy to fight again and that really worries me. The lower back pain and pain in my legs is so tiring. I just feel weak and pathetic but I'm trying to hold it all together for everyone else, especially Sophie and James. Rest In Peace Emily – I love you.

24 December 2008

Christmas Eve. Had a super day. Went to watch James at squash and he came third in the tournament. Then we went up to London. We saw Spamalot and it was hilarious. Great views of the stage but seating was a bit cramped! James and Sophie both laughed a lot and James got a 'fetchez les vaches' t-shirt, but I resisted the urge to buy the t-shirt and badge with 'I'm not dead yet' slogan on it! Went up to Regent Street and Carnaby Street to see the lights. Regent Street was poor, Carnaby Street had some very lovely giant snowmen. Came back on the train and went to Iain and Emma's to swap pressies. Lovely, lovely family day. Watched Gavin and Stacey Christmas special, then waited for the kids to go to sleep.

25 December 2008

No one woke up till 7am! Had a lazy morning opening stockings and Santa did very well. A DVD each so whilst Si and I were sorting out, Sophie and James were quite happy to watch those. Had a generally lazy day. I felt really tired and a bit nauseous but hey, what's new. Kids loved all the pressies. James got very excited and wanted to open everything at once! Sophie was a bit quiet but I think the reality of Christmas is with her now!! Cheer up Moo, you'll get excited again, promise. Iain came over and we did pressies and Si, bless him, did ALL THE COOKING and was FANTASTIC. That's why I love you babe. Liz, Rog and Alister, and Mum arrived. We Skyped Debs and the crew in France which was lovely. Had more pressies and then lunch. I didn't feel like eating loads. We staggered pudding till 4pm! Watched TV and fell asleep. Really nice lazy day. Kids played on new games and listened to music. Love my new PJ's and statues of the family. Really touched by Sophie and James' 'red room' gifts. I hope everyone had a good day. I felt so odd inside. Must shake this and find the fighting side again. Don't want to be beaten, no way, not yet, still have goals to reach: MoonWalk, James going to secondary school, next Christmas and being 42!

26 December 2008
Had Boxing Day at Mum's which was lovely. There was the 'Christmas of One Carrot', well this was the 'Boxing Day of Dodgy Gravy'! Taste the difference... hmmm! Then there was the trifle... oh how we laughed with the introduction *"You won't like it because the sponge is the rubber roulade that went wrong and the cream is too runny but it has a real vanilla pod in the custard!"* Iain and I just creased!

In the week, I went to the sales in Luton and there wasn't much out there. The Chairman's Drink was fun, with a treasure hunt over Harpenden. Lovely to get out into the fresh air. Getting scared about going out too far in case I'm in pain. Stupid really as I am only taking mild pain killers once a day.

31 December 2008
New Year's Eve. Went to Paul and Julie G's. Did a murder mystery. It was a good laugh. Dressed up head to foot in black to play Kitty Killer, a spy/journalist! Including a wig! Si was an East End gangster Champagne Charlie Bunson. He looked like my Uncle Keith with a moustache and porkpie hat! All the kids were very well behaved and watched DVD's all night.

Angels

At midnight I took the wig off. Didn't want to start another year in a wig. That'll come eh?! Glad to see the back of 2008 but dreading 2009. Phoned Mum, Iain and sent some texts. Mum coined the phrase 'hopeful' New Year. Well, ain't that the truth. So scared of 2009. Going to talk to the kids on Sunday. Dreading that.

1 January 2009
Hopeful New Year Mum said... Didn't get to bed till 3am so didn't get up till 11am! Went to Iain and Emma's at 2pm and went for a walk. So many folk walking around Harpenden, walking off hangovers no doubt. Walked all over the Common then popped into the Engineer for a drink and then back to the Sinnotts. It felt much later although it was only 4.30pm! Had an early tea of chilli and bits. It was lovely. Just relaxing and laughing. Watched some TV and came home at 8pm. Need to get back into an early night routine. Watched some TV at home but couldn't get to sleep... strange thoughts in my head but also not sleepy.

3 January 2009
Kids practising Gang Show all the time! Went to Amanda's to see Rachel and Ricky and their kids. Can't believe it's five years since they came over from Oz. It was really nice and the chat just flowed. All the kids got on and we ended up staying for a curry! Got home at midnight. What was so great was for a whole evening I was Fi again and nothing reminded me that I had any issues. It was so wonderful. Dreading tomorrow and shattering my kids... AGAIN!

10 January 2009
The kids were OK, they took it very well. James had a wobbly on the 5 January but it's because he's older now. I'm so proud

of you James and Sophie for the way you deal with this. I'm the one feeling guilty that this has been a huge part of your life too. So NOT right.

Well, one treatment down now. Didn't think I'd find the strength to deal with it but all the wonderful uplifting texts I got really helped. Plus, Nicky, my fave nurse, found a vein first go and it gave blood and so it all went OK. They give Piriton as a pre-med so I slept through the chemo! I was so tired. Feeling tired and a bit achy like normal today so managed breakfast. So good, so far!

3 April 2009

Well, went for scan results thinking good news but oh, so, so, so wrong. Chest lump hasn't changed but worst of all, despite chemo, I now have spots on my LIVER. Lots of little spots and that isn't good news. So I sat stunned as Dr A explained she needs to change to a Gem Carb *(a type of chemotherapy)* routine: two weeks treatment, one week off. This should control and shrink spots but I WILL NOT be cured. So I asked the dreaded question and the honest answer came back. It could be six months, it could be eighteen months. So it's official. I'm dying. Not terminal as there is still treatment, but we are running out of options. The plus point is I have no liver symptoms yet (!) and I am well. Have asked to see MacMillan counsellor as to how to deal with all this. New treatment starts 17 April and I see Dr A on 5 May.

Mum was brilliant. Don't know how she holds it together. James is poorly and off school so he was lying on the sofa. Liz and Iain had looked after him and Mac! When I got home my head was a mess. I went and sat in the garden with Mac. My gorgeous puppy just ran around the garden and as the sun was shining and the birds were singing, I thought how strange the world is. Has anything really changed? Yes, I suppose it has. I now need everything to count and mean something. I sat and wrote letters to Emma, Iain *(Fi's brother)* and Debs. I watched TV with James and it hurt me so much just to look at him. Sophie came back later, having been to the park with her mates. She was red faced and laughed as I asked her if she'd been snogging?! Just like Simon and me. OMG. Hils came over and I told her but said no one else must know, as I don't need the sympathetic pitying looks I had off the chemo staff today. That was horrid.

The MacMillan nurse is coming after Easter to see me. Never thought I'd do that, but need some advice. Shit, that makes it real then. I'm not invincible, nor will I live to be 43! Hey, life, the universe and everything – the answer is 42! I guess I knew that all along.

Told Simon and that was so hard. We need to talk a lot now and do it honestly. Lay in bed tonight, so many thoughts going round my head. I can't get the guilt out of my head. I want time and that's something I can't control. This wasn't supposed to happen yet. My kids are too young. Those words still haunt me: *"Its bad news... it's serious... you need to prepare your family."* I'm 41. What is all that about? We've just bought a puppy, booked holidays. No, this isn't right.

So now every moment counts and my head is full of things I need to sort and say to people. Guess that's why I've started writing again. I remember Dad putting stickers and labels on stuff, to show who he wanted to have stuff.

Reflecting, I guess I've been lucky! I have spent my whole life with the boy I fell in love with and we had three great kids. He even bought me a dog! Poor Mac. Must make the most of you too.

4 April 2009

Em phoned this morning. I made light but said I'd pop in for a coffee later. She knew. She always knows. That's what best friends do. I arrived at hers and we chatted, then I told her. We cried and cried and then I made her promise that she'd be there for Sophie – a surrogate mum as she is the only one I trust to do that. She is the person closest to Sophie. I trust her as godmother and my almost sister. See Em, when you and Iain agreed to be godparents, you weren't expecting that! But hey, you were always there when we had Emily, rushing to London and various hospitals to help and support us. We certainly chose excellent friends. For all of that I thank you from my heart, mate.

13 April 2009
I met you 25 years ago today my darling Simon. It only seems like yesterday. Those dodgy hairdos, that flying jacket, boots and you all in black! Me – I was wearing my mum's trousers and heels, and some dodgy jumper ready to make myself look older to get into the Empire Night Club for John's 18th. Drank Cinzano and lemonade, how sophisticated! But it worked, I landed you! And even with the ups and downs, so glad I did. Eighteen years married and three great kids and a dog. Not bad eh?! So I've known you more than half my life and that makes me so thankful.

21 April 2009
Really achy today. Can do chemo and APD when I'm not in pain. Si worked from home this morning which was great. Mind you, Mac had been up at 3am whinging! Feel like an old crock. Pain makes you so low and today I feel really low and depressed and it all comes down on me what is happening. Just have no energy to deal with anything. Can't curl up, too painful. Just want to sleep but too much to do. Need to make books for Sophie and James, sort out lots of other things too. So scared about the holidays I've booked now. August

seems so far away but then if things don't go 'my' way, it's not far enough. Scared about the MacMillan Nurse coming on Thursday as that's like me being put on the final path. As the movies say: 'Dead Man Walking'. If I could have a wish or three I just want normal back. I envy all my mates who are rushing about. I don't have the energy. The sun shines but I have to be uber-careful, as I will burn. I desperately want to do The MoonWalk and that is my next goal. Mind you I need to walk ten miles in the next two weeks and today I struggled to get round the block. I'm 41 for heaven's sake. Kids have been great but I'm dreading it when they begin to see me deteriorate. I'm the one who is supposed to do the looking after, not vice versa. Still have this horrid cough. Can't shift it.

8 May 2009

Today is my Friday 'off' hospital. I have had a cycle of Gem Carb. I just feel odd and can't really explain it. My appetite is off and not really interested in eating anything. Feel bloated and full. How strange. This in turn means I feel tired so can't win. Glad we have Mac so I am going out for a walk every day. Need to get Sophie and James' baby negatives on digital to add to their books I'm making. Have transferred all of Emily's negatives to digital so I'm pleased about that. Went to Shirl's for a catch up with curry club last night but all the small talk seemed so odd. Talking about kids and how fast they grow up, then onto weddings and family holidays.

16 May 2009

The MoonWalk! Woke up so excited about today and sharing it with Sophie. Dreading my back giving up and me not being able to do it. This is one of THE most important events for me to share with Sophie.

We got to Hyde Park at 8.40pm and headed for the Pink

Tent. Mum was at home, looking after James and Mac. We found Norma and Steph and bumped into Liz who was being a marshal. Time flew by as we waited. We ate our pasta and went into the tent to listen to Nina. I'd built this up so much in my head as to how I'd share it with Sophie. Part of me felt let down as the event seemed to lose it's meaning and become a race. We had a cry during the minute's silence.

Then we were off. Paul O'Grady did the countdown. Norma and Steph strode out quite fast. I didn't want to and couldn't go that fast. I was rather pissed off by two miles as my back hurt and they had gone ahead with Sophie. Hils stayed with me. Every so often they'd wait and we'd catch up! Sophie didn't know what to do, so I said to walk with me, albeit a little slower. Missed seeing Liz at three miles. The group spread out and we got an even pace. Sophie and I held hands and although my back was aching, we were doing it together. Me and my baby. Before we knew it, we were at seven miles – still jostled by fast walking Full MoonWalkers but making good time at 3-4 miles per hour. At nine miles we called home and split from the Full Mooners. I popped a painkiller and we were on the home stretch. We really walked fast into Hyde Park. Despite the chill in the air we'd done it in our bras (thanks Mum, they were ace) and I took off my mac to do the final mile. Simon, Mum and James missed us finishing by two minutes as we crossed the line at 3.25am. Four hours of walking. We got our medals and photos. So very proud of Sophie. She walked so well. Got a final surprise when Iain turned up with Debs! Shame no one saw us finish but then we had really paced it for the last miles!

17 May 2009
It was a real surprise to see Debs. Didn't do much today. Just lazed about. Really tired and my back hurts but otherwise all

OK! Got to bed at 4.30am! Liz B made an amazing boob bra cake. Had dinner with Mum and Iain and Debs and us. Really lovely. Mum surprised me with THAT Radley bag – the dog on the gondola! She is SO naughty, I love it, but she didn't want me to buy it. It's mad I feel well and look well so I don't want special treatment because of this 'situation'.

I heard Debs and Si discussing it tonight. She told Si she knew as we had talked about it on Mac's walk. I'm glad Simon opened up to Debs. Simon knows I want to stay at home. I HATE hospitals and DON'T INTEND TO DIE in one. I've spent too much time in them in the last seven years. I know it would be hard to live here knowing I'd died here, but if that were his wish I would do that for him. The kids WOULD cope. As for telling the kids now – NO WAY. They don't need to know yet. I WILL PROTECT their childhood. I don't want my life or death status to be public. So much of my treatment is discussed among friends. I WON'T DO IT.

20 May 2009
Had a chat to Simon. I guess I'm just scared. I don't want to be treated any differently which will happen when people know. He promised me he'll do what I want.

22 May 2009
Seizing up again but today I spent the day in bed. Not just muscular but deep down bone pain, my right rib and left pelvis especially. Hurts when I breathe. I have no strength to move and even sitting up puts pressure on my back. Si took a day off and worked from home thank God. All I could do was apologise for being useless! The kids have been fine. I stayed in bed all day as don't know what else to do. I'm moving like a snail.

23 May 2009

Typical. On a sunny bank holiday weekend, I'm laid up. If this is how APD reacts to chemo, can't do that again together. Feel a bit more mobile. I managed to sleep OK but my ribs and pelvis are still really achy. Fed up with being in pain or spasm. It's been on and off for a week now. Only saving grace is that it wasn't the MoonWalk tonight as there was NO way I could have done that at all.

24 May 2009

So very frightened – still achy but a bit more mobile. Was sick this morning and have so little energy. Feel so trapped in my body. Just want to feel OK again, like me. I need more time. So worried and scared that this is the beginning of it all. Trying so hard not to and to gather my fighting spirit again. Si and the kids have been fab. Me, I'm just sitting about being useless. I miss walking Mac so much. It's been three days now.

11 June 2009

Enjoyed Debs' return visit. We walked Mac and had a laugh. She is never still. I get tired just watching her! I missed her when she flew back to France. Half-term came and went and the kids occupied themselves really. We didn't do anything special.

My muscles in my back still ache and twinge. It's not just 'me'; it's the effects of the chemo and APD. It's been a month now since my back has been painful. I'm so sick of waking up everyday in pain. It affects my mood, appetite, what I can do each day. It's so wearing.

Anyway, today, despite the Tube strike, I went up to London with Emma and Hils and we went to see Calendar Girls. They had a special gala night and we got to meet the original Calendar Girls. I got my programme signed and got their photo too. Bought a calendar and should have got that signed but never mind. The story still makes me laugh and cry! The Calendar Girls were lovely and I had a chat with Angela, the lady who lost her husband John and started it all. She was lovely.

Oh – I have been selected to do the Cancer Research advert! Liz H came over a week ago, did an audition tape and now I am to do some filming for them! Strange isn't it that 'having cancer' has given me these opportunities – WNTW etc! Mind you I'd give all of that back to be healthy and clear.

Mac got his first haircut yesterday. He looks like a real Schnauzer now. He's such a cutie and so loving. Porch update... it's nearly done!

21 June 2009

Father's Day! Simon and the kids have been at family camp this weekend. They left on Friday as I was up in London filming the Cancer Research Advert. I took Emma with me. We had to hang about a lot! We got the train to St Pancras and then a car took us to Greenwich. We met up with Liz H and spent two hours sat in Café Rouge waiting for my slot. We filmed in a block of flats! Urban chic!! Finally finished at 7pm. It was weird. Lots of repetitive phrase saying and certain facial expressions. So who knows if I shall make the cut. It airs 12 July for two months. Finally got home at 10pm! Very achy this weekend. Taking a couple of hours to be less stiff and I get up. Poor Mac didn't get a walk till lunchtime.

Popped over to Chalfont to see Si and the kids at camp. Stayed for a couple of hours. It was really lovely to be sat outside and just chillin'. James did the high wire and I stayed to watch him. I thought he was very brave. Sophie was funny. She was 'hangin' out with her mates. Mind you, they made a bird box! Wish I could've camped but my body just won't let me. This is what I find so frustrating.

I'm so bored of feeling aged 110 and so achy. I'm 41 with the body of an old crock. Mind you at least it makes me rest up a bit more. Just need more energy I think. So my kids woke up in a field in a tent with their Dad on Father's Day!

Took Mac to Jane C's last night when I went for dinner. He and Tilly *(Jane's dog)* were funny! He was very good considering he's a puppy and she's an old lady. Did keep sniffing her bum so good job I've booked him in!

22 June 2009

Not a great start to the week. Still achy and feeling really depressed. Reality is kicking in. I'm three months down the line from when Dr A told me 'the news'. So am I 'holding' or 'folding'? Didn't get chemo as my iron level is too low! So this week's treats are a CT scan and blood transfusion. When I left the Unit on Tuesday I just lost it. Cried all the way home. Scared I have no fight left. Scared the CT is going to bring more bad news. How do I carry on? I know I can't give up because of Simon and the kids but I'm so sick of being in a losing battle. I'm jealous as hell of all those who take life for granted, their kids, their health. Right now I can't see a bright side.

26 June 2009

Had my blood transfusion. Really weird. Hilary came with me and it took ages. Had my line put in at chemo at 9.30am and then went to St Mary's Day Unit who despite having loads of staff were confused by the fact I had a port and line inserted! Eventually I got my first unit of blood at 11.30am! Crazy waste of time. It was so warm in the Unit and no TV. Anyway each unit took two hours and so we finally left at 4pm. Mind you, I did feel better. More lively and with it. I hadn't thought about what happens when someone gives blood. I just thought about operations and accidents, not the fact that two people gave blood to help me carry on my treatment. So thank you to them.

6 July 2009
Still really achy and although feel better and less tired, I feel physically tired because I am in pain. Taking Co-codemol and Nurofen but it makes me constipated! Joy. So I got some Senna and now I'm 'not constipated' but my stomach aches now as well as my body.

Oh wouldn't it be good to wake up one morning and NOT be in any pain. Oh I dream of that as, although I sleep well, my body isn't truly rested.

7 July 2009
Off to Luton Hoo with Hils for afternoon tea today. Can't believe James is off for his trial day at secondary school on Thursday. My baby is growing up! Luton Hoo was nice. Mind you we got soaked as the heavens opened!

9 July 2009
James had a great time at school. He said lunch was good and he enjoyed the Science lesson with the Bunsen burners! Started to get some of his uniform too.

10 July 2009
James had his leavers' party. Aqua Splash and Party in the Park. I felt really awful today, nauseous and so achy. Getting a bit depressed by all this now. Sophie went into town with her mates after school and I met up with James and the Y6 lot in the park. Helen and Cath sorted out lifts for James which really helped. He's staying in the park until 8pm. Not eating much at the moment.

I am so scared now, this pain and feeling sick, the not-really-eating. So scared this is the beginning of the end for sure. 6-18 months hmm! Already three months into countdown. So scared about getting the results of CT and MRI on Tuesday. Dreading more bad news as after last time I thought it was all going so well.

Anyway CRUK *(Cancer Research UK)* advert DVD arrived today. What a powerful, tearful ad that is, and my contribution... "Breast" in one ad and "but things can get better" in another. Flash of my face and that's it. Blink and miss it! But hey ho. I'm on the poster that is going to be in the shops too. Well I hope it helps raise cash to save other children from losing their Mum before they should.

Emma came round. We were supposed to go out but I wasn't in the mood. Need to get out of this depression.

11 July 2009
Si and the kids are being great but I can feel the tension. Poor Si is doing so much and working, so I worry about him too. I don't want to be a burden. I don't want them to hate me.

Results Day
Well it's holding.

The scan said liver was no change so that's great as I was dreading that outcome changing too soon. There is some increased bone activity which explains the pain in my back and shoulder. Dr A wants to change APD to Zomat which is more money! But it rebuilds and inhibits bone decay. Still feel so tired by it all. Think I do have depression as can't get motivated or excited about much these days. I'm looking forward to the end of this chemo. Only five more sessions but then what? If I was in the USA I'd be on permanent chemo. Dr A says I need a break, some radiotherapy and monitoring with scans.

24 July 2009

Back from our week in Wales. It was really pretty there and taking the dog was great. It was relaxing and wonderful to spend time with Simon, Sophie and James, oh and Mac – just us. Mind you it gave me time to think. Sitting there on Poppit Sands Beach watching the kids playing so carefree as I'm thinking all the wrong things. How many people take life for granted? The simple things – sunshine, laughter, silly chats. You don't need flash gestures. People are what's important and letting them know how much they mean to you and how much you love them.

We did beach days, looked around St David's, ate ice creams. I wanted NORMAL and despite being in pain and now having headaches, I tried to do normal. I know I'm slowing down and lots of activity leaves me breathless but that's fatigue and hopefully when chemo stops it should too. Not sailing through the Gem Carb quite so easily but at least not nauseous all the time. Taking Mac on holiday was great fun. Thanks Simon for all the driving, cooking and just being a great husband and Dad.

26 July 2009

Liz and Rog did the garden whilst we were away and it looks fantastic. The house is great. I love the porch but need a smaller step outside as it hurts my back! Sophie and James are off to Scout Camp today. God, how I'll miss them. They have no idea. I know they'll have a fantastic week whatever the weather in Dorset. I'm so proud of them and I love them so much. I hope that in heaven you really can look out for the ones you love. I want to know that they are OK. I hope that they will 'chat' to me just like I do to Dad and Emily.

I watched the Farrah Fawcett story on TV and her fight against cancer. It was so moving. She tried everything and fought so hard. She was 62 and not ready to die. Hey and I'm 41 and neither am I. She said the hardest question is 'How are you?' What are you supposed to say… 'I'm fine'? Well I have cancer, I'm still alive so yes I guess I'm fine as things go. It's getting harder each day not to keep thinking about the cancer. When I had chemo before, there was an end to treatment and usually a reaction. I so want that again. I'm NOT ready to walk into that dark goodnight. I still want my life back. I want normal again.

27 July 2009

Got a letter from school saying my contract isn't going to be renewed but I shall be offered supply as and when. Six sentences/lines and that's it. End of my twelve years at that school. Maybe a natural end. James has left and I can't see me in front of a class again. Even if I am the greatest teacher according to James and his memory mat. Poor Love! His leavers' assembly was emotional and his play was great too. Can't believe in September he'll be at secondary school.

Need some new goals.

- Did Moonwalk.√
- James' school uniform.√
- James to secondary school.
- Iain's 40th.
- Sophie's 14th birthday.
- Si's birthday/Mum's birthday.
- Christmas.
- Mac's birthday.
- James' 12th birthday.
- My 42nd birthday.

- Our 19th wedding anniversary.
- Sophie's option choices.
- NEXT summer.

Have to focus on getting them ticked off. Took Mac to the vet to be castrated today. Poor Boy, I feel so bad for him. Won't be straightforward as one testicle is undescended. Now I'm worrying about him. Thankfully he'll have a quiet week as the kids are away. Lead walks only for four days around the garden.

Picked Mac up at 3pm. He bounded out to me! I was amazed at how well he was. He has a lampshade on to stop him licking and picking his stitches. It all looks very neat. They found the rogue testicle in his canal so it wasn't a prop. I gave him a roast chicken breast for tea as a treat and bought some pigs ears. He doesn't like the lampshade but he's getting used to it and walking like John Wayne!

28 July 2009
Very achy today. Dropped Mac to Hils today so he could be looked after. Got chemo and new bone stuff but it took ages. Had a chat about getting some more blood as HB *(haemoglobin blood count)* was 9.5 so before it drops too much. So now in my week off I'm having a transfusion again on Friday. But I know it will help me so I'm OK with that. Just annoying that it takes all day.

29 July 2009
Slept OK and woke up feeling less achy so maybe bone stuff is working already! Missing the kids as it is so quiet but then Mac and I probably need the rest. Shame that Simon and I haven't really made the most of the kids being away. Could have nipped off on Eurostar for a day somewhere.

31 July 2009
Really achy today. Meant to meet Chris F and Co but couldn't face it. Simon stayed off work. He ended up taking Mac back to the vet as he was still swollen. But Mac does seem more like himself again. Kids are home today and I have missed them. Mind you I've felt so crap the rest for me was good. They had a great time at camp and I'm glad they went so they could do lots of fun stuff that I'm just not up to.

4 August 2009
Went to see Dirty Dancing with Liz B, Felix, Flora and Sophie. Had a fantastic evening and the show was brilliant. Sophie really enjoyed it. My neck now aches and feels really stiff. Wish I could have physio or something as I seem to be seizing up. I'm getting tingling in my legs and a pain in my knee which makes me feel tired and sick from it all. Hope it is the chemo and not cancer spreading as I feel that in the last three months I am less mobile and upbeat. Getting bloods again on Friday. At least that makes me feel more energetic.

7 August 2009
Blood went OK. Another long day at L&D. Si took the day off work to be at home with the kids. Defo feel more with it. Shame the pain's still here.

8 August 2009
Had to get up at 5am as our Balloon Flight was finally going to happen. Typical, I thought, I feel less than great and it's now. Anyway got to Knebworth at 6am and there it was, this huge balloon. Si and James helped to inflate it and there were sixteen of us. Getting into the basket was fun for me! But they had seats in it so at least if my legs gave up I could sit. We took off at 6.15am. It was so effortless and gentle. We flew over Codicote

and towards Welwyn and Brocket Hall. The houses looked tiny. It was so peaceful apart from the burst of the burners. We flew for 45 minutes and the morning was so perfect. Sunny and clear, you could see for miles. We landed smoothly on Brocket Hall Golf Course! We flew over the lake and the bridge. The boys helped pack up the balloon and then we had champagne, even Sophie and James. They loved it too. Sophie got some amazing photos. What a way to start a weekend. It was well worth the five attempts! Thanks Mum, Liz and Roger.

12 August 2009
No chemo today as my platelets are too low, so second delay! Mind you, blood HB *(haemoglobin blood count)* was 11 so that was good. Now means chemo 5a whilst away in Norfolk. Feel crap. Neck still achy and getting tingling in my legs. Right knee very painful. Just want chemo to be over but so scared my body is shutting down on me!

14 August 2009
Norfolk Broads here we come! Have had a terrible week. So much pain, didn't think I'd be going anywhere other than L&D. Started to wear Simon's knee support and think that is helping. Mind you, I am living on Co-codemol and it's barely touching the sides.

Boat is lovely. It's got two loos and a three quarter poster bed!! Kids are sharing a cabin with Mac! It's roomy and has a removable canopy.

15 August 2009
First night, slept a treat. Must be all the fresh air. We drove/sailed 4.5 hours yesterday to Acle Bridge and moored there. Went out for tea. I'm not eating much these days and am the lightest I have been in fifteen years. Weather has been hot

and sunny. Sailed all the way to Great Yarmouth. We saw the beach and the sea. Moored at St Olaves. Really peaceful.

16 August 2009
Felt really awful today. I hate this pain and the fact it doesn't stop. I stayed in bed for a while today and then felt worse that Si and the kids are doing everything and I'm not. Sophie has been brilliant. I need to get to L&D to sort this pain out. Moored at Horning tonight.

17 August 2009
Met Mum at Coltishall. We got there by 1pm and secured a mooring. Weird to think we'd done that with Iain and Emma. Still in loads of pain. Get a phone call from L&D saying Bilirubin is up and so may not have chemo! Spoke to Nicky and explained about pain. She said as I was coming back to have a blood test, we could sort pain relief out. Said it's been three weeks and can't live like this. I'm so desperate to have a pain free afternoon! Saw Roger, Margaret, Gilly and loads of dogs. Toured Limes and went out for tea. Mum, bless her, drove me home at 8pm so I could be in my own bed tonight for L&D. I had a dreadful night. I couldn't sleep, I was in agony until at least 4.30am when my body was so exhausted I slept.

18 August 2009
I spoke to pain management nurse and she said there was no need for me to be in agony. Only trouble is, any medication has to pass through the liver to be processed! Rock and a hard place. Typical. Didn't get chemo today as Bilirubin still too high and rising it would seem. Now have a scan booked for Friday so will have to drop the boat off a day early. I'm so sick of this disease ruling my life. I can't plan or enjoy anything anymore. I hate the effect it has on my family, Simon and especially the kids.

Thank God the new meds and morphine (Oramorph) seem to work. Went back to boat and slept well tonight.

19 August 2009
Had a fabulous day. No aches, no pains, almost normal. Yeah! Still have no appetite and feel nauseous which worries me, and my eyes seem a bit yellow. Sunny and peaceful on the boat. We cruised and sunbathed and life was good. I'm so sad this holiday has been mucked about.

20 August 2009
Home today. Took Oramorph and felt sick and was sick. Cruised back to boat yard and we unpacked. So sorry Simon that it wasn't the restful break you deserved. Sophie has been really helpful. I worry about James. He's so young and seems so angry. I don't want him to be like this. Got home at 5pm and felt tired AGAIN! Had to drink horrid Contrast – couldn't do it. Threw up.

21 August 2009
Back to hospital for the scan. Managed 300ml of Contrast but no more. Spent all day there. Poor kids and Mac home alone. Had scan and went back to chemo for blood test. Bilirubin now up 30 points! Not good. Sat about ALL day. Scan results reported verbally – no new tumours as far as they could see in liver (good news) but liver seemed damaged by chemo – overloaded. Didn't look at other areas as most concern was about the liver. Must get Bilirubin down. Have decided not to go to France. Don't think I'll cope and what if I get worse? How will I get home and what would happen to me? Again, no control. Spoke to Debs. Really gutted both of us but she understood. Need to have another blood test on Monday for levels. Then if still going up, guess I need treatment and to be

admitted. Saw Liz B and their new puppy tonight. She cooked tea for Simon and the kids. She's very kind to us.

Like Emma says, stop putting on a brave face and let people know how you feel. The pretence of it all being fine is hard to maintain. I worry about Simon as this is going to get harder as I get worse.

22 August 2009
Spent most of today popping pills and lying in bed. When I sleep I forget. Bliss. Simon told Liz and Rog about the scan. I stayed out of it upstairs. Emma came to see me this afternoon (just as well so it made me get up and shower). Mind you after two hours chatting I needed to lie down again! I've asked her to talk to Iain and see if he'll talk to Simon as he has no outlet, no one to say how he feels. I do worry for him as I'm trying to be practical and set things into place to help him. He accused me of giving up last night and maybe I kinda have. I'm tired of feeling sick and like this. Need to get focused on my Goals Checklist and tick some more off. Extra goal... need to eat!

24 August 2009
Went for another blood test today. Didn't go to France. Just waited all day at home. Well no news was supposed to be good news. The Registrar for Dr A phoned and apologised that I never got to go on holiday but...

- My levels are up AGAIN.
- If it was chemo it should have recovered by now so they are now thinking it is the liver deteriorating due to cancer (so April to August is five months!)
- So, treatment... I need Epirubicin chemo (which means bye bye hair again) which is less liver toxic.

- Need heart echo too as it can affect the heart.
- Need radiotherapy possibly to bone areas.
- Need less harsh painkillers.
- Need to monitor my hydration levels.

BASICALLY, she never said, but outlook grim.

When Dr A told me in April that it was 6-18months, I don't see it being 18 months anymore. I remember Maureen lasting four months after it took hold again. I shall be lucky to see Christmas at this rate. Phoned Mum and that was horrible. I know everyone wants to be helpful and positive but it's so hard. At least the word terminal hasn't been mentioned yet! But it's so not looking great anymore. Iain is going to take me to the cardiogram tomorrow.

Feeling bruised due to cardio ultra sound. Nicky's husband did it for me. Nice guy. Only trouble, feel like I've been kicked in the ribs!

Spoken a lot to MacMillan nurse Claire. Now on Haloperidol (mental health drug) to try and sort the vomiting out. Still eating very little and tend to throw up last thing. Wish I could eat as I look so skinny (my mind's going!). Don't think I can face chemo on Tuesday feeling like this. But the pain in my legs has gone. Just lower back pain and ribs! Haven't taken morphine since Tuesday. Been sick Tuesday and Thursday. Eating very little all week. Managed more over Saturday and Sunday. Fruit salad, bacon sarni, biscuits, jellies! Trying so hard not to vomit.

30 August 2009

Woke up with terrible neck pain, otherwise would have felt SO much better. Stayed in bed all day.

31 August 2009

Still feel awful. Stayed in bed all day. So weak and don't know how I shall get to hospital. Need a wheelchair and haven't eaten without being sick. Poor kids, they are terrified. Don't have the strength to read my book either.

1 September 2009

Took me ages to get up. Phoned L&D and almost cancelled. Mum came too. Thank God we had two cars. Got to the top of the stairs and was sick. Kept nothing down. I read somewhere that if you don't eat for two weeks you die! Had bloods taken at Unit but needed a wheelchair to get there. Spent from 10am to 1pm lying on a bed in chemo. Feel so much pain in my neck. Had a chat to Nicky B, Head Nurse. Saw Dr A at 2pm (2 hours late). She ordered loads of painkillers and more or less said that was it. Ball park! Could be days – weeks! So many tears from Mum and Si. I had no energy so couldn't cry, almost felt relief. Neck still agony so came home. Told Liz, kids and sent texts to Liz B, Em and Hils. More visits, more tears and then sent THE email to EVERYONE. So now that's done. Emma came over and that was nice. Very emotional. Had family conference and James wanted his book to see. Began making plans of what we need to put in place now. Gonna see the vicar about the funeral this week. Skyped Debs too.

2 September 2009

Woke up feeling OK until I lifted my head off the pillow and worked out it wasn't that way. Started taking pills. Had a busy day. Lots of visitors. Saw Revd. Chris at 2pm. Had a super meeting planning the funeral and felt so uplifted and in control. Really helpful to do that. Stayed downstairs. Emma came over. Walked the dog with Sophie and did stuff for my L&D hamper. Printed out amazing responses to emails, so many caring messages to me. Hils popped in and Liz C came and thoroughly cleaned bathrooms and kitchen. Liz B came and bought me a gorgeous PJ lounge suit, a chocolate champers bottle for James and a good luck card. So cute. Planned days for kids to go for tea and put in place. Lots of tears, then Trisha came and was so sad but also arranged tea for Sophie for the rota routine. People have been so amazing and want to help me and ultimately Si and the kids. Mum came by again and I got my pain patches. Got my pallbearers chosen: my brother Iain, Al, Sam, Iain and Pete and they were all in tears about it. Iain and Si went out on a Round Table bike ride so Emma came to babysit me! My bro and Lisa popped in and we had a lovely evening. I forgot about everything and life seemed NORMAL!

3 September 2009

James up early for school. So emotional this morning as he starts 'big school'. So scared for him. He looks so gorgeous. Lots of photos taken. Made another goal. Yeah James.

> *For Mum: my grey Radley bag to remind you of being my Friday friend!*
>
> *For Sophie: all my other Radleys and Abercrombie gear!! Tiffany jewellery and Beatrix Potter figures.*
>
> *For James: Granddad's police medals, ring and necklaces.*
>
> *For Emma: a Radley and jewellery*
>
> *To Do:√*
> - *Wedding cards and letters for Sophie and James*

- *First baby letters*
- *18th and 21st letters*
- *Photo story book for the kids*

My Christmas Wishes
- *Remember how we used to always decorate the tree with Christmas music playing!*
- *James knows which ornaments are special and Sophie knows that you have to wish upon the star at the end of decorating the tree.*
- *Stockings need to have fun presents but also practical things. Oh, and different wrapping paper from the other presents.*
- *The stocking advent calendar has two chocolates on 21st and 22nd for Simon and Emily! Remember the Watching Santa decoration.*
- *Believe in Santa and the magic of Christmas for as long as you can.*

My Wish List
- *I'd like flowers on my birthday, Mothers Day and our anniversary and a holly wreath at Christmas.*
- *A balloon message on special birthdays.*
- *Don't take my pictures and hide them away I'd like to be around you.*
- *Think of me and remember me with a smile.*

We will certainly remember you with a smile Fi. No doubt about that.

Angels

As hard as it all was, incredibly there were still lots of smiles and laughter from Fi and those around her. Fi's best friend Emma, her husband Iain and their children spent a final day in August, the two families together just fooling around as always. Fi's favourite kind of day. *"It felt good to be together,"* Iain and Emma remember, *"even though we knew the clock was ticking."*

But most of all, those final, tough and heartbreaking days were full of loving events remembered fondly by those who shared it with her.

Her brother Iain encouraged cousin Debs to visit Fi earlier than planned, arriving on 5 September which was also her birthday. Traditionally for birthdays, Debs and Fi would Skype each other and sing 'Happy Birthday'. This year, understandably, Fi had told Debs she wouldn't really be able to as she wasn't feeling good but she would try and catch up at some point. No one, except Iain, knew that Debs would be coming over for her birthday. After picking her up from the airport, Iain brought Debs and a birthday cake over to Fi's house, creeping through the back door and into the living room where Fi was sitting. *"What the fuck are you doing here?!"* exclaimed Fi as they all burst into laughter. *"Her words were great."* said Debs *"It's so strange how sometimes humour, when well placed, can bring you even closer together, even in the face of death."* Debs had explained her sudden arrival due to the fact that Fi hadn't sung to her on her birthday. *"I'm dying!"* retorted Fi, *"I'm excused!"*

For her brother, Fi's black humour surfaced again when she told him that at least she would be dead when Mum died and he would have to clear out the house and do everything on his own. *"Cheers for that!"* answered Iain *"You'll be up there pissing yourself laughing! This dying early with cancer malarkey has got a lot to answer for!"* But he also remembers some bizarre coincidences. Six months earlier, for reasons he can't recall, he had taken the 10 and 11 September off work. That meant he was at home and able to be with his sister on the day she died. Strangely too, Sophie and James had decided that they didn't feel like going to school on that Friday. All around them thought that was fair enough, given the circumstances. So it meant that they were there too, along with Iain, Debs and her son Sam, Jean, Liz (Simon's mum) and of course, Simon. Sam was Fi's last visitor. The day before Fi died, she had been asking for her godson and he arrived late in the afternoon. His mum, Debs, states that although Fi was drifting in and out of consciousness, *"she knew he was there in those final few hours. I remember her saying to me that once she'd seen him, she'd be happy and then she could go. And she did, the following morning."*

Iain describes Fi's final moments:

> *"I woke up on that morning and thought I'll go over to Fi's about 10am. I got round there at 10.15am and she had a fit about 10.30am till 11am and slowly drifted off. The window was open and there were cards on the bedside, and the second Fiona died there was a gust of wind and a card fell over and it was almost like she was going out the window."*

A few days earlier, Iain had got a tattoo. He had told Fi about it. It was a five point nautical star with a banner around it with the words 'Angels do exist'. *"It's all to do with speaking to Fi and Dad when they were dying, basically saying look after Mum etc, and I said 'Yeah, who's gonna look after you?' and they both said 'Oh we'll be with the angels, angels do exist'... that's why I got this on my back, it's almost like Fi's watching my back."*

Angels

On the days when he thinks how losing her is such an irrational waste, Iain gains strength from his family, particularly Debs who is now more like a sister to him than a cousin; the same family that provided Fi with the strength and courage to carry on as she did. They are all truly remarkable people. Debs goes further, *"Although Fiona was the most amazing and courageous woman I know, she got it from one person, her mum Jean. What a wonderful, amazing lady. Not many women could have done what she did, and carry on. Incredible strength and faith."*

Fi had called upon her mum to ask the Rector to visit so that she could discuss her funeral plans. Jean remembers,

> *"Her plan was perfect, just like her teaching plans, and she even invited him back to the reception after the service. That was the first time he had had such an invitation from the 'about to be deceased'. We all decided she needed a dress rehearsal for her funeral, like you do for weddings, so 'we' would get it right. She was in control right to the end. The night before she died she said 'I have no regrets, I am ready to go'. She was at peace with herself which made her passing so much easier for the rest of us."*

Jean's resolute honesty is a trait obviously inherited by Fiona. It also has been passed on to Sophie, Fi's daughter.

> *"Another thing she said to me a few months before she died was 'If you keep talking about someone, they never die' and that's one of the best things she ever said to me and the one I'll never forget because it's true. She will always live on in our thoughts and this book is the best proof of this, ever."*

14

Amazing

Amazing, awesome and inspirational actually. Or 'apparently', according to Fi herself. That is what everyone who knew her thought of her, although she never quite believed it.

Facebook messages give an idea of how special she was to those who knew her. Fi's diary entry of 26 July 2009 expresses her hope that Sophie and James will 'chat' to her, as she did with Emily and her Dad. Well she got her wish, everyone is chatting to her!

> *SE: Gorgeous lady you've just brightened another place, selfishly I miss your sparkling light here – love to you all xx*
>
> *BS: You were amazing, awesome and inspirational and we will miss you. So sad I am so far away xx*
>
> *NS: Hi, I have decided to do a sponsored run for Cancer Research UK. I HATE RUNNING!!!! I know I'm pretty fit but running is one thing I*

do NOT do. My training starts tomorrow. I've registered my intent to run the 10K in May 2010 and the half marathon in September 2010 via the Cancer Research website. Very happy for anyone to run it with me as long as you'll slow down to my pace!

ZW: There's the Great South Run in Bristol – a group from Walk the Walk do it. It's a half marathon – all money raised goes to Cancer charities – too late for this year – but I'll do it if you will (although I don't know you, any friend of Fiona's must be a great person to know!)

LR: God must have needed a very special angel to have taken you Fi. An inspiration to everyone who knew you, we will miss you xxx

SB: You were such a brave lady and will be sadly missed. xxx

DS: Courageous to the very end – love you so much xx

DC: If there's a Facebook in heaven, I reckon you're already logged on. You will be missed by so many Fi.

GR: You were so strong and brave. We are all going to miss you so much xxx

CR: Guess I'm just selfish, I want you back here. I never thought it would happen. I always thought it would be you who would be the miracle. You are my inspiration of how to be better and I thank you deeply for that. I will never forget you. Your beautiful family are a legacy to be proud of Fi. Love and miss you xxx

FB: Fiona you were an inspirational person. You will never be forgotten. I wish I had known you for longer. I will help to beat cancer. I love you. Why did it have to be you? Lovely, beautiful, kind, inspirational – there are so many nice things to describe you, but I know you had a good life and I swear I will look after Sophie till the end.

RDC: You were a very special person Fi and you touched so many people. We'll miss you xxx

SM: Heaven got better this morning with a special angel. I know you are always gonna be with your family and help them when they are in a difficult situation. Rest in peace.

PR: This isn't fair :'(You are an amazing person... everyone loves you to bits... we will all be here for Sophie, Simon and James always. You have inspired a lot of people :) and we will all do The MoonWalk on behalf of you this year. Rest in peace, we will all miss you so much and I wish you were back xx

HL: We will miss you so much Fi. You have left us with treasured memories of a beautiful, brave, amazing woman. I am a better person for having you in my life and I owe you a debt of gratitude for bringing Jonathan and I together. xxxxxx

Amazing

BG: The most easy-going, genuine friend ever. What a great teacher you were, in more ways than one... xxx

SS: My love to Simon, Sophie and James – your wife and dear Mum was amazing xoxoxox

HF: An amazing inspiration to so many people, you touched the hearts and lives of so many people, your memory will live on in everyone who knows you. Brave, strong and beautiful. Forever in our hearts. All my love xxxxxxxxxxxxx

IM: I know I can look to the sky and see three bright stars now, say hi to Dad and Emily for me – till the day we meet again I'll miss you so much and I promise I'll always be there for Simon, Sophie, James and Mum. I would have been proud to be just your friend but to be your brother was an honour xx love you xx

LM: I am honoured to have been lucky enough to be a part of your life and family. You were so strong and brave, a true inspiration to us all. I will miss you dearly. Simon, Sophie, James, Iain and Jean, I am so sorry for your loss, you are all in my thoughts and prayers. Please know that I'm here for you all. Fi will live on in our hearts forever xx

SF: Yo Yo GMFC lol. I'd just like to say that you've proven angels do exist and it was an honour to have lived by you.

DR: The emptiness you have left in all our lives can only be understood by those who knew and loved you. Fi you were an inspiration to all you met. We are all so very proud of you and feel honoured to have had you as our friend xxxx

HC: Dearest Fiona. You touched so many people with your zest for life. We are so proud of you and were so privileged to have been your friend and colleague. I have such fond memories of working with you and sharing our reception classes together. You will always have a special place in our hearts and you inspire us daily to be better people. We love you and will miss you so much. You will always be our special princess FiFi La Crompo xx

TS: You were always up for the craic and always smiling... it was such a laugh working with you even when the going got tough! My love to Simon, Sophie and James x

BG: Hey Fiona. We will all miss you so much; whenever I came round you were always smiling. You were so brave and I admire you so much. Me and loads of people will do The MoonWalk for you and will do all we can in the fight against cancer x

JC: Hey Fiona. I've only known you a short old while but within that time you have shown me how caring you are. To not only your family and friends but to others around you. You don't realise how much people look up to you and see a fighter.

Amazing

JB: Dear Fiona. You were an inspiring and lovely person. A truly wonderful mother, a superbly energetic and kind teacher, and forever kind, jolly and fun to be around. I love your cheeky sense of humour and your practicality. My love and prayers.

BC: I know it's been a while, but that doesn't mean you were forgotten, or will be. We had lots of good times back at school, and some really tiresome School Governor Meetings when you and I were Head Girl and Boy, and that was a good 20 years ago! Thanks for some good times.

JL: Read what everyone before me has written and that sums up all my thoughts as well.

KJ: So very sorry you've gone Fi, the world is a poorer place without you. I'll always remember your brilliant sense of humour and indomitable will.

NG: Well Fi, its taken nearly a week before I could face looking at this – and several boxes of tissues – but then I remembered that you always smiled and joked even when life was not going so well for you darling. Every time life gets hard I'll think of you and will smile and laugh in the way you always managed to. Miss you lots.

CS: Fiona, it was a very touching service today and I was honoured to be there as a friend. Will always remember your smile, wise kind words and your strength.

DS: Just wanted you to know that your godson qualified today as an AET, he PASSED his final exams this morning – I told him you would be very proud of him, I knew you would be. Miss you loads... xxx

CR: Keep popping in to see your gorgeous smile x

JC: I miss you so much – we had so so many fab times in Notts and you have left me with so many good memories! You were so talented and inspirational. Thought about you even more than usual today – was eating a choc hobnob – remember those revision sessions sat with tea and biccies listening to Simon Mayo?

DS: We're in!! I was up, poised at the computer keyboard, ready for the off – I was bloody determined to get a place for 2010. Me, Hannah and Iain are all doing the Full Moon – Iain reckons it's well worth £45 to see 15,000 pairs of boobs in one night!!

HL: So am I! Meet you in the big pink tent!

GR: Still waiting to hear if I've got a place Fi. Started training already though. 10k yesterday and another 10 today. Fingers crossed aye. Miss u x

SF: Read your letter again last night. It's becoming a regular thing now lol. I'll know it word for word soon. I'm always thinking about you, still missing you but I don't think that will ever go. Love you GMFC xxxx

Amazing

CR: Still expecting the pink puffa jacket to appear around the corner in this rain! Thinking of you babe xxxxxxxxxxx

SF: I'm off to make you proud soon GMFC. Just wish I could tell you. I miss you so much tho I do talk to you every night at work. Love you and miss you. And you're right; it is a great career xxxx

SC: I miss those days when I would curl up in your arms, and you'd tell me everything would be okay. So much has changed since then and things couldn't be more different :(xxx Time to move on now :/ :) xxxx

And so the messages continue to be sent to her. On her birthday, along with dozens of birthday greetings, are these messages from Sophie and two of her many devoted friends. Never did the phrase 'out of the mouths of babes' fit so well. These posts show how amazing a mum and role model Fi was to the all-important kids around her.

SC: Happy Birthday Mum, I never know what to say when I write on here because I find it so difficult to write things down :P but I know if I was writing you would be shouting at me for my pencil grip and how scruffy my writing is, not to mention, my spelling! Can't believe it's your birthday already. It was a weird day but went on a dog walk with Liz and that was really good fun, nice to get some fresh air to clear the head! I miss you so much and I can't believe that I've even managed to make it this far, but as you said, take each day as it comes.♥ I remember when you asked me how to do a heart on Facebook and what (8) means, oh how I laughed :) you always said to me if you keep talking about someone then they never die, it's amazing because this is so true, and I know I will never stop talking about you! I miss you so much Mum, I love you xxxx ♥

FB: Happy Birthday, we all miss you so much in our household, it seems like yesterday I remember walking to get Sophie for school and you always shouted at her 'Will you ever be ready for this poor boy?' :') I can still remember your voice, and I hope I always will be able to. Sophie's doing so well, but everyone misses you Fi, it's like you're the missing piece of the puzzle, we need you to help us sort things out. I was in some trouble for something ridiculous, and I know what you would have done, and for that I miss you, I miss everything about you, your personality, your smile, your lovely kind heart ♥ I'll post something again soon, I miss you and I love you ♥ xxx Forever in my memory ♥

PR: happy birthday :) if that's the right thing to say... thought about you a lot today... kept thinking this time last year :') brought back some nice memories :D...me and Odette went to St.Nick's after school and saw Soph and Liz coming out. Standing in there it really felt like you were standing right beside us! The minister came out, Heather, to say hi and said a few things :) missing you tonnes and still keep expecting to hear your voice when I come in to see Sophie. She's amazing... keeping strong

Amazing

> *and just carries on with everything and I know that everyone's so proud of her! and James and Simon too* ♥

As I write, people are still talking to Fi on her Facebook page, keeping her up to date, commenting on how much they miss her and letting her know about MoonWalk and fundraising events that they are doing in her honour. But as her brother Iain so eloquently put it:

> *"I know you are here, but I miss you so so much. Why have you not set up Facebook Heaven yet?"*

But really, it wouldn't be necessary (although her photos would be interesting!) because all of her Facebook (and non-Facebook) friends are having conversations with Fi anyway, be it every day, in their dreams or at those little moments when we think of her and smile.

And her smile was so strong, so powerful and so dazzling that it will stay in our minds and hearts without a doubt.

Amazing.

15

Sweet Disposition

2011

Hi Hun,

Well, time is racing by and I've thought about you every day since we said goodbye back in September 2009.

That first Christmas without you, there was a Gavin and Stacey Special which you would've watched and loved. Doris, Smithy and Gavin sang that magnificent Smiths song 'There is a light and it never goes out'. There seemed to be reminders of you everywhere in the immediate months after your funeral. This was one such reminder, not just because you loved a bit of Gavin and Stacey, as well as The Smiths, but also because I wrote those words in your book of remembrance. That title just summed you up. Your smile shone through all the stuff you had to deal with and there always seemed to be a light around you. That light still seems to be here. It's the Fi effect again.

Sweet Disposition

There's been tons of stuff we would've gossiped about: Big Brother finishing, the final Ashes to Ashes series (now it made sense!), Robbie Williams no longer a bachelor and even our beloved S Block being demolished! They were all things that came to an end, as if to emphasise the fact that you were gone too.

But happy stuff happened too. Take That got back together! More amazingly, I met, shook hands, chatted, hugged, snuggled slightly and got a photo with none other than the genius singer-songwriter-musician that is Lloyd Cole!!! OMG!!! Cue girly screams!!! If I didn't have a photo of it I wouldn't have thought it really happened. I am now part of his team called the Young Idealists (it's the title of one of his 2006 songs) who go to gigs and sell merchandise for him! Lloyd always comes out afterwards to sign stuff and chat. Predictably, I was awestruck and gushing, and forgot how to form coherent sentences. But it could have been worse. At least I didn't dribble. So now, in my forties, I'm officially a Young Idealist, and whenever I can get to his gigs I'm there selling his CD's! These lyrics from 'The Young Idealists' remind me of you and how we met all those years ago.

"The Young Idealists
Raging through the coffee shops and bars
Make believe the world was really ours
Still supposing we could make a difference"

And you have made such a difference to so many people! That's what I hope this book will do too.

It's not just a remarkable record of my remarkable mate and her remarkable family. I hope that it might make a difference to those that read it, whatever their life is throwing at them. I hope they experience a little of the 'Fi effect' by proxy. Everyone should benefit from having a 'Fi' in their lives. Simon hopes that your honesty about what happened and how you shared your feelings so openly, will help people understand just a little more of what it is like for those suffering from this evil disease, as well as for those around them. I hope they will read this and see how you found the strength to brush aside the anger and make happy times with those you cared about, despite the terrible things that you have had to deal with in your life. Emma and Iain see the book as a way of you fighting from beyond the grave in an everlasting battle to raise funds to find a cure and support those affected by cancer.

Incidentally, that song is from Lloyd's album 'Anti-depressant' and you were certainly that in human form. Your smile and laughter was better than anything on prescription (or otherwise) and lifted me out of a depression many a time. So I hope that this book acts also as a reminder that fun, laughter and mischief should be part of everyone's life. We can't control everything, as much as we would like to, but we can at least try to influence our own happiness.

When your birthday came around, which always follows James' birthday, it was a time of mixed emotions. I was happy for James. He's getting all grown up and stylish, with girlfriends on the scene, and loves his iTunes account as much as Arsenal.

Brilliant boy. He and Sophie are just as sociable and surrounded by friends, as you were when I first met you.

But I was sad at the same time, because you weren't here anymore to celebrate your birthday or your son's. I'd have sent you some choccies and had a Skype chat to see if there were any more photos that Time On Your Hands Productions could make into a moviette for you. Instead, I donated to your Just Giving page set up by Simon for your funeral. Wish I could pay something to have you back. Bet you wished something similar at some point. I bet everyone left behind is wishing you could magically return and laugh with them again. The closest they get is checking out the smile on your Facebook profile picture.

Happy Birthday seems odd to say to you on your Facebook page, but everyone's saying it, remembering you, missing you. All the special occasions and birthdays will continue to pass by, along with the years, and we will all still miss you.

The one thing that frightened you the most was missing those moments. But nothing can change this and we all have to go along with what has happened. As bad as it feels to us, it was bad for you so very much more. It was hard enough saying goodbye to you, but you had to say goodbye to everyone. We can only keep reminding ourselves how you dealt with the unfair situation you were put in, follow your example, try our best to be strong and live life to the full.

I've been wearing something pink and purple every day since you asked for it for your funeral.

It wasn't a deliberate act but I came to notice the pink bow on my bra or my purple nail varnish and automatically thought of you. Then I realised there was always a bit of pink or purple, a reminder of you, on me every day. I like it.

It's starting to dawn on me that you haven't actually just gone away somewhere where you can't be contacted and I can save up all the news until you get back. I can't share the memories or make new ones with you either.

And that is the reality of it.

So I'm putting all my memories together with your story to make this book. Another little project for you from Time On Your Hands Productions/ Publications. That way it feels like we're still in touch. Like one big long email, but one that I won't get a reply to. Although, actually, maybe, I might. Like that time in one very vivid dream where you showed up at a house party I went to. We had a chat (and a boogie) and you gave me some photos to use for the book. I'd asked how you were able to be here in Belgium with me considering you were dead. You just giggled and said, "I get around!" and carried on dancing. When I woke the next morning feeling as if I'd really seen you, it didn't feel sad. It was just like all the other times we had got together when you were alive – great fun, let's do it again soon, must arrange another meet up. The only difference being it wouldn't be me doing the arranging. I'd have to leave that up to you. In the darkness of the morning, emerging from my reverie, in the back of my mind I heard you say "You know what? 'I woke up and it was all a dream!' It's that classic Year 2 story ending!"

In the meantime, and in case I don't have any more dream visitations, I have this book to hear you speak and see your smile. I also have the soundtrack from all the chapter titles – plenty of chick songs just for you. I shall be here with my hairbrush and when I dance with my eyes closed you will be boogie-ing right beside me. Unless I fall over, and then I'll just say "For fuck's sake!" like you always used to. I only have memories from now on, but at least they are fanbloodytastic ones to have.

So life goes on, and I have to say that life is all the better from having had you in it. We all wanted that time to be a fair bit longer but hey, we had you there all the same. Better than nowt, as we say up north.

Thanks to you I smile more, have a better attitude, am more determined to enjoy life and have even watched (and cried at) a few chick flicks! I haven't found the motivation yet to accept the challenge of The MoonWalk, but you never know. All of this has made me realise that if you talk and laugh about something then it's not as scary as you might first think, and when there is something negative in life, it is often met with the opposite to rise to the challenge – positivity of such magnitude that it can be quite astounding.

The random strike of the 'Beast' has affected so many. It's made your 'Giant Four' just one. You all braved the Beast with immense courage and inspirational positivity. You are a hero to so many, but as you said, giving £2 a month towards Cancer Research UK can make anyone a hero too. Seeing how you coped with such strength, dignity and humour, Iain says he will never again moan about having a bad day at work. That doesn't really constitute a 'bad' day, given what you went through. Your brother Iain told me exactly the same thing.

The news is saturated with reports of death and heartache through war, natural disasters or at the hands of another, with a distinct lack of positive, inspirational features. It is the reality of life that we are surrounded by death. But if we look hard enough, the very things that help us deal with adversity and suffering also surround us. You helped me see those things.

On those days when I am being shadowed by a melancholic glumness, when even the sunshine pisses me off, I will keep on looking.

Forever, Bobs xxx

16

Starlight

This entry was found tucked away at the back of Fi's final diary. At first glance it looks like a letter to all her friends and family. A final goodbye. But in actual fact, it was a script. Fi had an idea to do a DVD of herself to show at her funeral, with a final message to us all. My first reaction was that it was so typical of her! (Up on the big screen – it's a natural move after you've done so much TV!) Sophie said it would be her mum thinking 'I'm there, but I'm not there!' But, on reflection, although it's not unknown for such a thing to have happened and although it is so 'Fi', it is also 'OTT Weird!' as Simon put it. Everyone would've been in a terrible state! We wouldn't have heard her voice, over the sound of blubbing and sobbing! But maybe if we saw it years later then it would perhaps be less a reminder of the pain of the final few months of Fi's life, the stress of those years coping with a cancer diagnosis and treatments, and more about the Fiona that loved being the centre of attention, who was never a wallflower, game for anything with an infectious laugh and phenomenal smile.

Hi Everyone

Yes. You know me. Always like to have the final word. So I didn't want to disappoint you.

So I am not invincible after all. I guess what I should start with is thank you. Thank you all for coming to send me off. I am hoping that the church is packed and it has been a celebration of me with a few embarrassing stories thrown in. I want everyone to know the way my family and friends supported me, kept me strong, focused and fighting.

As I said on my 40th, all those comments about me being inspirational, amazing, awesome, I couldn't have been without strong and loving people around me. Wow what a party that was! I never saw myself like that. I'm a mum, a wife, a daughter, sister and friend. Those were the most important things in my life. The things I am most proud of.

I was so lucky when I met Simon at 16. Sitting on that signpost near Queensway. Cigarette in one hand, lager in the other and what can only be described as an atom bomb haircut. Never in a million years did I think I was looking at my soulmate. They say after your dad, your husband is the next most important and special man in your life. Well Simon, that's true. Dad thought the world of you even if he almost made you sleep in the spare room when we came back off honeymoon! All of my adult life I have been with you Simon and for that I have been truly blessed. You are my rock, the other half of me and I love you more than you'll ever know.

You gave me three beautiful children. Our special Emily Bean and my mini-me Sophie – Mrs Moo, and the gorgeous James, our Jimbo. Kids, you have made me so proud. The way you have lived with all of this and coped, makes me realise I have done a good job. All I ever want for you is for you to be happy and know how much I love you. It's hard to find the words to tell you how much I love you and how special you are to Daddy and me. In all my life Sophie and James, you are what I am most proud of. I am still amazed that from the love Dad and I had, came you guys. All I ask and want for you both is to live happy and wonderful lives. Take every opportunity offered to you, see the world, make amazing memories, great friends and remember to tell it to the brightest star in the sky... that'll be me watching over you.

So Mum, where do I begin? 'Thank you' is so pathetic. I couldn't have got through this alone and without you being my Friday friend, well, words can't express what that has meant to me. To watch someone you love going through all that, you have amazing courage and strength. Maybe that's where I get it from. Hey, at least it meant in our busy lives we got to spend time together and talk. Great! A positive to come out of this!

Liz and Roger – you have always been so supportive and wanted only the best for us all. You've always been so kind and generous. You welcomed me into your family and then welcomed my family too. Thank you for all you have done for me and my children. That's why Simon and I moved back to Harpenden – to be close to our family.

I NEVER had any regrets. I'm grateful for the way cancer changed my life. So many opportunities. It made me realise what a wonderful life I had, with amazing friends and a supportive family. It made me make the most of it.

I'm hoping you all have your own memory of me which will make you smile.

17

My Beautiful Friend

Are you now a Fi fan too?

Do you wish to choose to be happy despite any bad, uncontrollable and downright unfair circumstances in your life?

Do you want to raise money for Cancer Research UK or Walk the Walk without involving exercise?

If the answer is yes to any of the above, then get all your beautiful friends together and have a Fi Party!!!

All you have to do is have fun with those that matter to you. But to make it an Official Fi Party there are certain things you must do.

- ♥ Everyone present at the party should have bought this book. You have therefore already raised money for Cancer Research UK and Walk the Walk. Nice one!
- ♥ Everyone should wear something pink or purple.
- ♥ Play Fi's all-time favourite chick flick 'About Last Night' (or any other film mentioned in this book, or any chick flick).

My Beautiful Friend

- ♥ There should be a bottle of vodka, a big bar of chocolate and a box of tissues present. Whether they get used or not is up to you. (But you know what Fi would do!)
- ♥ The party should start with the exclamation "C'mon groovers, let's rock!"
- ♥ If any manifestations of slushiness result in someone starting to blub, give them a tissue and say "For fucks sake!" or "For Gods sake" followed by their name. Fi is remembered by her friends for always saying the former as in "For fuck's sake Simon!" on regular occasions, and by her family for the latter as in "For God's sake Mother!" directed at Jean whenever she said something that exasperated her daughter.
- ♥ Download/acquire the songs listed as chapters in this book as a soundtrack to your party. They fall into two categories – Hairbrushes and Handbags.

Hairbrushes

If you don't know the words to any of these songs then print off the lyrics from the Internet (just Google the title, artist and 'lyrics' and up they pop). Grab a hairbrush for a microphone and belt them out!

HAPPINESS IS AN OPTION by the Pet Shop Boys. Sing along to the anthemic chorus and hear the lovely Neil Tennant having a rap.

SHE'S GOT A WAY by Billy Joel. Listen closely to these lyrics. It's as if this song was written especially for Fi. Warning: may cause manifestations of slushiness.

YOU'VE GOT A FRIEND by The Housemartins. All together now. Friends forever. If Paul Heaton happens to be at your Fi Party then give him the hairbrush and get ready to do the oop oop's.

LOVE IS ALL AROUND by Wet Wet Wet. The classic chick love song. Nuff said.

BACK FOR GOOD by Take That. Made for karaoke. But no one does it like Gary.

POSITIVITY by Suede. Worth learning the lyrics for. Makes any day a sunny day.

CHANGE by the Sugababes. Don't take anything for granted.

WALK ON by U2. For all those amazing people out there who show such strength, courage and determination to achieve their goals, especially when that goal is survival.

ANGELS by Robbie Williams. Fi's fave member of Take That sums it all up in this epic song.

THANK YOU by Duran Duran. This is a cover version of the Jimmy Page and Robert Plant song. Dedicated to Fi's ability to surround herself with love.

CARAVAN OF LOVE by The Housemartins. See if you can sing all the way through without giggling. You need someone to 'bom bom', someone to 'aaah aaah', someone on backing vocals and someone to sing lead vocal (obviously Paul Heaton if he's there). Don't forget the finger clicks. Or the peas.

Handbags

Boogie on down to these tracks. When you're dancing, you'll be smiling and a room full of smiles will make you happy. Putting handbags on the floor to dance around is optional but nostalgic (and sometimes dangerous if you're 'arseholed').

(I'VE HAD) THE TIME OF MY LIFE by Bill Medley & Jennifer Warnes. Chicks, you know what to do!!

YOUNG GUNS (GO FOR IT!) by Wham! Those 80's dance moves coming back to you yet?

GOOD LIFE by Inner City. Smoooooooooooth.

WHAT IT FEELS LIKE FOR A GIRL by Madonna. Go Girl!

KIDS by Robbie Williams & Kylie Minogue. Can you flirt as good as Fi could?

I NEVER FELT LIKE THIS BEFORE by Mica Paris. How could we not include the soulful Ms Paris in our boogiefest?

AMAZING by George Michael. Funk it up with gorgeous George.

SWEET DISPOSITION by The Temper Trap. Feeling good.

STARLIGHT by The Supermen Lovers. We're really grooving now!

MY BEAUTIFUL FRIEND by The Charlatans. My type of music for my type of friend.

GIVE IT TIME by The Woodentops. A bit of 80's indie for any Indies out there like me.

YOU AND ME SONG by The Wannadies. It's THAT song. Do it for Fi for fuck's sake!

DON'T LEAVE ME THIS WAY by The Communards. Dancing to this is the closest I get to doing exercise.

SOMETIMES by Erasure. Get ready to act out the first verse!!!

RIO by Duran Duran. Sing 'Fio' very loudly whenever you hear Mr Le Bon sing the song title.

Dedicated Fi fans can add more to these basic essentials of a Fi Party. Maybe have some pink and purple balloons (inhaling helium is always fun especially if singing along to 'Don't Leave Me This Way'), have someone doing nail art, take lots of photos (which can be lovingly put together in a Photobook or iMovie afterwards), do fancy dress (80's themed or perhaps a Sex And The City glamour night) or host a 'make your own Elmer Fudpucker' competition. You get the idea - anything inspired by Fi's life. Flirting should be actively encouraged (even if it's towards no one in particular) and if at any point someone has a 'ruck' then deal with it and move on. A Fi Party is no place for Timewasters.

Just enjoy the moment of being with those you love and do whatever makes you happy, but please do something during the party to raise money for Cancer Research UK or Walk the Walk. If, in a moment of wild abandon you sign up to do the next MoonWalk, The SunWalk or a Race For Life, that's entirely up to you.

Happiness IS an option in life. It's up to you whether you choose it or not.

18

Give It Time

If you, like me, have some Time On Your Hands then have a peek at these websites, inspired by Fi.

Be Happy

- www.walkthewalk.org
- www.photobox.com
- www.travelcounsellors.co.uk
- www.pauledmonds.com
- www.trevorsorbie.com
- www.radley.co.uk
- www.facebook.com
- www.mayaangelou.com
- www.youtube.com (Kid's Rock by Tim Hawkins, Max the Dog by John Hegley)

Find Out More:

- www.breastcanceruk.org.uk
- www.cancerresearchuk.org
- www.amoena.co.uk
- www.macmillan.org.uk
- www.gosh.org
- www.blood.co.uk
- www.ocado.com

Fi's Links:

- http://www.stalbansreview.co.uk/news/4526376.Harpenden_cancer_sufferer_on_national_TV_advert/?ref=mr
- www.justgiving.com/ForFionaC
- www.wikipedia.org (David Chadwick footballer – Fi's Uncle)

19

Thank You

Thanks go in shedloads to Simon, for loving the idea of this book, and entrusting me with Fi's journals and files. They felt like a huge and priceless diamond (Tiffany of course!) in my suitcase when I brought them back to Belgium, not least for their weight but because they were so precious. I know it's been painful at times Si, but you were so generous with your time and have been an absolute star.

To Sophie and James, thanks for being you guys; so great, funny, cool (is it not cool to say cool these days?) and MEGA incredible in the way you both deal with stuff which is in part due to your amazing Mum and wonderful Dad, but mostly due to YOU. To fellow Gemini, Emily – I never knew you lil' babe but I feel I do. Thanks also to the lovely Jean, the Apostrophe Queen, for being happy about the book (despite some surprising discoveries about your daughter in her youth!) and being the inspirational, amazing woman that you are. Fi truly inherited all her amazing-ness from you. Thank you to the brilliant Debs and Iain, and to Emma and Iain, for their willingness to contribute, and although we never met, supreme respect goes to John, Fi's dad and inventor of the chocolate button tree. Thanks to Roger, Liz and Ali who all made me feel welcome.

Thanks also to Hils, to Normski for getting my facts right and letting me call you Normski and to Chris. Cheers Hels for all the encouragement, the contacts, the spare bed and the Brit Packs, you really helped to make this book happen. Thanks Jon and Dave too.

Thank you Diane, Liz, Sarah, Ceri and Tracy for taking time to talk to me. Your contributions were very, very much appreciated. Also to Mary at Cancer Research UK, and to Nina and Guy at Walk the Walk for your time and enthusiasm for the book.

Thanks to my sister Sue who finally got me started writing instead of just thinking, to the lovely Ian, Lord of all proofreaders, to Bethan who is the closest thing to having a daughter but without any of the serious grown-up stuff, to my Mum for her unconditional and totally biased love (back at ya!) and to Dad who always said I should be a writer. I wish I'd listened to you when I was an obnoxious teenager.

Iain, my soulmate, I couldn't have done any of this without you and now I'm going to sound like a true chick but I-don't-care-because-Fi-would-be-proud, I love you for all time, for ever and ever and for keeps. I will never take you and your love for granted.

To Fi's Facebook friends, thanks for all your contributions, albeit unknowingly given, but very much appreciated.

To my good friends (you know who you are) thanks for being my good friends and cheers to those of you that gave me feedback on the book.

Thanks to New Writers UK for giving me the information to get this book off the ground, and especially Claire Kinton for all your emails (buy her fab book 'Dead Game' on

Thank You

www.clairekinton.com - which donates to Help For Heroes and SSAFA Forces Help). Cheers Andy at the Writers Bureau for the reassurance. Thanks Frankie and John at Chandlers for the personal touch. Also to Brooke, thanks for giving your time for free and helping me set up the website for this book (www.bjgidman.com).

Thanks to Lloyd Cole for not being in the least bit disappointing which can happen when fans meet their idols and for agreeing to let me quote your lyrics (thanks to Chrysalis too). I cherish my autographed prints, posters and albums and wish I had your way with words. Despite what people say, I am not a stalker, you are completely safe.

Finally a HUGE and MASSIVE thank you to Emil at D-R-ink (www.d-r-ink.com) for doing all the graphic design work so wonderfully and totally for FREE which is just amazingly generous and made such a difference. I am truly grateful for your talent, time and patience.

If I've missed anyone out – sorry and thank you.

Rather than a stuffy reference section, which is way too much of a reminder of doing assignments back in the S Block days and way too conformist for my liking, what follows is where I sourced the factual information used in this book. All the telephone and email interviews with Fi's family and friends are not individually listed but are hereby acknowledged and greatly appreciated. The poems mentioned throughout this book can be found in general circulation on the Internet and as such are viewed as 'in the public domain' and not requiring any individual referencing.

> Brosnan M., 2006. Fiona gets TV lesson in What not to wear. *Herts Advertiser*, 5 October. Page unknown.

Cole L., *Young Idealists*. Antidepressant. Chrysalis, 2006. Lyrics reproduced by kind permission of Lloyd Cole and Chrysalis.

Collingham D., 2006. Wearing Wisdom Lightly. *Radio Times,* 21-27 October. Page 151.

Hotchin, L., 2009. Audition interview for Cancer Research UK advertising campaign. Interviewed on film in London. June 2009 (exact date unknown).

Unknown Author, 2003. Moonwalkers raise cash for cancer. *Herts Advertiser*, 15 May. Page 3.

Unknown Author and date. *Nina Barough*. Online. Available at http://princescharities.org/stories-people/1731 (Accessed 27 January 2011).

*" It's **about** friendship, good times, bad times, last times, decisions, honesty, dancing, fun, a single day, **a crazy** night, hugs, **chick** flicks, laughter, music, memories and a smile... "*